# Praise for
# *Master Your Workday Now!*

"This fast-moving, practical book is loaded with great ideas that help you to focus, concentrate, and get more things done faster than ever before."

—Brian Tracy, author of *Time Power*

"*Master Your Workday Now!* presents a cutting-edge and foolproof solution to your overwhelmed workday and to mastering a productive life. If you follow these practices, your daily tasks and e-mails will be well managed, your goals will be clear and achievable, and your career will be on purpose. I highly recommend this book for anyone seeking to catapult their life to higher levels of success and fulfillment."

—Jack Canfield, author of *The Success Principles* and co-creator
of the best-selling *Chicken Soup for the Soul* series

"I love the profound principles and brilliant tools offered in *Master Your Workday Now!* The strategies are easy to apply and yield fabulous results. Following this program will transform the way you approach your workday and your life—you'll be able to get more done in less time and with greater happiness and fulfillment. This book is a life-saver!"

—Marci Shimoff, *New York Times* best-selling author of
*Happy for No Reason* and featured teacher in *The Secret*

"In a world of information overload and constant interruptions, this book brings sanity to an overwhelmed work life. If you want to get your workday totally together, buy, read, and use the tools in this book."

—Stewart Emery, coauthor of *Success Built to Last*

"Master Your Workday Now! offers a fresh and practical approach to getting control of your workday, reaching your goals, and enjoying your career."

—Greg Thomas, Sr. Director for Corporate Positioning,
Cisco Systems Inc.

"In *Master Your Workday Now!* Michael Linenberger shows an incredibly clear and practical model of work that will help you get control of your chaotic work life. I highly recommend this book."

—Al Howard, NASA Engineering Consultant

"In my 20-year career of transforming top and bottom lines for businesses, I know unequivocally which businesses will turn-around results rapidly—those that master the art of execution. This book provides an easy system to make the *Thank God It's Monday* magic happen. Buy this book and start getting results faster."

—Roxanne Emmerich, CEO, The Emmerich Group and
author of *Thank God It's Monday*

"Using Michael Linenberger's system I am much more relaxed, knowing that I have a handle on all the items I need to work on. I am no longer seriously stressed out about the great cloud of ill-defined and perhaps unknown tasks, or worried about what I might be missing. In short, this approach has transformed my work life."

—Kyle Vickers, CIO and VP of Knowledge Management,
American Health Care Association

"Living with purpose and passion is critical to success in life. *Master Your Workday Now!* offers a clear, simple, and amazingly effective system for freeing up your workday and connecting your daily activities to your bigger goals and purpose, so you can live a passionate life."

—Janet Attwood, *New York Times* best-selling
coauthor of *The Passion Test*

"Michael's approach to task management has saved me at least 30 percent of my time. It is so easy to understand and implement. It has also reduced my stress level. *I* am now in charge…not my calendar!"

—Bill McDaniel, CEO, McDaniel Consulting

"If you've ever felt overwhelmed by your workday, get this book. From cover to cover, Michael Linenberger reveals original, straightforward, powerfully effective strategies to completely mastering your tasks, e-mail, goals, career direction, and even life in general."

—Ivan Misner, Founder, BNI and the Referral Institute and *New York Times* best-selling author of *The 29% Solution*

"Michael's approach to getting your workday under control is powerful, effective, and easy to learn. Engage these techniques and watch the stress flow off your day."

—Andrew Hartnett, Vice President, PCubed

"This book presents a holistic approach to putting work into perspective. It gives you tools to control the daily deluge of action requests, and new ways to successfully create your goals and to connect more meaningfully with your career. If you want to get your workday totally together, get this book."

—A. J. Rachele, President, MPS

"Michael Linenberger's *Master Your Workday Now!* steps you through a powerful, highly practical system for taming the millions of demands in life. How we *think* about life is what causes stress. Michael shows you how to organize task lists and goals to produce a life that feels spacious and relaxed, while still accomplishing everything you need to get done."

—Stever Robbins, host of *The Get-It-Done Guy* business podcast

"In the process of any kind of business there are those hidden activities that result in very clear wastes of time and money. Michael's simple approach helps expose those unseen actions and simplifies them for greater productivity and smoother outcomes. Imagine having workdays that consistently end up more productive and joyful. Identify the problems of productivity, solve them right away, and still have some time to celebrate!"

—William R. Levacy, Human Performance Improvement (HPI) consultant

"In our complex world of infinite demands on our time, Michael Linenberger's book integrates sound task management with psychological theory to create techniques that are new and powerful. His methods get tasks done, on time, in prioritized order, without overwhelming us. This is a breakthrough book that makes both intuitive and practical sense."

—Dr. Chris Wagner, Professor of Industrial and Systems Engineering
and creator of *IdealFlows* work flow tools

"Michael Linenberger's incredible system has brought order and sense to my tasks and e-mail. Now I can focus on getting my work done instead of just managing my work!"

—Devon Johnson, Portfolio Management Lead,
American Automobile Association

# Master Your Workday *Now!*

Proven Strategies to Control Chaos,
Create Outcomes & Connect Your
Work to Who You Really Are

*By Michael Linenberger*

New Academy Publishers
San Ramon, California

For information on bulk purchases, please contact info@napubs.com.

Although the author and publisher have made every effort to ensure
the accuracy and completeness of information contained in this book,
we assume no responsibility for errors, inaccuracies, omissions, or any
inconsistency herein. Any slights of people, places, or organizations are
unintentional.

First printing 2010

ISBN-13: 978-0974930442
ISBN-10: 097493044X

Library of Congress Control Number: 2009913686

Visit the publisher's website at www.newacademypublishers.com for
additional information.

The following trademarks appear throughout this book: Workday Mastery,
Workday Mastery To-Do List, Workday Now, Workday Now Horizon,
Now Horizon, Now Tasks, Critical Now, Opportunity Now, Target
Now, Over-the-Horizon Tasks, Defer-to-Do, Defer-to-Review, FRESH-
Prioritization, Now Goals, Locking In New Beliefs, Microsoft Outlook.

Cover photograph by Joe Burull
Cover design and Workday Mastery Pyramid by Sara Clarehart

# Contents

Introduction

    Attaining Workday Mastery...................................................... 1

    The Three Layers of Success................................................ 5

    How To Use this Book ......................................................... 8

PART I: Controlling Your Workday Now

    Chapter 1: Control Your Work Before Work Controls You ...................... 11

    Chapter 2: A Quick Start for Gaining Control......................................... 17

    Chapter 3: Why Are We Out of Control? ............................................... 23

    Chapter 4: What is Your *Workday Now?*.............................................. 33

    Chapter 5: The Power of Urgency Zones.............................................. 45

    Chapter 6: Mastering Your Urgency Zones.......................................... 57

    Chapter 7: Task Management at the Next Level................................... 83

    Chapter 8: E-mail Mastery ............................................................... 103

    Summarizing the Control-Layer Solution........................................... 117

PART II: Creating Your Workday Now

    Chapter 9: Rising Above Control ...................................................... 123

    Chapter 10: Step 1, Vision—The Missing Component
                  from Workplace Goals................................... 131

Chapter 11: Step 2, Merging Vision Goals and Target Goals
to Create "Now Goals" .................................................. 143

Chapter 12: Step 3, Activating Now Goals—
The Key to Goal Success ............................................... 159

Chapter 13: Step 4, Taking First Action on Your Now Goals ................ 187

Chapter 14: Stretch Your Now Goals ............................................. 195

Conclusion to the Create-Layer Solution ......................................... 213

PART III: Connecting Your Workday Now

Chapter 15: The Overlapping Circles of Life and Work ..................... 219

Chapter 16: Connecting to a Larger Vision or Purpose ...................... 227

Chapter 17: Connecting with Yourself ........................................... 253

Chapter 18: Connecting to Your Life's Work .................................. 277

Chapter 19: Connecting to Your Personal Mission ........................... 297

Conclusion to Part III: Thinking Big ............................................. 305

The Workday Mastery Toolkit ...................................................... 309

Recommended Resources ............................................................ 321

Acknowledgments ..................................................................... 332

Index .................................................................................... 333

Free Workday Mastery Tools ........................................................ 343

# Attaining Workday Mastery

Workday Mastery is that feeling and knowledge that work is flowing smoothly, that workday chaos is a thing of the past, that your goals are clear and obtainable, and that your career is developing just the way you want. Using this book, you can attain that experience of Workday Mastery.

But as you may imagine, very few workers have that. Most people describe their workday as a jumble of too much craziness and too little accomplishment. This book is the answer to that craziness—and that lack of accomplishment—that so many of us feel.

It provides proven solutions to the questions so many of us have: "How am I ever going to get all this done?" "Is my life nothing more than e-mails and meetings?" "Why do I feel so overwhelmed with work?"

It also offers solutions to deeper questions about accomplishments: "How can I create goals that feel right and actually work?" "How can I progress beyond a seemingly dead-end job and into a meaningful career?" "Will I ever find truly inspiring work?"

Solutions to all these questions, and more, are found in this book.

### Most of Us Are Bogged Down at Work

Think about your average workday. Do you find it's an urgent race that you often lose? Are you falling behind with too many e-mails flooding in, too many action requests piling up, and too many meetings robbing you of valuable work time? The resulting stress—from missing obligations and falling short on responsibilities—can be intense. And the frustration can be constant because you see little progress on your important tasks.

It's likely you are making little or no progress on your goals either. Most people have given up on setting goals (they never seem to work). But even if you do have them, finding the time to work on goals is nearly impossible these days. Even more disappointing, the goals on your list probably don't inspire or motivate you.

You see, goal setting in the corporate environment is in a flawed state. Work-assigned goals these days are usually harsh measures you are dinged with at review time, rather than aspirations that inspire you to reach for more accomplishment. The idea of a goal as a pathway to higher achievements seems to be lost.

And finally, can you honestly say you're progressing in an inspiring career? Can you call the job you're currently working at your "life's work" or even progress toward it? Probably not; it is rare anyone can these days.

This book can solve those problems, and a new solution is badly needed. That's because the typical solutions that attempt to rise above this sorry state are not working. Time-management training has not helped the out-of-control workday. Goal-setting training and the use of SMART goals has not raised goal planning to a productive science or inspiring art. And career planning—when was the last time you saw help on career planning within your corporate walls?

### The Solution: Mastering Your "Workday Now"

Obviously we need a new approach. The stagnation we see is unnecessary, especially given the easy solution in this book. There *is* a solution and you will find it here. A large part of this solution has to do with first recognizing the differences across *tasks, goals, and career*—and meeting that three-level problem in a *holistic* way. It has to do with understanding that universal principles are at work—principles that before now have been undiscussed and untapped. Once you tap them, you will see a greater ease in your workday, and a much greater motion forward. You will in fact see that you can manifest in your workday the unfettered and inspired career you have always longed for.

The solution is a concept I call your *Workday Now*. The title of this book, *Master Your Workday Now!* has a double meaning. On the one hand, it means the book will show you how to manage your workday—right now; it will show you how to get control of your workday and increase your productivity quickly. In fact, take a look at the Quick Start chapter of Part I—there you will learn one immediate path to workday control that takes only minutes to implement.

But the term *Workday Now* is also a concept that refers to a specific period of time within your work. As you will soon learn, it represents your immediate now at work, plus about a week or so in the future. This is a very important time period at work, and this book will explain why in detail. *It is your power period,* the span of time across which, if managed correctly, you can most influence your productivity, your work outcomes, and your satisfaction with work. This book will show you how to improve your experience and performance in that period, so that you are essentially happy, satisfied, and successful with work. By focusing on this period you will see that you can get control of work, achieve your goals, and ultimately build a more satisfying career. This is what I call Workday Mastery.

## Source of the Workday Now Solution

Where does this Workday Now concept come from? It comes from more than thirty creative years in the business world, where I witnessed similar issues to those above and found solutions. I then taught the solutions in books, seminars, and speeches. Over 25,000 people are using elements of my solution with great success.

Starting as a civil engineer when I designed foundations for some of the largest buildings in California, I have seen workplace productivity at its best and at its worst. I later held senior management roles such as the head of the IT Department at the United States Peace Corps, and as a Vice President at the large management consultancy firm Accenture, all the while fascinated by the problems of the productive workforce. My work at Accenture was especially enlightening. It was common to arrive at a new client site and see projects stagnated because staff members were buried in the noise of their workdays.

Project management became my specialty as I kept working to solve the problem of stifled productivity. I managed very large projects for Accenture clients such as UPS, Sun Microsystems, Applied Materials, eBay, and others. After Accenture I led the creation of project management centers at AAA, Safeway, and other organizations. Yet even with the best project management tools available, I would still see many client staff members hobbled by the minutiae of work: too many e-mails, too many meetings, and too many requests for low-priority actions.

Since e-mail and task overflow were some of the central immediate causes, I started my march toward an overarching productivity solution by developing work-control systems using Microsoft Outlook—the most commonly used e-mail and task management platform across all companies. That led to two books on workday control using Microsoft Outlook. They both became #1 best-selling Outlook books and instant hits because the solutions worked so well.

This book now extends such solutions into an overarching theory of workday management—one that goes beyond e-mail and tasks, and hits at the heart of the productivity issue.

### The "Workday Now"—The Path to Workday Mastery

The Workday Now refers to a new way of looking at your work, a new way of addressing the tasks you work on, the goals you long for, and the career you aspire to. It is an exciting concept; one that requires just a small twist in the way you approach work, but one that will have a huge impact on your effectiveness and enjoyment of work. It is not at all hard to implement—easy, in fact—and yet once you do, the sense of relief and forward momentum will seem remarkable.

Once you do implement the Workday Now solution, you will attain that Workday Mastery. Again, Workday Mastery is that feeling and knowledge that work is progressing smoothly, that workday chaos is under control, that your goals are being reached, and that your career is unfolding just the way you want. Using this book, it is achievable.

Shortly, you will see that a large part of the path to Workday Mastery is a mental one. It is a new way of looking at your work using the Workday Now concept so that you concentrate on the right things in an effective way, easily. In a way, it shows that work, like golf, for example, is largely a mental game, one that can be won with the right approach.

The Workday Now concept can be examined on three levels, which I call Control, Create, and Connect—and these are the main divisions of this book. Let's look at that three-layer model and how it can help transform your workday.

## The Three Layers of Success

### The Workday Mastery Pyramid

The three parts of this book—Control, Create, and Connect—represent what I find to be a natural delineation of managing your success in the workplace. The three-part delineation also describes how to study the Workday Now concept. My Workday Mastery Pyramid shows this well.

As you can see in the Workday Mastery Pyramid, the Control layer, which forms the foundation for the layers above, is all about getting control of your

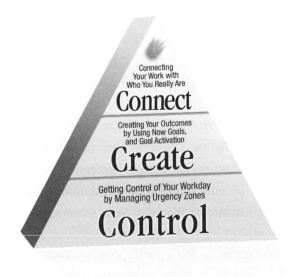

**The Workday Mastery Pyramid**

own workday. This includes managing through a powerful concept I call *urgency zones,* defined by the Workday Now. It is a major consideration when getting work under control, which we'll explore in Part I.

The Create layer, layer 2, is all about formulating and achieving work outcomes, usually by setting and managing goals. Workday Now tools are also used there, as you will see in Part II of the book.

And the Connect layer at the top is all about connecting your work with who you really are. True productivity cannot be achieved unless your activities match you. In essence, this is about aligning your work with your life. Once again, the Workday Now concept provides answers on how to do that and is covered in Part III of the book.

## The Three-Layer Sequence

So the Workday Mastery Pyramid starts with the Control layer—before you get to working on goals and a larger mission in life. "What?" you may say. "Haven't I been told for years that I'm supposed to start with mission, and then goals, and only then assign goal-based tasks to gain control?"

While that sequence is ideal, unfortunately it has not been working for most people. When you are so consumed with trying to deal with urgencies, you can't even begin to consider goals or mission; you are too overwhelmed to do so. Most people cannot get even their minimal daily tasks off their plate effectively enough to have time to focus on visualizing and planning their goals, much less take time at work to consider their work's role in their lives.

That is what sets this system apart from the rest. You start where you must— by using *control* as a foundation and then working your way up the Workday Mastery Pyramid in a holistic and powerful way.

There are several ways to look at this. First, the Control, Create, and Connect sequence identifies the natural progression that a person's career takes as they work from entry level to higher levels of responsibility. For example, a new employee just entering the workforce will probably be working more at the Control layer. They might be asked by their supervisor to do very simple and specific tasks. The main abilities that a supervisor might expect of them are doing what they are told, and accomplishing tasks on time. These are very much Control-layer expectations.

As the employee matures and perhaps takes on a manager role, they will be asked to think more for themselves and find their own ways to create outcomes; this is a Create-layer activity. And, finally, if the person reaches upper management or even ownership of a company, they might be creating the vision for the company and its products, through their own sense of how they see their work and the business interacting with the world. That's very much a Connect-layer action.

But the reader does not need to wait for a promotion to benefit from the later sections of the book. The Control, Create, and Connect sequence also represents what I think is the natural order of *tools* people should apply at *whatever* career level they are currently on. At the Control level, for example, they should make sure they first have their control structures in place. By this, I mean tools for self-management of their tasks, e-mail, and calendars, and perhaps also tools for delegation tracking and even project management. Next, at the Create level, tools for setting and managing goals come in; even new employees can use those. Tools for the Connect layer come next; they are at a whole other level, a very personal level usually, but still applicable for those new to the workforce.

## Starting with Control

As I said, this order is different from what you may have seen in other management books. For example, most productivity books ask you to write your mission statement (a Connect-layer activity), then identify goals that help achieve that mission statement (a Create-layer activity), and then identify tasks after that (Control layer). That is a very top-down approach.

However, while it is an ideal approach, I strongly feel that you should start at the Control layer first. First perfect your system of tracking and working tasks, because tasks are how you take action, and action is the mechanism for achieving everything you do at work. Getting tasks under control is how you get your workday under control; if your workday is out of control, you cannot take the next-higher-level perspectives.

In fact, you may see some resemblance in my Workday Mastery Pyramid to Maslow's Hierarchy of Needs, which takes a similar pyramid form. Abraham Maslow was a psychologist who in 1943 proposed a natural order of human needs. This similarity to Maslow's pyramid is no accident, because the theme is similar; in Maslow's pyramid you also start at the bottom.

Maslow states that the basic needs of human physiology—food, water, and shelter, which are at the base of his pyramid—must be met first before moving up to feelings of love, belonging, and self-esteem (middle of his pyramid). At the top of his pyramid are experiences of self-actualization, which describe higher-level thinking and experiencing. This lines up well with the Workday Mastery Pyramid in this book, and you will find the Workday Now teachings to be as core to your work as Maslow's are to your life.

## How to Use this Book

If you're interested in improving your work life and becoming more productive, this book is for you. You will find that each of the three parts of the book fills these needs in a different way.

Part I is called "Controlling Your Workday Now," and is for the extremely busy person. It is for someone who feels that their workday is nearly out of control, and is feeling frustrated by the inability to stay ahead of tasks and e-mail. You will find techniques unlike those in any other approach for managing time, tasks, or e-mail, ones that are unusually effective.

The same methodology that is used in my number one best-selling Outlook book called *Total Workday Control Using Microsoft Outlook*, is used here, but presented without Outlook; in this book I show you how to do those techniques using merely a type of paper to-do list that you can carry with you. Thousands of people have studied or used these techniques and found them remarkably powerful. I think you will too. Graduates of my seminars routinely report a 25 percent or more efficiency boost from these techniques—some even say 45 percent—so I urge you to try them out and see the improvements in your day.

Part II is called "Creating Your Workday Now" and is for anyone who wants to achieve their goals. It is especially for people who have tried other goal books or techniques and become frustrated with them. Goal setting and achieving is shrouded in mystery. On the one hand, the word *goals* has become common parlance in management-speak for *targets* that managers expect their organization to meet. On the other hand, goals also represent higher orders of achievement at the personal level. Sometimes those two uses seem at odds.

If you have been looking for a secret ingredient for how to make work goals work for you, you will like Part II; it teaches a new and profound Workday Now approach to fulfilling your work goals.

Part III is called "Connecting Your Workday Now" and is for those of you who may be starting to question why you are working in the career you are in, or wondering if there is anything more that you can do to be more satisfied with your career. It's about creating a vision for your work that matches your life. It provides tools for identifying your life's work, then making it happen. It is for anyone who is not fully satisfied with their career, and it is particularly useful for someone wishing they could make a bigger mark in the world.

So let's get started on this adventure, an adventure that will introduce you to techniques to control your work, achieve your goals, and, ultimately, achieve satisfaction with your career. This is the journey to Workday Mastery.

# PART I

# Controlling Your Workday Now

The Workday Mastery Pyramid

CHAPTER **1**

# Control Your Work Before Work Controls You

"Oh, crap! I cannot believe I forgot to do this!"

It is 6:45 p.m. and you've just left a marathon late-afternoon meeting with Engineering. It's been a day full of meetings, and you are finally back at your desk glancing through your e-mail, and your attention comes to an unread e-mail you jumped over this morning. The e-mail is reminding you that the quarterly sales report is due at 8 a.m. the next day. It is late and this is a two-hour job!

"Man! That has been on my radar for three days and I completely let it go!"

You know your boss is not going to be happy if you just postpone it, because this is a critical report.

"Okay, looks like a long evening tonight. Darn, I stayed late last night working on the Quality Project emergency. My wife is going to be angry. Why can't I get these things lined up? I just have way too much to do."

This is typical for today's workforce. That overlooked or postponed item is often in e-mail and scrolled off the bottom of the page, but it could just as well be in meeting notes that have gotten buried, or in a sticky note on your monitor under three layers of other sticky notes.

And even if you do not overlook items, the tasks you know about seem like they are just too numerous to get done in the work hours you have. You have

13

a nagging feeling you are not using your day efficiently, but your main problem seems to be that you have an unending flow of requests for action, especially in e-mail, and you still have a "day job" too, with meetings to go to and phone calls to answer. How do you sort all this out?

It doesn't need to be this way. That is what Part 1 of this book is for. It presents a proven method of controlling tasks to get ahead of all that the workday throws at you, and to get home on time (for a change). The section is also about getting things done, but, more fundamentally, it is about making peace with your workday. You *can* control your workday rather than it controlling you.

## The Over-Clocked Workday

You probably know people who seem to manage well in their over-clocked work world; they may even thrive on it. Maybe your boss is like that. But for most of us, an over-clocked pace is frustrating because the workload and e-mail become a blur. As a result we start missing things: opportunities, obligations, desired outcomes. And then we regret those misses; we feel guilty about not keeping our commitments and not being more productive. We freak out a little bit every time we miss an important promise or deadline. And the stress and hours it takes to stay ahead just does not feel worth it. As a result we dislike or even hate our work. This is especially true if our missed deadlines lead to criticism by stakeholders or especially by our boss.

But even without others' criticism, that feeling of blur scares us. We are not sure at any given time what we are missing, what we should be doing. It leads to a constant undercurrent of anxiety, a self-talk that says, "I am not keeping up with my work," "I am getting farther behind," or "I am missing something important."

The constant feeling of possibly missing something important is as bad as or worse than actually missing the thing. That underlying anxiety is very destructive. It eats away at our sense of ease and appreciation of work. A missed promise can be remedied, but a constant state of anxiety robs us of our quality of life.

So Part I of this book really has two goals. First, referring to the Workday Mastery Pyramid, it provides a Control-layer system, which enables you to regulate and lessen the load you focus on at any given time, to make it more reasonable.

But equally important, it provides Control-layer tools to help you be much clearer about what is on your plate at any given time, so you can eliminate the blur and that *feeling* that you are out of control. The improved feeling level that results may be the most important outcome, as it greatly improves your ability to enjoy work. After all, that is why we work in the profession we do, because we want to feel satisfied with our work and career. So, in many ways, this section is about improving your psychology and improving the way you approach your mental engagement in work. It is the first step toward Workday Mastery, and uses the Workday Now model to do that.

## If You Have Microsoft Outlook

If you use Microsoft Outlook I encourage you, after reading this book, to read my Outlook book called *Total Workday Control Using Microsoft Outlook*. It provides a step-by-step guide for how to use Microsoft Outlook to implement the Control-layer solution you are reading about here in Part I of this book. In that book, I showed readers how to get ahead of their workday using principles of e-mail and task management similar to the ones here in Part I, applied exclusively in Microsoft Outlook. Tens of thousands of individuals have implemented those processes, either from reading the book or taking one of my corporate seminars. There has been an overwhelming response with a clear message: these principles, when applied to Outlook, really work. They help people for the first time get their workday and e-mail under control.

If you have already read that book, you may be wondering, "How does this part of this book fit in with that?" After all, that Outlook book was about getting control of the workday too.

This book is needed even for Outlook users because some people who use Outlook still prefer a paper system for tracking tasks; Part I of this book provides that. And Part I takes the principles taught in that Outlook book well beyond what I covered there. So even if you have read my Outlook book, you will want to read Part I of this book too.

## If You Don't Have Microsoft Outlook

Many people do not use Microsoft Outlook, yet still want to benefit from the underlying theory and system from *Total Workday Control Using Microsoft Outlook*. So I extracted the basic principles from that book and included them here, but expanded the material into a universal theory of work that has never been discussed in any other book. It is a theory that deserves a separate treatment of its own and expansion into broader topic areas such as goals and career management. This book fills that void.

If you do move on to my Outlook book after this one, make sure you get the latest edition of that book, since it has been updated to reflect a considerable amount of new information. And before you contact me and ask, no I do *not* have specific written material for implementing these principles within other e-mail systems, nor on the Macintosh version of Outlook. However, I think you will find the general principles in Part I applicable to all e-mail systems, so do not be discouraged.

Enjoy the lessons here in Part I; they will help you to, perhaps for the first time ever, get your workday completely under control, and quickly. With that in mind, the next chapter shows you an especially quick way to get started.

CHAPTER **2**

# A Quick Start for Gaining Control

The underlying principles of the Control Your Workday Now solutions can be applied in a variety of formats. As I have said, my first choice is to use Outlook, but if that is not practical for you, or is not your preference, you can pick pretty much any medium you want and implement the solution. On your computer you can also use Excel, or even a word processing program. You can use a brainstorming program called MindManager, which is one of my favorite computer software applications. Or you can use any other program that allows you to create multiple lists.

However, what I emphasize in this book is how to use the solution on *paper.* It's the simplest approach and more mobile than any computer-based solution. It lends itself to a variety of work environments, and it may feel more natural to many of you who already use a paper-based calendar or task system. You can create the pages described below with a pen or pencil, or create them on your computer and then print them out. You can use the pages by themselves, or insert them into an existing calendar planner system. Whatever approach you use, I call this Control-layer solution the *Workday Mastery To-Do List,* and you will start using it in a very simple form right now.

## Try This Now on Paper

As a quick start, using paper, let's explore rapidly the underlying principles of the Workday Mastery To-Do List. Using this quick start, you can actually begin to get your workday under control within a few minutes. Follow the steps below to manually create the Workday Mastery To-Do List. Or go to MasterYourWorkday. com for free downloadable templates (navigate to the templates page and choose the Level 1 Workday Mastery To-Do List).

1. Take out a piece of paper, either lined or blank (or open your word processor or spreadsheet program), and at the very top, centered on the page, place the label "Now Tasks List." See Figure 2.1 at right.

2. Just below that, flush left, write the label "Critical Now (must do today)."

3. Then about one-third of the way down the page, write the label (also flush left) "Opportunity Now (start this week or next, review list daily)". That's it for the first page.

4. Then take another piece of paper, and at the top of that page, write the title "Over the Horizon (Review Weekly)."

You've now got the basic Workday Mastery To-Do List in hand, all on only two pages. See Figure 2.1 on the next page for how this will look (with some sample tasks entered).

### Populate the List

Let's start using it. Pull out any existing to-do lists that you might have, say in a journal or a collection of yellow sticky notes, or whatever else you are using now. You will be copying tasks from there into this template.

From those sources, or from your head, enter into the top section of the new template any tasks that you know you need to complete today. You should also glance at your e-mail in-box to see if there are any pressing actions in there. Write down a one-line summary for each action due today.

Write into the next section (the one titled Opportunity Now), those tasks that aren't due today but that you would like to start as soon as possible. Write

---

**Now Tasks List**

**Critical Now** (must do today)
- Send Artwork to Mary for review
- Complete book review writeups
- Set meeting with Suzanne
- Call Ted regarding print quote

**Opportunity Now**
(start this week or next, review list daily)

- Start arlternate printing quotes
- Study joint venture opportunities
- Call Donna re: review service
- Decide on interview timeline
- Figure out who does print media
- Decide on new website url
- Create quotes list
- Schedule copyeditor next phase
- Discuss YouTube strategy with Penny
- Update project schedule

---

**Over the Horizon** (Review Weekly)

- Investigate galley printing options
- Find overseas licensing options
- Find painter for house
- Designer for new office space
- Set meeting with planning commision on streets
- Decide on Spring party venue
- Create manual for invoice processing
- Find copyeditor for ad hoc work on newsletters
- Invite insurance salesperson to next monthly mtg
- Identify best sources of temp staffing
- Create hiring plan for next quarter
- Call Office Depot about bulk purchases
- Conference room furniture: replace
- Set meeting with executive committee re: planning
- Buy books for library
- Assign Printing project to Sally

**Figure 2.1**   The Workday Mastery To-Do List (Level 1).

down any tasks you would like to work on if you had the opportunity to fit them in today or soon.

And then, on the next page, the one labeled "Over the Horizon," enter any tasks that are fairly low-priority and you know you don't need to get to for a few weeks or more. That could be a big list.

That's it; you have now started using the Workday Mastery To-Do List.

## How to Use This List

So how to use this list? Most of it is fairly self-explanatory. Obviously, Critical Now tasks must be done today. The rest of the tasks on page 1 you will then work on as the opportunity arises, when you find time in between or after your critical tasks (and in between any meetings or other work).

Finally, Over-the-Horizon tasks (page 2) are just that; they're beyond your concern right now, and so you need not attend to them until a weekly task review (we will discuss that weekly task review in a moment). This second page is a great place to store tasks you do not want to lose, but may not get to for a while.

There are some subtleties to using this system. Here are some recommendations that describe those.

Try to put all your tasks into this list. There are many benefits to listing everything in one place. Adhering to that means if an e-mail comes in with a to-do item in it, as soon as you read it, make a note of it on this task list; same with voice mail. With one place to list all tasks, when the end of the day comes, you can tell with one quick glance if you can go home or not, without leaving any critical things undone.

My next instruction is don't over-use the Critical Now section. Use the following test when placing items on that list: would you stay late at work tonight to complete this task if it were not finished at your normal departure time? If the answer is no (you would not stay late), then don't put it inside the Critical Now tasks section. Reserve that section only for tasks that really must be done today.

Next, the Opportunity Now list will build up rapidly, and you need to keep it relatively short so that you can review it easily. You should be reviewing that list completely at least once a day if not more, and I have found that if this list exceeds 20 items, you will not be able to do that. So once that list starts to exceed 20, take the lowest-priority items off of that list and move them to the second page, the page titled "Over the Horizon."

Next, if an Opportunity Now task has a specific deadline, enter the date of that deadline right at the start of the task description. For example, you might write a task as follows: DUE August 16, Sales Report. You can also put tasks with distinct due dates like that on your calendar if you like. But only do this for real deadlines; do not create artificial ones.

And finally, you should review the Over-the-Horizon tasks list (page 2) once a week. I recommend setting a Monday morning appointment to review that section. During that task review, if you find any items on that list that have become important, move them onto the front page.

That's really it—that's the Workday Mastery To-Do List in a nutshell, and I encourage you to start using this new system today. I think you'll find that it has a remarkably powerful effect on getting your workday under control.

I will present more about the theory underlying this system in the chapters ahead. What you just learned I call Level 1 of the Workday Mastery To-Do List.

You will also learn some additions to the system that make those pages a bit more complex (called Level 2 and 3), but they are just as easy to use. And you will learn a number of fine points that allow the system to cover more situations. But for now, please do start using this new, simple to-do list approach. I think you will find it very powerful.

## Why the Word *Now*?

You may be wondering why the emphasis on the word *Now* throughout this solution.

There are a couple of reasons. First, all the tasks on the first page of your tasks list ought to be eligible to be done now. That means they are not dependent on other tasks, they are not waiting for a future date to arrive, and they are not such a low priority that you really don't intend to do them for a week or more. So the idea is that they are current tasks; you might even call them "as soon as possible" tasks.

The other reason for the term *Now* is that these are tasks you want in your awareness now. You only have so much mental capacity to consider to-do items. You don't want to try to consider too many tasks at once; doing so will add too much stress to your day. You cannot get to them all anyway, so there would be no sense in cycling through hundreds of tasks every time you consider what to do next. Instead, this is the small subset of tasks you want in your mind, or close to your mind, right now, and no more. Identifying this small Now Tasks list is a great stress reducer.

Also, the word *Now* is right in the title of this book. It comes from the concept of the Workday Now that I addressed at the start of the book; it is a key part of the workday mastery theory in this book. It is applied differently at each of the three layers: Control, Create, and Connect. As you will see in a moment, in the Control layer it refers to that period of time that you need to focus awareness, concern, and management attention on. That is your Workday Now.

CHAPTER **3**

# Why Are We Out of Control?

Continuing your path to Workday Mastery, in this chapter I will explain the problem many of us have of feeling like we have too much work. You see, to get to a solution for your overwhelmed workday, first you should ask yourself, "Why do I feel overwhelmed (or possibly even fearful) about the amount of work on my plate?"

Most people of course will answer, "I have too much to do." For some of you, I think that is an accurate answer; you *are* overloaded. But for many of you, I suspect the answer may lie more in the way you approach your work; perhaps you are approaching it in an inefficient way. Considering the time wasted on e-mail alone, there may be rich opportunities for efficiency improvement to explore. I coach all my students to look first at efficiency before declaring to everyone around them, "I am too busy."

## Are You Overwhelmed at Work and Why?

Whether you really have too much to do, or are just being inefficient, a solution to both problems can be found in the Workday Now Control layer. This first third of the book focuses on the basic question, "How do I control my workday so I do not suffer the angst of getting behind, of feeling overwhelmed,

23

of not meeting expectations—both others' and my own?" Clearly, the solution at this level has to do with showing you ways to get your most important work attended to, and how to deal with what you cannot.

First, let's talk more about the Control layer. When we talk about controlling anything, we are usually talking about using fairly basic management styles, ones usually based on "Do this and good things will happen, don't do it and bad things will happen." In other words, it is often all about rewards and punishments as a management style. While some may say that sounds a bit old-fashioned, for many job roles, tasks, and outcomes, the reward/punishment model is very effective; it works. Ask any sales manager pushing their staff to meet their monthly goals (and thus bonuses), and they will say it works.

And even for those of you not in sales, a rewards-and-punishments approach is still usually necessary, especially for organizational "administrivia." For example, withholding some pay if a time sheet or expense report submission is incomplete is a punishment that leads to tension, and creating such tension is sometimes the only way to get people to do even small, seemingly trivial tasks.

My point is that the Control-layer management style is often just the right thing to do. A little tension can help get people moving. And whether you put tension on yourself or others impose it on you, that emotion can be useful to motivate you to get things done and stay ahead.

Another useful form of tension is tension that comes from advancement. Psychologists point out that most humans get accustomed to the status quo and often resist change, even good change. So a feeling of tension may be an indication that you are experiencing a change that could in the long run benefit you. A new company, a new job assignment, a new boss, or just new and more challenging work can all cause tension at first, but could be an improvement for you.

However, when applied tension becomes overwhelming, it needs to be fixed. Here I want to mention the difference between tension and stress. James J. Mapes describes this best in his book *Quantum Leap Thinking*. There he states, as I do, that tension in the workplace, especially creative tension, can be good. Such tension is often what drives us forward, allowing us to do tasks that may not be our favorite things to do, but that need to be done nevertheless. Mapes also says, however, that when tension turns into *stress,* we need to make an adjustment. Stress can be destructive and counterproductive. Stress is tension taken too far.

## Urgency Is a Fact of Work Life

At the busy workplace, both tension and stress usually come from urgency. What I am referring to here is the feeling you have when you are pushed to move too fast on something, either self-induced because you are getting behind, or induced by others who want things now.

Some say that in the ideal workplace we could avoid urgency. If we plan out work and staff it correctly, and have systems in place to manage it, we could smooth out the peaks and circumvent urgency.

Others say that urgency is just fine, that it's an unavoidable fact of the workplace.

And still others say urgency is fine as long as you are sure to apply it only to important things. For example, Stephen Covey's book *The 7 Habits of Highly Effective People* is famous for its interpretation of a well-known four-way grid with high and low urgency on one axis and high and low importance on another. The book states we should take urgent actions only on things that are important to our goals and values and minimize activity in the quadrant called urgent but not important. Doing that may free up much of your day and lessen the number of urgent things you do.

I say urgency is normal and *needed.* I feel *reasonable* urgency can be a management tool, even a self-management tool. Urgency motivates, it stimulates. Think of the classic case of the student who won't study for a test till the last minute, when urgency is high. We all use that same last-minute approach for many of our tasks at work. We do so perhaps because we are very busy, but we often do it because we like the push that urgency gives us. This is true for all kinds of tasks, whether small administrative tasks, or larger mission-critical ones; a sense of urgency helps get us moving. Brian Tracy, the well-known management guru, states that the ability to feel and convey urgency is one quality that identifies a good executive. That's because such people are able to get things moving.

We thrive on urgency in our personal lives as well. Think of how much we enjoy movies with a plot that creates tension and urgency. Think of the physical sports we play that impose urgency. Or the mental ones: card games, video games, board games—anything that moves fast and forces us to think on our feet—we enjoy that. We like urgency; at times we even thrive on it.

## Urgency Taken Too Far

So, no, we should not try to eliminate urgency from the workplace. But urgency, if taken too far, also wears us down. Clearly, we need timeouts from urgency. Even a good action movie has slow parts where you catch your breath, where the tension is resolved. And you do not want the urgent episodes to last too long or become too intense.

What is an example of urgency taken too far? Many of us have those scenarios at work where all the exciting urgent things pile on top of one another all at once. At that point they lose their glow, and what was at one moment stimulating, now instead becomes overwhelming or even fear inducing. If this continues hour after hour, and then day after day, all zest for work is lost. Rather than feeling like a cavalry leader conquering all our work tasks, we feel like an injured soldier who fell off his horse and is being dragged behind it.

And that is the main symptom of the out-of-control workday, when too many urgent items pile on top of us, day after day, and we feel we cannot come up for air. We feel like we have lost control.

What typically leads us to this? Well, certainly, it is a high volume of things to do in proportion to the time we have. If we try to do them all at once, it feels overwhelming. If we instead try to spread them out, that doesn't work either because some things that start as reasonable requests become urgent later because we cannot get to them quickly enough. More things to do are coming in every day, and the pile-up gets worse.

This leads to a perceived need to learn time management. Or a request for more staff. Or a request to direct new assignments elsewhere. We feel if we only had more time, then we could get it all done.

The feeling of being out of control is also caused by losing clarity about what is on our list. When the list gets too big, the fear of missing something important can lead to stress.

### Working Low Priority First Is the Biggest Issue

In addition to a feeling of stress it causes, the other problem with the lack of clarity about your list is that you do not see or measure the true priority of things on it. That leads to you working low-priority items at the expense of high-priority ones just because they are in front of you. This then leads to wasted time, which itself then leads to a time shortage. Then you really do have a time management problem! Things that were not urgent before become urgent because you are not getting to them in a timely manner.

In fact, I would say that working lower-priority items first is probably the largest cause of an out-of-control workday and the resulting buildup of too many urgent items. When you do that, the things that get put off or even dropped at the end of the day are your most important things, and the stress from not finishing those is high.

E-mail is the largest low-priority culprit these days. When we read and react to e-mail as it comes in, we are usually doing low-priority work at the expense of our core higher-priority work. Many people spend hours and hours per day doing this, and then wonder why they don't get their main work done.

## Is Prioritization the Answer?

Proper prioritization will obviously be a big part of the answer. But how do we prioritize correctly?

Making a prioritized list is something we have all tried, and, if volumes are not too high, that can work. It's a good first step. In fact, I would say this is what separates an average worker (who merely complains when they have more to do than time in the day) from a better worker. The better worker knows that too much to do is just a challenge and learns to prioritize within that work, and "manages down" the lower-priority items to do later.

Knowing what tasks are important to do will help solve the lack-of-clarity problem I just outlined.

However, once work reaches a certain volume, a simple "do the important tasks first" approach will stop working. What often happens is you end up with 40 to 140 items, all marked high importance, and so you will find many important things are falling through the cracks and your sense of being overwhelmed returns.

In fact, because the list gets so big, most people skip many of their high-importance tasks; they end up sitting on those tasks for weeks or months. Eventually people stop using a task list because of the overwhelming size it reaches.

Maybe the problem is with how we measure importance? Yes, that is a major cause. Many of us end up skipping tasks we mark important because we don't fully buy into our own importance rating. Why is that? Here's my theory. In identifying importance, even when using our values and goals or some other thoughtful measure, we often come up with an inaccurate identification of what we really should be doing.

There are a couple of reasons for this. One is that many of the things that we call important really are not important to us, but rather are marked important because we think others want them to be done. We are responding to others' priorities that we do not own ourselves, for example, tasks assigned to us by our boss, or promises we have made to others. So when we reach the decision time of whether to do the task or not, we end up skipping it. We would be doing it out of guilt, which feels lousy, so we avoid it. We'll talk in Part II about how to better own these types of goal-generated tasks.

Another problem is that importance is a very subjective thing, and we often identify something as important merely because we are enthusiastic about it, or fearful, or frustrated. Someone tells us a scary story about the perils of low insurance coverage, say, and we write down a task to increase ours. Then later, when we see the task at a less emotional moment, we don't buy into the importance, and skip over it.

Or the importance of a task may drop over time, but we don't consciously acknowledge that drop, and leave it marked high. That's a common result of reacting to the crisis of the day and writing a task to fix the underlying problems; a few days later the crisis has dissipated, but the task to improve things remains.

All of these issues can lead to an excessive abundance of "important" tasks, and an unusable system. In that case, you will fall back on just doing urgent items right in front of you. You see, compared to the murky and subjective world of importance, the fact that an item is due now is so much more clear. It is so definitive. Urgency demands action. This is why most of us like urgency (if not taken too far); it is motivating and action inducing.

Many people still insist that if we just make sure to identify as important only those tasks that are truly linked to our goals and values, the problem will sort itself out. If these tasks truly are from our own passionate goals, we will be motivated to do them, right? And we then will be doing only high-value tasks and the low-value ones will fall by the wayside.

However, while many of us have tried this, most people in a very busy environment find it does not solve the problem. Why is that?

One reason is that, for most of us, our ability to identify goals and work toward them is impaired. I discuss the reasons and a solution in Part II.

But the main reason is we are simply too busy. The freight train of work has run over our best intentions to focus on high-minded goals. If you try to do only tasks related to your goals, you will start dropping urgent things for your boss or clients, or drop other tasks that don't make the goals cut, and you will soon feel the pain of that. But more likely you will find that there are just too many urgent tasks—so many that you never even get a chance to even think about goal-based tasks that are not urgent.

However, I feel the answer still lies in finding a "right" way to prioritize down to a short list—identifying what we really need to attend to now, what we can put off, and how to put those things off in a manageable way.

## Is Getting Organized the Solution?

Maybe there is a way to organize our work such that the correct priority of tasks becomes more evident. Perhaps there is a way to organize our work lives so that the most important things to do at any moment will float correctly to the top of our lists.

That may be too much to ask, but certainly if our work were more organized, the feeling of being overwhelmed would diminish, and that could have a positive effect on our work, right?

There is some truth to that second statement. Being surrounded by chaos can drive many people to feel more overwhelmed than they actually are. That negative feeling can then lead to a vicious cycle in which they truly start to become less effective with work. But getting and then feeling organized can certainly help break that cycle to some extent.

However, others say that the time and money many of us spend getting organized is mostly wasted.

*A Perfect Mess*, a well-researched business book by Eric Abrahamson and David H. Freedman, states that much of what people and organizations do to get organized is ineffective. It asserts there is no viable economic case for most organization efforts.

My gut check on the book is that the authors are spot-on sometimes, and miss the point of organization at other times. As an example of the latter, while some organization efforts may not pay off in terms of direct efficiency gains, I do think there is a value to the *feeling* of being organized; and that feeling can translate indirectly into more efficient work. Certainly, getting organized can make you more efficient at finding things. And prioritization is a form of organizing that helps you focus on the highest-priority items first.

One of the places *A Perfect Mess* is correct is that the cost of getting organized—the amount of time spent—may exceed the savings in efficiency. I believe many of us recognize this, and that is why most people give up on complicated organization systems they try for a while. It feels good when the system is first put in place, but after that good feeling wears off, the actual efficiency gains are hard to find. Same with spending hours filing e-mail in layers of folders; the true payoff is often not worth the time spent doing it—we just feel compelled to eliminate the mess (I show better e-mail filing systems in Chapter 8).

Whatever organization method you use, it needs to be lightweight; that is, it needs to take little effort to keep it in place. Then the payoff will be worth it.

## Summary

So let's wrap up this survey of why we may feel overwhelmed at work, even after trying many solutions.

Most of us feel out of control at work because we have too many urgent items being presented at once. The healthy tension of having a brisk work life has been overrun, and we now feel bad about the unhealthy amount of stress we experience.

Our inability to clearly see our list of tasks and easily identify the most urgent ones is the main problem; solving that is one way to gain efficiency. Prioritization is the key, as it allows us to know the next high-priority task we need to accomplish and helps us avoid wasting time on low-priority actions. But basing prioritization on importance usually does not solve the problem. Importance is too subjective, and with so much to do, our "Important" list gets too big.

In the midst of lots of urgent things to do, organizing our work can make us feel better, but it doesn't always actually make us more efficient. Many systems take more effort than they are worth, and so we give up on them.

In the next section I present the solution taught in this book. It has to do with meeting urgency head-on, since urgency is the main problem here, and since the standard importance-based solutions are not working. Let's see why recognizing urgency ends up being the key to the solution.

CHAPTER **4**

# What Is Your
# *Workday Now?*

When everything at work seems urgent, how do you tell which tasks are more urgent than others? How do you get the list under control so you can think clearly about your priorities?

What if you had a system that clearly told you what was most urgent and what wasn't, so you could pace your workday? What if that system gave you ways to shorten your list down to a reasonable level, and ensured nothing critical was dropped?

In this chapter and the next two, Chapters 5 and 6, you are about to learn such a system—it represents the Control-layer portion of the Workday Mastery Pyramid.

It is not a system of organization per se, but you will feel organized once it is in place. Certainly it adds order, but is not like other organization systems with complex filing and classification approaches. Rather, it is very lightweight, meaning the amount of time needed to maintain it is very low.

It is not a prioritization system based on importance, but it does prioritize the urgency of your work. It allows you to focus on the most critical tasks first, so that you do not waste time on low-value work. This frees up time for goal-based tasks, should you choose to devote some time to those. It is not a time-management system, but you will find yourself saving time.

The solution is based on the Workday Now concept in this book. It removes that feeling of being overwhelmed and shows what needs to be done, now.

## About Mental Models

The concept behind the Workday Now solution is as much psychological as logical. One reason for this is that the solution was derived by analyzing how we think about work. What makes us feel anxious at work? Why do we worry about some tasks more than others? Why do we work on some things first and put other, even more important, tasks off until later?

Since it is a partly psychological solution, I am going to use a concept called a *mental model* to explain how this system works.

Communication management experts have for years been saying that if you want to manage conflict and improve communications among staff members, you need to help them understand one another's mental models of how they perceive work and their place in it. Better communication is fostered by making one another's perspectives more apparent.

In the same way, if you want to manage stress in a company, you need to understand the mental model that staff members apply to their workload. It is often the application of their mental model that causes them to feel stressed, and that feeling of stress then leads to poor judgment, which in turn results in inefficient work. In many cases, managing the mental model will solve the stress and performance issues without needing to significantly reduce the workload.

So what exactly is a mental model? Perhaps the best way to explain a mental model is to give an example of one that many of you may be familiar with.

### A Visit to Fisherman's Wharf

When friends and family come to visit me, I often take them down to the Fisherman's Wharf area of San Francisco. The area is beautiful, but is also full of tourist shops, most selling sweatshirts, since on a typical foggy summer day, San Francisco can be the coldest spot in the Lower 48, and summer tourists rarely come prepared for that. You probably recall tourist shops selling T-shirts and gifts at vacation spots you have been to, and you may recall seeing for sale in them what I call *cartoon maps.* They are reproductions of hand-drawn and hand-colored maps that highlight the special spots of an area, often exaggerating key landmarks to make their location and importance stand out.

You may recall a particular version of one such cartoon map of the United States. It shows a sketch map of the country from the standpoint of a "coast dweller." The map shows the West Coast states, mostly California, as huge— occupying about 40% of the country. The same exaggerated treatment is given to the East Coast states on the map. And completely wrong dimensions are given to the rest of the country in the middle, which is only shown occupying about 20% of the map.

## Mental models often don't match reality

The humorous point of the map is that many people living on the coasts think this is how things are; their image of the U.S. doesn't even include much, if any, of the Mountain and Midwest states. That is because they fly from one coast to the other, and never stop in between. This is a mental model that many people hold in some way. It is not geographically accurate and it is completely unfair to those who don't live on the coasts, but that does not matter; it is simply how some people think of the U.S. due to their experiences and the way they think. It is their mental image, and, most importantly, it impacts their opinions and actions.

Another classic mental model is from the medieval times. In those days nearly everyone assumed the sun rotates around a stationary Earth. That was how everyone pictured it, but it was wrong.

So mental models are mental structures we create of reality that often do not *match* reality.

A mental model, therefore, is our mental image or assumptions about how things in the world outside of us exist. It can in fact be about the world—the earth and geography—as the two examples above show. But it can also be about people, organizations, work, or any variety of intangible things as well. It is how we think about something, or picture it, based on the limited information we have. By this definition our model is usually incomplete or inaccurate when compared to the actual thing we are modeling. We can only know about a thing from our own perspective, which is usually narrow and colored by our previous experience.

---

**Source of the term *Mental Model***

The person who first invented the concept of mental models was Kenneth Craik in his 1943 book *The Nature of Explanation*. Also, Professor Jay Wright Forrester has the most commonly quoted definition. Here is how he defined, or discussed really, the concept of a mental model: "The image of the world around us, which we carry in our head, is just a model. Nobody in his head imagines all the world, government or country. He has only selected concepts, and relationships between them, and uses those to represent the real system." *http://en.wikipedia.org/wiki/Mental_model*

Finally, the person who brought the concept of mental models to the modern management forefront was Peter M. Senge, in his book *The Fifth Discipline.*

---

What I found in my task management research was that understanding how we mentally model our workday will help us solve this problem of being constantly overwhelmed at work. Undeniably we hold tens or even hundreds of mental models about the workplace that represent our interpretations of various aspects of work. Aspects such as positional authority, time pressures, rewards, colleague competition, and even things like equipment ("that copy machine hates me") all capture our imagination in ways that twist reality. But one mental model stood out to me as having a strong influence on how we interpret work urgency. That model defines largely why we approach tasks inefficiently at work.

And there lies the value to us. In defining how we picture our workday urgency in our mental model of tasks, we can identify a way for us to manage the urgency thrown at us.

# The Workday Now Mental Model

So let's look at this model of urgency. In our typical out-of-control workday there are two harsh realities.

#1 As a busy professional, you cannot possibly get it all done. You will think of, and be handed, way more tasks, meetings, and e-mail than you can possibly act on fully.

#2 While you know that your most important outcomes and goals should rule your activities each day, usually it is *urgency* that rules what you do at work every day.

Let's talk more about how prominent urgency is in guiding most people's work activities. As busy professionals we all collect a very large number of near-term responsibilities and tasks. In a busy office we tend to focus first on immediate emergencies. Next, we focus on urgent things due soon, and then on slightly less urgent things that are due a little farther out, and so on. In the midst of that are meetings, interruptions, and diversions, and hopefully some importance-based tasks. In general, though, our focus is based on time and urgency, and there is one aspect of this mental model that stands out the most: something I call your Workday Now Horizon.

## *Identifying Your Workday Now Horizon*

To define that model, consider this. If someone (not your boss or an important client) tried to insert a half-day project into your currently very busy schedule, giving you no permission to drop other items, and then asked you to complete it tomorrow, I am pretty sure you would say, "No, I am too busy right now." However, even with the same workload, if that request were due, say, two months from now (and you had some interest in it), you would probably say "fine." Somewhere in the range between tomorrow and two months is the date after which you stop feeling too busy, as you mentally gaze from now on into the future.

To refine that time frame, I have posed this same question to hundreds of groups at nearly all my speeches, over several years. I ask people to raise their hands if two months is fine. Almost all raise their hands for a yes. I then ask, "What about one month?" and nearly all hands stay up. I work the time frame in more, asking three weeks, then two, and then one. In nearly all cases most hands are still up at two weeks, and most hands are *down* at one week. So somewhere between one and two weeks is this threshold of work concern. I call it the Workday Now Horizon, or Now Horizon for short.

The Now Horizon helps define the mental model of your current workload. It delineates which commitments you consider when you think about what is

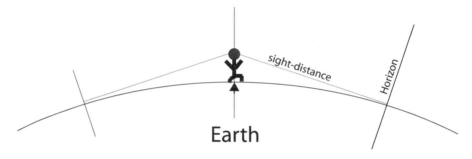

**Figure 4.1**    Horizon as a *sight-distance*.

on your plate now. Most very busy people, when they think about work inside that horizon, feel anxious or stressed about their workload. When they consider work beyond that horizon, however, they usually mentally relax, even if there is no change in their job or commitments. However, unless your work is seasonal, you don't in reality become less busy; you just imagine that you will. This is a classic mental model where our mental image does not match reality.

Again, it is interesting that across all the busy knowledge workers I have interviewed, that period is, on average, 1.5 weeks. Most of them feel as if work will relax for them after that time period. There are exceptions, of course, and it varies by industry and job type; for example, it is longer for senior managers, and shorter for administrative staff. But 1.5 weeks is a typical average.

Take a minute to consider what your own Now Horizon is, and keep that in mind as you continue reading.

Think of what the word *horizon* means. If you imagine yourself standing on a flat beach and gazing out over the ocean, the horizon is that line on the ocean where, due to the curvature of the earth, you can see no further. It's a sight-distance (see Figure 4.1).

Similarly, your Now Horizon is that time edge of work beyond which you do not mentally see your future work clearly, and so it seems less troubling. Now, imagine placing categories of tasks on this horizon-like time frame in Figure 4.2, where the past is to the left and the future is to the right. Let's focus on the future side of this picture, since that should be our primary concern in the

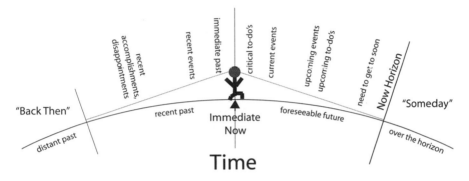

**Figure 4.2**    Horizon as a *time* concept.

Now Horizon mental model. Note that the closer the items are, the higher the urgency of the tasks.

## The Conveyor Belt and Treadmill

Let's convert the horizon concept above into another mental model that many people have when they think of their work. Factory workers typically work next to a conveyor belt in which physical objects are brought to them, perhaps machine parts they need to assemble or pack. Their speed of work is controlled by the speed of the conveyor belt.

Knowledge workers who work in offices do not have a physical conveyor belt, but they often describe their work as like being on a treadmill—workers say they feel like they are running in place and barely keeping up with the flow of tasks and requests coming their way.

Combining all the above, here is a useful model. Imagine a man or woman walking in place on the left end of a moving treadmill-like conveyor belt that stretches a far distance to the right; for simplicity of discussion we'll assume it is a man for now. He is facing and walking toward the right end at a speed that just keeps him in place above the left end of the moving belt (see Figure 4.3).

Coming toward him on the belt are workday tasks and meetings that he needs to keep up with in order to "do his job." Those things immediately in front of him are what he is working on now or that are due now; as he accomplishes these,

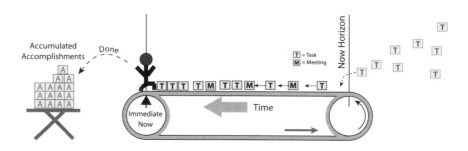

**Figure 4.3**    Treadmill mental model.

he tosses them into his mental "accumulated accomplishments" pile shown in Figure 4.3 and moves on to the next item in front of him. A little beyond his immediate tasks are things that are going to impact him soon and that he may need to get ready for. And beyond that are less urgent things, but they are still in his awareness. Typically, the man works on tasks as they arrive to him on the belt. But occasionally he reaches out and picks up items farther ahead, to get them done ahead of time, either because he wants to be proactive and get ahead of his work or, more likely, because the timing of related circumstances might be right to get them done now.

# Workday Now Defined

At the far right end of the conveyor belt is the limit of what he can easily see coming. It is the Now Horizon we described above. It is not that no work exists beyond that horizon; it is just that work beyond that point is out of sight and therefore out of mind, and so the man is not anxious about it and probably does not think much about it.

This is a good model for your workload and how you react to it. That time period between the immediate now and the Now Horizon is what I call your Workday Now (see Figure 4.4). It is the time period you are thinking about now

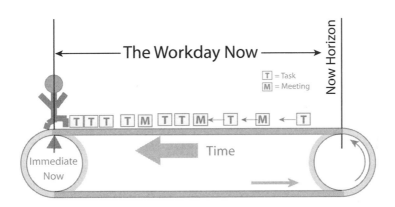

**Figure 4.4**  The Workday Now defined.

at work. It is a very important period of time because it is the period we put nearly all our energy and attention on. If someone asks, "What's on your plate now?" you look inside that period when you answer. The volume of things you perceive to be due in that period is what determines if you feel you are too busy or not. The impact of this period is so important that it is at the core of the title of this book, *Master Your Workday Now!* Your ability to manage that period well affects whether you are happy with your work.

## *The Rate of Work Is What Matters*

In this model, being too busy has to do with the rate of work. If the rate of work entering and leaving your Workday Now is the same (as in Figure 4.3) you

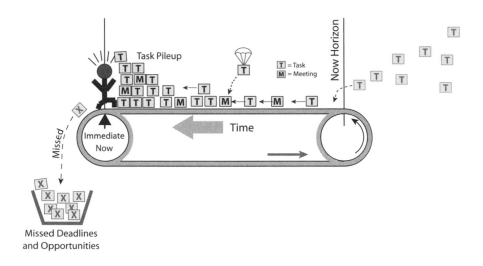

**Figure 4.5**   Workday overload.

feel good. Similarly, if you complain about being overloaded with work, you are
most likely complaining that the rate entering is too high and pileups of work
are occurring within your Workday Now. If the speed and resulting pileup of
new tasks in your workplace is *too* great, you start to miss opportunities and
deadlines, and that leads to your sense of regret or anxiety about work (see
Figure 4.5).

On a lighter note, you may recall a funny episode in the classic television
show *I Love Lucy* that illustrates this well. In that episode, Lucille Ball and her
cohort are newly assigned to a chocolate factory and they are supposed to
wrap all chocolate candies passing in front of them on a conveyor belt. The
belt is fed from the other side of a small door, through which they cannot see.
The conveyor belt starts out slow and reasonable, with Lucille declaring, "This
is easy. I can do this all day!" However, the belt soon speeds up and the two of
them anxiously lose control as unwrapped chocolates slip by their hands. All
their stress comes from the increasing speed at which new tasks are coming.
In the television show, the character's reaction to getting behind is very funny;
Lucille Ball is hiding chocolates under her hat and even in her mouth, so she
does get caught with unwrapped chocolates when the supervisor comes to

check on them. But in real life, getting behind like that is anything but funny; it is a very stress-inducing experience as workers worry about not keeping up with their work.

### Over-the-Horizon Tasks Are Out of Sight

Again, whether overwhelmed or not, in this model you still do not think much about work outside, or "over," the Now Horizon. In the Lucille Ball episode, the Now Horizon was the door through which the chocolate candies entered on the belt; she could not see beyond it.

In the office it is the limit of what we have our attention on when gazing into the future, normally about 1.5 weeks out. Because we are not thinking about tasks beyond then, we just don't worry about them. And, as I said, most of us assume we have less work beyond that time frame.

### Surfing Your Workday Now

Again, this is just a mental model. In reality, your workload does not decrease after 1.5 weeks. Like a wave on the ocean, it is a *rolling* time period—your holy grail of a more relaxed work pace is always just a week or so away, and remains that way. You are likely constantly thinking, "If only I can get past this week, I can take a breath." And that thought repeats itself, week after week.

But that is not a bad thing. It actually gives us the basis of a tool to solve our workday overload by, in a sense, surfing that wave. You see, the true power of identifying the Workday Now is that it allows us to define what I call "urgency zones" within this model, which I will describe in detail in the next chapter. This is what turns this mental model into a powerful task management tool. Identifying these zones is extremely useful since doing so provides a way to be specific about the way we work tasks within the various zones.

For example, if we consider everything inside the Workday Now (left of the Now Horizon) separately from everything beyond the Now Horizon, we can start to get a handle on work. Specifically, if the task list we study daily represents only tasks within the Workday Now period, and if we can control the number of tasks we place on that list, we may be able to control our stress and anxiety about work. The Workday Now period is the period we worry about most. And since there are only so many things we can do in the next week or so anyway, why not admit that and adjust this list accordingly? Just selectively move more items off that list and onto the Over-the-Horizon list (page 2 of the Workday Mastery To-Do List from Chapter 2), the list you study only weekly. Doing that small step alone can control a huge amount of chaos, and I will show you how in the next chapter.

But we can do even better than that because there are even more urgency zones that will help your workday control. For example, the harshest urgency experience any of us can have is when a task is due today and we forget or miss the deadline—usually because we don't have a clear and timely view of the commitments we've made. That's negative urgency at its extreme. As you will see in the next chapter, using the urgency zone called the Critical Now can get us ahead of that as well.

## Summary

So that is an overview of the Workday Now theory, and the background of where it comes from. As you can see, it is based on a recognizable mental model of how we all process urgency.

To review, we all tend to focus nearly exclusively on activities that are either due today or coming up within the next 1.5 weeks. The existence of that 1.5 week time period represents the central premise of Part I of this book—that we all have a Workday Now, a unique chunk of time in our mental model about work.

Many of us say that period is like a conveyor belt or treadmill, with tasks continually coming at us as fast as we get them done. Overload in that Workday Now period happens when new tasks come *too* fast, and that is what causes us to feel overwhelmed at work, and to miss deadlines and opportunities. You learned that by being aware of that zone you may be able to manage your work much more appropriately for greater productivity and much less stress, for example, by moving more items to your Over-the-Horizon list.

Let's see additional ways to get that control, using the concept of urgency zones, next.

CHAPTER **5**

# The Power of
# Urgency Zones

In the previous chapter you learned the theory of the Workday Now, that key piece of time in our awareness that controls so much of our experience at work.

As I stated at the end of that chapter, the true power of identifying the Workday Now is that it allows us to define what I call "urgency zones" within this model, and I cover those in this chapter. Using urgency zones intelligently is what turns this mental model into a powerful tool, because these zones provide a way to be specific about the way we manage and work tasks on our list. Tasks in each zone require different management intensity. We can reserve our energy by limiting our most energetic reactions only to those tasks that really deserve it.

### Crazy Busy

If you do not do this—manage your work focus selectively—you can easily get into an "everything is a fire" mentality. You have probably seen this happen. You are extremely busy one day; perhaps the end of the day is approaching and you have worked yourself into a froth, trying to get it all done in a superhuman way. Your pace is so fast and imbalanced that everything you see seems like an emergency; even minor e-mail requests hitting your in-box throw you into action mode. You have lost your sense of reason about what the real emergencies are, or even if any truly exist—you just try to push through as fast as you can, thinking velocity alone is your answer.

In periods like that—and they can last days or weeks at a time, whether we are aware of them or not—we tend to make bad decisions. In fact while you may feel like your superhuman velocity is needed and effective, it usually is not. Research shows your effectiveness decreases greatly during those periods. An article in the January 2005 *Harvard Business Review* by Dr. Edward M. Hallowell asserts that people under those conditions can enter a state with near Attention Deficit Disorder (ADD)-like symptoms. You may have seen this in yourself and others—being so busy you feel "scattered." Well, it's not just a feeling—you *are* scattered. Your brain functionality is dropping. Dr. Hallowell asserts in this article, and in a book he later wrote called *Crazy Busy*, that as we make a habit of this, the degraded brain functionality can grow worse, month after month.

Managing tasks using urgency zones as taught here can balance these imbalances in our chaotic day. It does this simply by bringing to the surface underlying distinctions in task urgency, and placing them right in plain view. That way we clearly identify what truly requires our intense focus, and use such focus only on those items; we can relax appropriately on the rest.

### Using the "Paper" System

Let's go over three of the urgency zones in more detail now and look at how you can use them in a workable day-to-day task system. You will see you were *already* using them to some extent in your paper Workday Mastery To-Do List from Chapter 2, if you have started and continued using that tool.

By the way, recall that when I mentioned in Chapter 2 that this system can be used on paper, I also mentioned you could create the system in any computer program that allows you to make lists. Depending on how much you sit at your computer, you may in fact want to create, view, and edit these lists entirely within such a program. Or, if you leave your computer a lot for meetings, you can print them out to carry throughout the day. In that case you can make small edits on the paper with a pen, and if needed, enter those edits periodically back in the computer version and then reprint the clean version as desired. Or just use the computer to print blank templates and refresh them by hand weekly. Clearly there are a number of options here for you; I leave it to you to decide which option to take. You may want to try this a few different ways and see what feels right to you over time.

No matter which approach you decide to use, if you have not done the Quick Start exercise from Chapter 2, stop now and create the Workday Mastery To-Do List identified there (either in a computer or purely on paper). The details below will improve on that introduction greatly, and make this system fully usable.

## Critical Now Tasks—Your Most Urgent Focus

The first and most important urgency zone I call the Critical Now zone. It sits at the top of page 1 of the Workday Mastery To-Do List. To see it in our conveyor-belt model from Chapter 4, we need to modify that model as follows. I am going to draw a line just to the right of where the man is standing on the conveyor belt, about one-fifth of the way across the belt; Figure 5.1 shows that updated model. This line represents the typical deadline for things you may be currently working on or worried about. For most knowledge workers in most

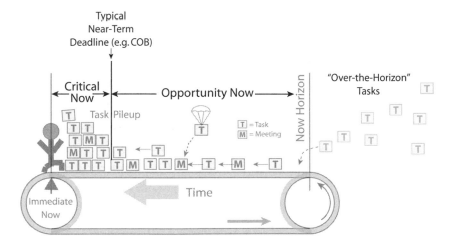

**Figure 5.1** Urgency zones.

industries, this deadline is typically at the close of the current business day (COB), but it varies across industries.

Naturally, tasks due inside that time frame have most of your attention and urgency. They probably have most of your anxiety as well. It is here where the typical task pileup occurs, which leads to missed deadlines and opportunities. Tasks due inside the Critical Now period I call Critical Now tasks.

For example, if your boss states firmly that he wants a report done by the end of today, that's a Critical Now task. If you absolutely must get a proposal to a client of yours by end of day, that's another Critical Now task. If a task created weeks ago is due today, it has now become a Critical Now task.

If you think back to your Workday Mastery To-Do List Level 1 from Chapter 2, this urgency zone occupies the upper part of page 1. First thing in the morning, you should brainstorm and populate that list with items due that day so you can track them and complete them in time. If your boss stops you in the hall and adds a new task due today, immediately add it to that section of your list. If any urgent e-mail requests come in with actions due today, you will want to immediately write a summary of the action requested on that list. Any aging tasks that have now become due, you should place on that list today.

More importantly, you should be very selective about what you put on that list. If you guard it carefully and use it only for true deadline tasks, then you can reduce to a minimum the number of truly urgent actions you take, thus reducing unneeded stress.

Once that list is created, you will want to check it often throughout the day, perhaps even hourly, to make sure you complete all such urgent work before the end of the day. As you start to leave at the end of the day, the last thing you should do is glance at that list to be sure it is all completed and that you can "safely" leave. Using this urgency zone on your paper list in this way is a phenomenal way of adding clarity to your day. I'll talk more about this zone in the next chapter; but what you have here is enough for now.

### Opportunity Now Tasks—Work Them More Comfortably

The next urgency zone I call the Opportunity Now zone. Tasks there represent everything else inside your Workday Now—in other words, everything other than tasks absolutely due today. In the conveyor-belt model they sit to the right of the Critical Now deadline, but to the left of the Now Horizon (review Figure 5.1, which I showed you a few pages back). Essentially, these are all the noncritical tasks that you are aware of and know you need to do soon, or as soon as is practical. However, since your urgent focus is on Critical Now tasks, you'd only do these less-urgent tasks if the right opportunity were presented to you, thus the name of the zone. For example, say the right person came by, or you had an inspired moment, or you completed all your urgent work; these are all opportunities that might lead you to work these tasks. In the Workday Mastery To-Do List, these tasks are written in the lower section of page 1.

Some practical examples of these tasks might be "Read and sign sales contract" that is due in five days; or "Complete HR request for new staff" that is due end-of-week.

Clearly, these are things you might need to do *within a few days;* however, you admit you are likely to not get to them *today* since other, more urgent, matters are pressing, and so you mark them accordingly by placing them in this section.

But note this: due to the right-to-left flow of the conveyor belt, these items may become critical if you put them off too long, so you want to keep your eye on them. Therefore, you should scan this list at least once or twice per day to see if any tasks there become eligible to fit into the day, or to see if any of them have jumped in urgency.

I will cover this zone in more detail in the next chapter, but the principles above should enable you to get started using it now.

### Over-the-Horizon Tasks—Chill Out

Any tasks to the right of the Now Horizon, beyond your current consideration, are called Over-the-Horizon tasks (see right side of Figure 5.1). By definition, you are not very concerned about them. There are exceptions, of course; there might be a big event a month out on your calendar that captures part of your attention. But regarding your current day-to-day responsibilities, you do not think much about these tasks.

These are your slower-burn tasks. Examples might be cleaning up your client list, starting a project due in one month, or even reading an article your colleague sent you. Some of them might be *important;* they just are not very *timely* for this week or next. You want them out of mind for now, given all else that is currently on your plate, but you *do* want to reconsider them later because many of these might become more urgent over time.

In the Workday Mastery To-Do List, these were tasks placed on page 2. You will review these tasks weekly to see if the time has come for any of these, or if any have jumped in importance due to changing business conditions. If any do jump, you should move them to page 1, into the appropriate section.

The fact that you need to check this list only once a week clears a great amount of management effort and concern from your workday. It helps keep your daily focus clear and unfettered.

In fact, in the next chapter, I discuss how to effectively move even more items into this zone to keep your workday relatively stress free.

Again, all these task types are shown in Figure 5.1.

Now that you understand these zones, think again about the Quick Start activity you did at the beginning of Chapter 2. I hope you now see the mapping between your Workday Mastery To-Do List and the mental model. Does your current written task list still make sense to you? Given these more complete

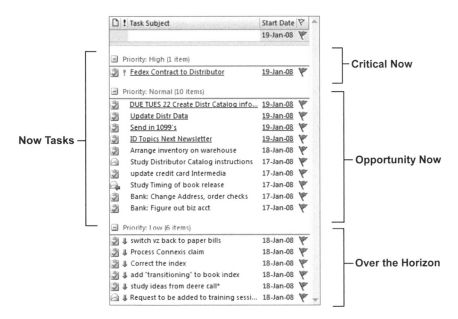

**Figure 5.2**    Urgency zones applied in a reconfigured Microsoft Outlook task window.

definitions, you may want to stop here and adjust your list, putting items in more appropriate places.

And if you are considering the Microsoft Outlook approach per my Outlook book, Figure 5.2 shows how these zones map into a reconfigured Outlook.

# Managing in the Urgency Zones

One thing you will see about this model is that everything is always in reference to Now. You know your Now is constantly changing; priorities change, events take over, time goes on. If you follow the basic management principles above, and ones I'm about to share, this system will reflect that constant change and keep your Now under control. As I stated at the end of the last chapter, you are essentially "surfing" these urgency zones as the days move by. Ultimately, that is why this system works so well; it is always up to date, nearly automatically.

We'll describe in the next chapters some fine points of how to manage within each of these urgency zones. For now, use the two most important rules, the ones you learned in the Quick Start and that I will repeat now.

## *The Two Most Important System Rules*

- First, only place items in the Critical Now list if they pass the going-home test: Would you work late into the night to complete these if they were not done? If no, do not put the item on the list. This stringent test will reduce that list to a very reasonable size—you will rarely have more than three to five items on the Critical Now list—and usually fewer. That greatly reduces your daily stress level, and allows you to focus better.

- The second management technique is to keep the Opportunity Now Tasks list to fewer than 20 items by moving the lowest-priority items to the Over-the-Horizon list. This represents a Control-layer activity and is probably the hardest part of the process, but it must be done to keep the list usable.

## *The Now Tasks List: All Your Concerns in One Small List*

Notice that at the top of page 1 of the Workday Mastery To-Do List I've labeled the two major zones—the Critical Now zone and the Opportunity Now zone—as *Now Tasks*. I call the tasks in this combined list your Now Tasks list because that's the list of everything you need to have on (or near) your mind right now; these are the tasks eligible to do right now. This is page 1 of your paper system. Once you start using the system, you'll see that it is very refreshing to know that everything you need to be concerned about is in one small list (fewer than 25 items). It is a phenomenally liberating feeling. It greatly reduces workday stress, and greatly increases the likelihood that you will get home at a reasonable hour.

By the way, Figure 5.2 shows how, in the Outlook version of this system, Now Tasks occupy the top two groups of tasks.

Here's another reason the Workday Mastery To-Do List is so useful: equally important to knowing what is on your list (the Now Tasks list) is the knowledge that there is nothing urgent that is *not* on this list. By having a list like this that you trust and can glance at quickly, you have mentally eliminated the sharks that might be lurking just off your peripheral vision, ones you think are there, but since you cannot see them, you worry they might take a bite out of you. Once you can clearly see your responsibilities for the day, it's a lot less scary. If you can see all your tasks neatly lined up in front of you, they look less like sharks and more like a line of trained pedigree dogs that do not bite—ones that are just waiting for your command. This is why, with a good system like this, even though you may not be "getting it all done" you can still feel good about your work and about your important accomplishments, and about going home on time.

### Urgency Based, Not Importance Based

Again, I want to mention and emphasize that this is an urgency-based management system, not an importance-based one. It's not that importance is not important; it's just that attempting to use importance as your primary decision tool in an urgency-based office environment usually leads to failure. Our frank admittance of the harsh reality that urgency rules the workday in most office environments these days allows us to provide this workable management solution.

You see, the theme of Part I is working within the Control layer to manage your Workday Now, to manage your experience of work. As I said earlier, the Control layer is all about basic management styles, such as, "Do this and you will be rewarded," "Don't do this or you will be punished." Working within the urgency zones is very much a Control-layer activity. The idea is to make a list of things you must do today (or you will not leave work), and then just get them done. And then a list of things you would *like* to get done, probably because they are work items you have committed to. With the time you free up by gaining this control, you'll then be able to use the more "enlightened" approaches in the next phase, Part II, where I talk about goals and how to set and achieve them. But for now, knowing that this level of self-management—focusing on urgency first—is needed and in place will help you get your workday under control.

## Intrinsic Importance: Rising Above Urgency

Even though I state this system is not importance based, you *can* apply an importance classification on top of this urgency-based system if you like, right here in the Control-layer system. It does not replace the urgency focus, but gives you additional information to use when choosing which tasks to do next.

But first you may ask, what do I mean by importance, now that urgency is considered separately? Well, once you separate out urgency, or the time element, from the measure of a task's importance, what is left behind is what I call *intrinsic importance.* It is a measure of the timeless value of the item to you. The best way to say this is, it measures how strongly a task relates to your ongoing important needs, desires, aspirations, core values, goals, life visions, and so on.

In the Outlook version of the system, I offered an optional column where you could score the intrinsic importance of a task from one to nine (nine being highest); this allowed you to see easily which tasks on your list might have more core value to you. I invite you to do that as well within this paper system if you like, by placing numbers next to your written tasks, and perhaps only against high-importance tasks. That way, as you scan tasks on the list, you may favor the ones with higher intrinsic importance.

So, for example, page 1 of your paper task system might list tasks like those shown in Figure 5.3.

The point of the numbers on that list is to direct your eye first to the more important items so you can consider them first. Note I said "consider them first," not "do them first." These numbers are not a commitment to the order in which you will do tasks—they only provide additional information.

That is because this is an *overlay* to the urgency structure, not a replacement for it. For example, you would never sort on that number across all your tasks— the urgency zones should remain your primary grouping. As I stated before,

**Figure 5.3**    Intrinsic importance notation example.

## Critical Now

- Send e-mail to team about upcoming conference

9 - Submit new goals list for review

## Opportunity Now

8 - Reply to HR request for staffing forecast

- Send meeting notes to Jane for distribution

9 - Apply for Director's position

7 - Start performance review format design

- Reply to e-mail from Stan on survey of user groups

6 - Schedule next project manager team meeting

importance-only task systems just do not work well in an urgency-driven environment. The primary need in an urgency-driven office environment is to manage the urgency, and that's what the system presented so far does. In fact, each time my colleagues and I use the intrinsic importance overlay described above, we usually end up ignoring the intrinsic importance scores, and give up on them over time. The urgency-based system is just so much more effective.

# Summary

Based on the Workday Now time period identified in Chapter 4, you can identify three key urgency zones and corresponding task-types within your present and future schedule: the Critical Now, Opportunity Now, and Over the Horizon. You will recall these were the task sections used in your Quick Start Workday Mastery To-Do List in Chapter 2. You enter tasks that are absolutely due today in the Critical Now section, tasks due in the next week or so in the Opportunity Now section (which you will keep to 20 items or fewer), and tasks due after 1.5 weeks on the Over-the-Horizon page—page 2 of your paper system.

The significant jump in productivity from this system comes from the fact that you now know how to use those zones to manage your work focus more appropriately. Specifically, you now know to check the Critical Now list many times a day, perhaps even hourly, so that very urgent items can be tracked closely. This prevents end-of day rushes or total misses of urgent tasks. The shortness of this list helps keep your intense focus only where needed, thus reducing the "everything is a fire" fervor we can sometimes get into.

You now know you will scan the complete Opportunity Now list once or twice a day—this allows you to work lower-priority tasks into the holes in your day, and lets you track near-urgent tasks with adequate care.

And you know you can ignore the larger Over-the-Horizon tasks list for up to a week at a time, which removes considerable unneeded distraction from your day-to-day work. On your weekly review of that list you are looking for jumps in urgency—if you find any, you will move those tasks to page 1 of your two-page paper task system and work them accordingly from there.

In this system, having such a clear and accurate delineation of urgency greatly reduces workday anxiety by focusing your daily work much more appropriately. Each day you just need to study your well-controlled short list (fewer than 25 items) called the Now Tasks list—page 1 of the Workday Mastery To-Do List—and work only those that are needed. In fact, each day you will only be really worried about the top 3 to 5 items—the Critical Now items; tasks worked after those are optional and can be done in a more relaxed stance. What a huge sense of relief and control this will bring to what otherwise could be an overwhelming workday!

I encourage you to use what you have learned so far for a few days within the paper template you started in Chapter 2. This way you can get familiar with the simple rules of use. Then, when you are ready, move on to Chapter 6, where you will drill down on the system, learning some additional elements and finer points that will help you get even more control of your workday, right now.

CHAPTER **6**

# Mastering Your Urgency Zones

In the Quick Start portion of this book (Chapter 2), I gave you a brief overview of how to use a paper list to implement the Workday Mastery To-Do List. In Chapter 5, I showed you how to use that system in detail.

The Workday Mastery To-Do List (Level 1) system consists of two paper pages, set up as in the diagram below. The top section of the first page is for your Critical Now tasks, tasks urgently due today. And the second section of the

---

**Now Tasks List**

**Critical Now** (must do today)
  -Send Artwork to Mary for review
  -Complete book review writeups
  -Set meeting with Suzanne
  -Call Ted regarding print quote

**Opportunity Now**
(start this week or next, review list daily)

  -Start arlternate printing quotes
  -Study joint venture opportunities
  -Call Donna re: review service
  -Decide on interview timeline
  -Figure out who does print media
  -Decide on new website url
  -Create quotes list
  -Schedule copyeditor next phase
  -Discuss YouTube strategy with Penny
  -Update project schedule

**Over the Horizon** (Review Weekly)

  -Investigate galley printing options
  -Find overseas licensing options
  -Find painter for house
  -Designer for new office space
  -Set meeting with planning commision on streets
  -Decide on Spring party venue
  -Create manual for invoice processing
  -Find copyeditor for ad hoc work on newsletters
  -Invite insurance salesperson to next monthly mtg
  -Identify best sources of temp staffing
  -Create hiring plan for next quarter
  -Call Office Depot about bulk purchases
  -Conference room furniture: replace
  -Set meeting with executive committee re: planning
  -Buy books for library
  -Assign Printing project to Sally

first page is for your Opportunity Now tasks, tasks due in a week or so. These two sections together are called your Now Tasks, since they are all eligible to do now, given enough time. That page provides one reasonably short list to put your primary attention on at work.

The second page of the Workday Mastery To-Do List is for your Over-the-Horizon tasks, tasks that you keep only cursory awareness of by checking in on them only once a week.

If you have had a chance to use that system for a few days or more, you have seen that the system is very simple and lightweight; it requires just a few pages you can easily carry in your pocket, planner, or handbag. Each day you will use the same sheets of paper and just modify them as needed to update new or completed tasks. You may find that you want to replace the front page periodically, because it will get a bit cluttered with completed and rearranged tasks, but other than that, you could get by with the same pages for days or weeks at a time. Compared to the thick planner-style binders many people use, this system will feel very refreshing. And if you do carry a paper calendar, you can easily slip these two pages into the front of that calendar set.

Let's review and then elaborate a bit on the main segments of the Workday Now task solution. By the way, if you have not done the Quick Start in Chapter 2 yet, please turn back and do that now, and then restudy Chapter 5. That way, you'll be ready for what follows.

## More about the Critical Now

The Critical Now section is for those tasks absolutely due today. Using it is simple but remarkably powerful. Let me tell you the story about how I first came to start using it and why it turned out to be such an important way to delineate tasks.

About seven years ago, just before I developed this system, I moved from a senior consulting role in a large company called Accenture into the role of Vice President of Technology for a new Accenture company. In that new role I found myself consistently putting in 12-hour workdays, and I was not happy about that. After a little self-analysis I found one root cause was that I tended to start work on important actions only after I got out of all my daily meetings, usually around 5:00 p.m. Before 5:00, I was so busy in meetings that I did not really know all that was due that day. It was not until I finally examined my meeting notes, my sticky notes, and my various to-do lists that I usually discovered a number of critical deliverables for the day. As a result, a major portion of my workday actually started at 5:00, and I had to work late nearly every day to get those tasks done. Of course I wrote this off to the reality of all the meetings a senior executive tends to have. But actually, that was not the core problem.

## Virtual Assistant

One way to illustrate the core problem is this. If I had an assistant who chased me around all day and collected my commitments, and then reminded me early in the day of things I had promised to complete that day, I probably would complete those tasks earlier. Knowing and seeing the list early, I would make the time to ensure that my promises were completed earlier in the day.

What I recognized was that without clear focus, I became a bit lazy about working tasks during the day. Instead I just went to meetings, reacted to phone calls and interruptions, and attended to my BlackBerry or e-mail, all day long. I consistently expected I would dig out of my task commitments later, after the hustle and bustle of the day had ended. By doing this, however, I was letting lower-priority items rule my day and ignoring my high-priority commitments. And I was extending my workday.

A sharp focus on current important commitments for the day is exactly what the Critical Now process gives you: a way to clearly record and easily see at a glance what your critical list for today is and to facilitate getting items on that list done early. I cannot emphasize enough how useful this is.

## The Critical Now (Must-Do-Today) Process

The Critical Now process is simple, deceptively so. From prior days, and then early in this day and throughout the day, identify urgent things that absolutely must get done today and enter them as tasks in the Critical Now section. First thing in the morning, review your Opportunity Now list, and if any tasks listed there are due today, move them to the Critical Now section. Reserve the Critical Now section only for items absolutely due today.

Then, throughout the day, glance at that list often, perhaps three or four times, even hourly, and ensure that you get all Critical Now tasks done as early as possible. To work those tasks, use either dedicated task time or gaps in your day. If necessary, use part of your lunchtime or time freed up by skipping a low-value meeting. Just try to get them done early.

That way, when the normal end of your workday arrives (whatever that is in your office), your critical commitments are done. With this new process, you will likely have the option to leave work on time most days of the week. Or if you decide to work late, you do so only to work on discretionary tasks, not because you have to stay. Working late in that case actually gets you ahead, instead of merely caught up. You will be able to control your workflow and your workday—not the other way around.

---

### Paper Planner Option

If you use a planning binder with daily pages, you might consider the following alternate way to emphasize Critical Now tasks. Copy your Critical Now tasks onto the current daily page in your planner. That will give them extra focus. It also allows you to schedule Critical Now tasks ahead to the future as appropriate.

---

Knowledge that using the system will get my pressing tasks done at a reasonable time is what makes this aspect of the system self-sustaining for me; when I look at my Critical Now task list I might think to myself, "If I get these done, I can make it to the gym today"—or if I am trying to get a leg up on my career and will be working late— "I can focus tonight on that new idea I had." In either case it is incredibly motivating. This also motivates me to find and write these tasks down throughout the day; I become somewhat obsessive about identifying them since I know these are what may sabotage my later plans.

By the way, when you do get these tasks done early, you have a sense of being ahead of the curve, which is a very nice feeling to have. It changes your whole work attitude and greatly reduces your level of stress. Work after that point feels more proactive, more self-motivated.

Also, by creating this list early in the day and managing it throughout the day, you should be able to tell early if your critical list really will exceed your capacity to complete it that day. That gives you time to reach out to stakeholders early and get permission to extend their deadlines, or compromise on the delivery. This avoids the sickening anxiety that can occur when the day's true deadlines tumble down on you late in the day, and it prevents an angry line of stakeholders from forming at your desk when you are trying to leave.

### Do Not Abuse

But be sure not to abuse this Critical Now category. It is easy to move items into the Critical Now section just because you are enthusiastic about them. This category is only for urgent items that must be completed today. The simple test I provided earlier is this. Ask yourself, "Would I work late tonight to complete this item if it is not finished by the normal end of the workday?" If the answer is "no," then do not put it in the Critical Now section. Instead, mark it as an Opportunity Now task.

Again, be conservative when using Critical Now priority. If a Critical Now task remains in that section for two or more days straight, what does that tell you about how seriously you are taking the phrase "must do today"? I usually have only two or three items in that section, perhaps occasionally up to five. If you have more, I suspect you have missed the point of the Critical Now section.

### Don't Confuse "Must Do Today" with "Important to Me"

Keeping the count small in the Critical Now priority section is essential; overloading it artificially will destroy its utility. One reason many new users load up the Critical Now priority section with too many tasks is they confuse the must-do-today concept with the thought, "This is important to me."

For example, I might really want to read an interesting *Wall Street Journal* article my colleague sent me about office productivity, and I am so excited about it I am tempted to mark it as Critical Now. However, unless it is time-critical for today, I need to keep it out of the Critical Now section. Instead, I use the optional Target Now section (described next) for tasks like those.

Some tasks are important but not urgent, and that can be good to know too. In this system those tasks are said to have high intrinsic importance, which I described at the end of Chapter 5. They link strongly to your goals and values. Again, you can mark those if you wish, as I showed in Chapter 5. But for now, unless tasks have an urgent deadline of today, keep them out of the Critical Now priority section of the system.

### Critical Now Next Actions

Another reason people load up nonactionable items that linger from day to day in their Critical Now section is they fail to delineate a task's next action. They put too large an item in the Critical Now section. You'll learn more about next actions later in this part of the book, but, in short, it is better to define for today only the small portion of a large task that you know you can and need to get done today. So instead of writing, "Quarterly Report Project," write, "Send e-mail to team about Quarterly Report." That task you can knock off quickly, and it really may be the only part of the project that is urgent for today.

## The Optional Target Now Urgency Zone

There is an optional subsection of the Opportunity Now urgency zone you may want to use in the paper system. It is identifying and using the urgency zone called Target Now tasks. Target Now tasks are Opportunity Now tasks that you would *very much like to do today.* Getting them done now might make a client happy or ease the timing on downstream tasks. Or perhaps you are just very enthusiastic about the task. In essence, they are your most important Opportunity Now tasks (see the left side of the Opportunity Now section in Figure 6.1). They are not absolutely due today, so they do not pass the test for the Critical Now, but they are likely the very first Opportunity Now tasks you will work on today, once other urgent items are out of the way. And they may be the very first Opportunity Now tasks that will graduate to Critical Now status if you ignore them too long (as the conveyor-belt flow in Figure 6.1 implies), another reason to do them first after today's Critical Now list.

I did not include these in the Workday Mastery To-Do List used so far (Level 1) because they represent an optional part of the system and could at first be confusing. But you may find this delineation useful and want to add it to the system, as shown ahead in Figure 6.3. This is Level 2 of the Workday Mastery To-Do List.

As an example of a Target Now task, I may very much want to write an e-mail to a prospective client today since the timing is right, but I would not

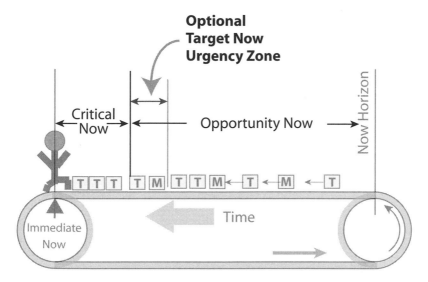

**Figure 6.1**   Delineating the optional Target Now urgency zone.

do it at the expense of a critical closing effort I am doing today. I want to *target* that e-mail for today since the timing is ideal, but I won't work late to do it.

This Target Now list sits at the top of the Opportunity Now tasks list, and so these are the first tasks you see when you scan that list daily.

If you are using the Outlook task system, my recommended way to show these in Outlook is to set a Normal priority task with today's start date on it. This, per configurations in my Outlook book, causes the tasks to be underlined and placed at the top of the Normal priority section, where they stand out nicely. Figure 6.2 shows that.

In a paper system like the one described in this book, there are a couple of ways to do this.

First, if you are using Level 1 of the Workday Mastery To-Do List, do this: modify the front page of your paper task system so that you create an additional section at the top of the Opportunity Now section. It ought to be either the same size as or just slightly larger than the Critical Now section. Title it Target Now, as shown in Figure 6.3. Check my website also; I will have page templates for you to download and print out, including ones suitable for use with MindManager.

**Figure 6.2**
Target Now urgency zone in Microsoft Outlook.

**Target Now**

Task Subject
Start Date
19-Jan-08
Priority: High (1 item)
Fedex Contract to Distributor 19-Jan-08
Priority: Normal (10 items)
DUE TUES 22 Create Distr Catalog info... 19-Jan-08
Update Distr Data 19-Jan-08
Send in 1099's 19-Jan-08
ID Topics Next Newsletter 19-Jan-08
Arrange inventory on warehouse 18-Jan-08
Study Distributor Catalog instructions 17-Jan-08
update credit card Intermedia 17-Jan-08
Study Timing of book release 17-Jan-08
Bank: Change Address, order checks 17-Jan-08
Bank: Figure out biz acct 17-Jan-08
Priority: Low (6 items)
switch vz back to paper bills 18-Jan-08
Process Connexis claim 18-Jan-08
Correct the index 18-Jan-08
add "transitioning" to book index 18-Jan-08
study ideas from deere call* 18-Jan-08
Request to be added to training sessi... 18-Jan-08


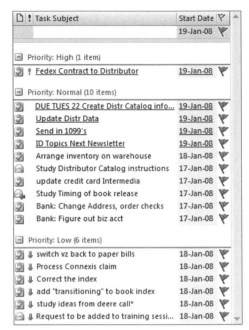

**Figure 6.3**
Target Now added to the Workday Mastery To-Do List (Level 2).

**Target Now**

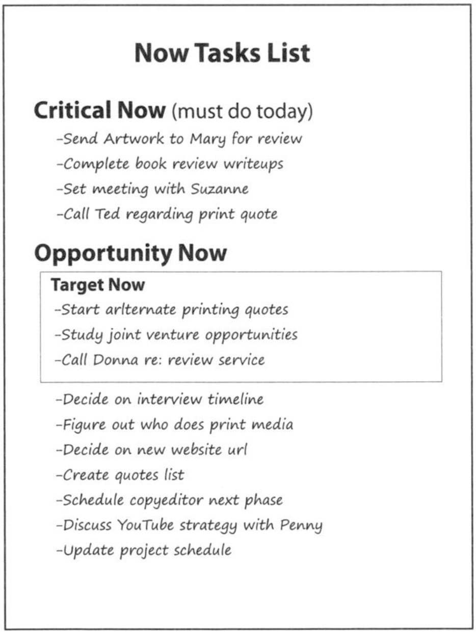

Now Tasks List
Critical Now (must do today)
-Send Artwork to Mary for review
-Complete book review writeups
-Set meeting with Suzanne
-Call Ted regarding print quote
Opportunity Now
Target Now
-Start arlternate printing quotes
-Study joint venture opportunities
-Call Donna re: review service
-Decide on interview timeline
-Figure out who does print media
-Decide on new website url
-Create quotes list
-Schedule copyeditor next phase
-Discuss YouTube strategy with Penny
-Update project schedule

Target Now tasks require maintenance since you need to reset the list each day. Because of that, many users of my system decide not to include it. But if the Opportunity Now section gets large, it can be a very useful way to focus your daily task time.

---

**Paper Planner Option**

If you use a planning binder with daily pages, you might consider the following alternate way to emphasize Target Now tasks, which is similar to what I suggested above for Critical Now tasks. On each daily page you can create a section called Target Now, just below your Critical Now section, and each day copy any target tasks from your main Opportunity Now list into that section. See Figure 6.5, ahead, for how that looks. Note I said *copy*. I want to make sure you still have a copy of that task on your main two-page list. That's because it is too easy to lose optional tasks in the older pages of a daily planner; you want to maintain these items on your main list.

---

## More about the Opportunity Now

As I said above, Target Now tasks are your most important Opportunity Now tasks. And, as you know by now, Opportunity Now tasks are tasks that are not due today but that you would like to get to this week or next. These are tasks that you work as the opportunity arises and time allows, and presumably after you have finished your Critical Now (and optional Target Now) tasks. They are not scheduled for any particular day because most of these do not have deadlines. In fact, I assert that almost no ad hoc, next-action tasks have deadlines. They are usually smaller steps to larger outcomes that themselves have the deadlines. So let's talk about deadlines for a moment.

### Most Tasks Do Not Have Deadlines

Somewhere during the history of task management training, someone created a rule that said, "Assign a due date to all tasks. If you do not assign a due date to a task, it won't get done." That rule sounds good, doesn't it? It sounds so *proactive*. That is why nearly all paper task templates and automated task systems these days include a due date field.

But I feel this is not a good rule. Why? Because the way the rule is usually used, which is to set artificial due dates on most tasks, is an attempt to trick yourself, and you are not so easily tricked. It reminds me of the person I once knew who set their wristwatch ahead ten minutes, thinking it would help them be on time to meetings. In reality, it only worked for a couple of days and then the person just mentally adjusted and started being late to meetings again. You do the same with artificial due dates; you just start to ignore them. Also, it can actually lead to more missed deadlines, because as you start to skip deadlines that you know are false, you suffer from the "cry wolf" phenomenon. Since most of your tasks have fake due dates, you get used to skipping them, and then you may not recognize a true due date when you see it, and you may skip that. Like Little Red Riding Hood, you get eaten alive, but in this case by missed deadlines.

That does not mean you should not apply a true deadline to those tasks that really have them, particularly those imposed from the outside (from your client or boss, for example); there are appropriate times to set true deadlines. And for those, use the technique I showed in the Quick Start: place the date right in the task name like this: DUE Aug 4 Status Report. Then when the deadline day arrives for any task, move the task up to the Critical Now section first thing in the morning, so you are sure to get it done that day.

But again, use deadlines only when they are true deadlines, not artificially. If you are entering next-action tasks, deadlines will likely be appropriate for only a few of your tasks.

---

**Refining Your List**

An extension to the deadline notation process is this one (it works only if you use a full-sized paper list): On the paper page, in addition to adding the DUE notation when you write the task down, place tasks that have a deadline later in the week on the right side of the Opportunity Now section, and position deadline tasks due early in the week flush left. If a task has an end-of-week deadline, but you want to start working on it early in the week, keep the task on the left.

## Opportunity Now List Grows Quickly

One of the harsh realities we discussed in Chapter 4 was how we will always have more to do than we can possibly do. I know that is true for me. Even though I am my own boss, I always think of more to do than I can do; I always bite off more than I can chew. I expect your world is like that as well, and it is especially true if you have one or more supervisors. As professionals and dynamic individuals, you and the people you work with will be constantly thinking of new things for you to do.

One result is that in an environment with constantly changing priorities, it is likely that when you start to work tasks on your Opportunity Now list, other urgent events may take over part or much of your day and you will not get the originally targeted list done; that is to be expected.

As a result, you will often be delaying nondeadline tasks to later, as other more important or more inspired items drop in ahead of them. I feel it is okay to delay tasks without hard deadlines; priorities and inspirations change, and you should react accordingly to the new priorities. Feel no regrets when you delay such a task; just allow it to sit on the Opportunity Now list a little bit longer.

Of course, as uncompleted tasks remain on your list from day to day, and you add new tasks each day, that list will grow. You will quickly reach a list size that is larger than what you can possibly consider in a given day. And that is good, to a point. It is good because you want your Now Tasks list to be a reasonably large list of tasks that you can pick from, using your business intuition about what is best to do that day. Having a choice like that increases the chance that you are picking the highest-priority things to do that day. Doing that also allows you to get the most urgent and useful work done each day, by having your prioritized list of top-candidate tasks visible at all times.

## The 20-Item Rule

But you do not want your Opportunity Now list to get *too* large. If you have too many tasks there, you will never scan the whole list and some important tasks might get dropped. And you may find the large size demoralizing. You need to keep the size of that list reasonable enough that it is not impossible to review and consider in one brief scan. I feel 20 tasks is the ideal upper limit for an Opportunity Now tasks list.

Keeping that list to 20 items may be the hardest part of this system. More than anything else in the system, this limit represents a Control-layer activity; it is work management by holding back and cutting out. It must be done to keep your list usable, and it is an appropriate activity for the Control layer. Let's talk more about that and the best way to do it.

First of all, this does not mean that once you reach 20 items you should stop adding tasks. No, you have to keep moving forward in work and life, keep the momentum of new ideas and passions going. So instead of stopping new tasks and ideas, you now need to start prioritizing your current and new tasks so that the 20 items left on your Opportunity Now list are your *best* ones, given current work priorities. You need to shorten it back down to 20 or so. The way to do that was discussed in the Quick Start section; you will move excess tasks to the Over-the-Horizon section until you get to 20 or fewer.

### The Simple "4-D" System: Do, Delete, Delegate, and Defer

In fact, if you have studied task management before, you may have noted that moving tasks to the Over-the-Horizon section actually represents one D of the standard "4-D" system of working tasks; it stands for Defer, which is one way to describe what you are doing when you move a task to the Over-the-Horizon section.

You might think the 4-D system would offer other ways to shorten your Opportunity Now list. However, in my opinion, the other "D's" are in fact not that helpful. Let's go over them briefly for completeness, since you may see this in many other resources on time and task management.

### Doing Tasks

The first entry in the standard 4-D approach is to Do the tasks. Of course this is an important choice, but if you are looking for ways to shorten a too-long Opportunity Now tasks list, I feel you would have done the task by now if it were doable and fit into your priorities; so this is not a very useful instruction to shorten a list.

### Deleting Tasks

If a task has lost all life, certainly delete it off your list. However, my experience is that very few tasks can be deleted early in their lives, so it is not a very good way of decreasing your Opportunity Now list either. I do not delete tasks unless I am confident they are really dead, and I usually delete them from within the Over-the-Horizon section, which is where my lowest-priority tasks end up.

## Delegating Tasks

Obviously, if you have staff or team members to delegate to and can do so, avail yourself of their help as a way to lighten your workload and reduce your effort on large tasks. But you still need to track delegated tasks, and you are ultimately responsible for them, so delegating does not really remove an entry from your list, it just reduces the amount of work you need to expend on it.

## Deferring Tasks

The last point, deferring tasks, is the only D that I really find useful as a way to decrease the size of a rapidly growing Opportunity Now task list. That's essentially what we're doing when we move the task to the Over-the-Horizon list. We are deciding that we will assess the task again later, and so we are putting it out of sight for now. In my opinion, of all the four D's, Deferring is the one you will most commonly want to use.

Keep in mind, though, if you are deferring a task that your boss or supervisor assigned you, or that you promised to a significant stakeholder, you should get approval from that person. One nice thing about having a clear list like the ones in this system is you can see what is coming and make the calls quickly. And if you are an administrative staff member who takes all your instructions from your supervisor, you can hand that list to your supervisor and say, "I need to keep this to 20 for this week. Which of these can I put off?" If they really have overloaded you, then this will put the burden on them to help you prioritize.

### *Review the Opportunity Now List Often*

You should review the entire Opportunity Now list daily, if not more often. Recall the conveyor belt model, where tasks are moving and changing in importance over time? Since many items in the Opportunity Now section are moving toward you on the conveyor belt in the model, some items on this list, if they go uncompleted too long, can become overdue Critical Now items. And even if that doesn't happen, with a list too big to review, knowing you haven't checked your full list for a while can lead to discomfort about what you might be overlooking. As I said earlier, it is often the unknown or poorly defined urgencies that are most destructive to our sense of well-being. That's why you want to make sure that section is no larger than what you can easily grasp in a quick visual scan; you want to see these items coming every day. Again, I recommend reducing that list so it has no more than 20 items, keeping your workload well visualized and potentially stress-free.

## Strategic Deferrals

So you will be using the Over-the-Horizon urgency zone as the place to put the least urgent tasks, once your Opportunity Now list gets over 20 items. I call this step "Tossing tasks over the Now Horizon" because in the context of the Workday Now mental model, that is what you are doing (see Figure 6.4).

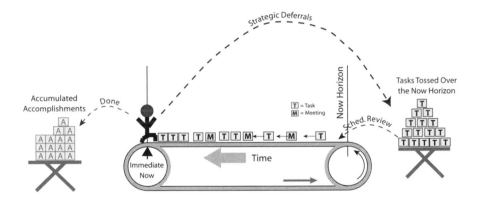

**Figure 6.4**   Tossing tasks over the Now Horizon.

By placing tasks there, you are essentially deferring the task to a task review at least one week out. When you do your next scheduled review of that section, you can decide whether the task needs current attention, or can be deferred even more.

I also have a formal name for this deferral process. I call it Strategic Deferral. Since we have only covered the process briefly so far, let's talk more about Strategic Deferral and the processes behind it. There is a lot more to it.

## The CEO Solution

One good way to talk about Strategic Deferral is to use what I call the CEO Solution.

Sometimes you hear about a CEO who decides to postpone projects or products their company is currently working on. The CEO often states, "We are doing this to allow the company to focus better on primary current priorities," or maybe, "We need to return to our company's core competencies." The CEO is usually hailed as "strategic," "decisive," or "practical," or as being capable of "making the hard choices." The CEO is not usually called a "procrastinator."

Similarly, when you postpone focus on certain tasks on your list because you honestly have too much on your plate, take pride in your decision. Do not think of yourself as weak or procrastinating; rather, think of yourself as making strategic choices. Think of yourself as being the CEO of your own workday.

I'm sure you've heard the commonly quoted story, that when on your deathbed if you were asked what you wished you had done more of in your life, you would not say, "more work at the office." The point is that when measured against life priorities, tasks at work are pretty low.

I bring this up because, in the greater scheme of things, for most job functions there is much more leeway on which action requests (including your own) you can choose to just not do. Once you put the frenzy aside and ask yourself, "What really will happen if I don't do this right now?" you will see that a lot of tasks can fall out, if you choose to let them.

Some people make a career out of ignoring requests, and they get a bad reputation for it. I am not suggesting you take that approach. Their problem is they ignore even important requests. But once you have a system for clearly prioritizing tasks, it is remarkable how many low-priority tasks you can put off without doing any damage. Just be sure to use the Strategic Deferral process. With this process you will defer intelligently, usually beyond your Now Horizon, with stakeholder approval, and using a scheduled review process so the deferral is done in a responsible way.

## Defer-to-Do: Deferring a Task to a Specific Date

There are two kinds of Strategic Deferrals in the Workday Now task solution: Defer-to-Do and Defer-to-Review. Let's start with Defer-to-Do since we have not talked about that yet. Compared to Defer-to-Review, you will use Defer-to-Do relatively rarely, but here's how.

Defer-to-Do tasks are tasks that you defer to a *specific* day on which you *really intend to do them.* On that future day, a Defer-to-Do task most likely becomes a Critical Now task, one you must do. Or it might become an Opportunity Now task that you very much want to do that day. (If you are using the optional Target Now tasks, it becomes one of those.)

As an example, let's say you have a task, "Write weekly status report." This task you may think of and record on Tuesday, but it's not due till Friday afternoon, and you know it won't take too long to do. You know Friday is relatively open so you want to do it that day, and you do not want to think about it until then; in fact, since it is a weekly status report for that week, you won't even have enough data till Friday.

If you are using my Outlook system with my configurations, to do this you simply set the start date to the day you want to do it—Friday, in this case. The task disappears and then Friday morning it appears at the top of your Opportunity Now list.

Assuming you are not using the Outlook task system, you have a couple of choices for using the Workday Mastery To-Do List.

One is this: if you carry a paper monthly or weekly calendar, write the task on your calendar for that day, indicating somehow that it is a task and not an appointment. Or if you carry a planner with one page for each day, just write the task on the Friday page in the tasks section.

In either case, continue to use the two-page Workday Mastery To-Do List as your primary task list, and only use the daily pages or calendar for Defer-to-Do tasks like this.

Also, be sure to mark whether the Defer-to-Do task you copy there is *critical* for today or if you merely want to consider it that day. If you carry a planner binder with a dedicated page for each day, use the approach I mentioned earlier: in the task section of that page, place deferred Critical Now tasks at the top of the task section and deferred Opportunity Now (Target Now) at the bottom (see Figure 6.5). Note: See my website, MasterYourWorkday.com, for availability of paper planner pages that are designed for use with this system.

**Figure 6.5**
Optional daily
planner page.

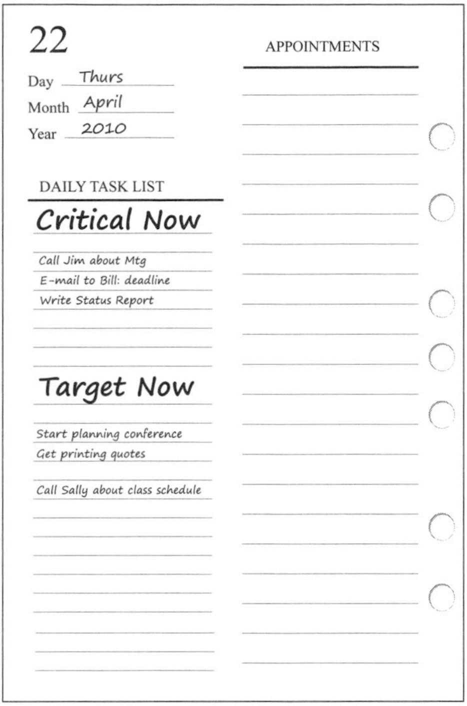

| 22 | APPOINTMENTS |
| --- | --- |

Day _Thurs_
Month _April_
Year _2010_

DAILY TASK LIST
*Critical Now*

Call Jim about Mtg
E-mail to Bill: deadline
Write Status Report

*Target Now*

Start planning conference
Get printing quotes

Call Sally about class schedule

If you do not carry a calendar or set of daily task pages, another way to create a Defer-to-Do task in your two-page system is to place it in the Opportunity Now section with the word *TARGET* and date in front of the task description. For example, "TARGET Apr-4: Call Fred About May Conference." You may want to place that near the bottom of the Opportunity Now section if the date is a ways off. Then move it into your Target Now section when that date arrives.

So in summary, Defer-to-Do tasks are tasks you defer to a specific day on which you really intend to do them.

## Defer-to-Review

Next, let's cover Defer-to-Review. This name is the formal name of what I taught in the Quick Start: placing tasks on the Over-the-Horizon list for later review. We covered much of that already, but there is more to it.

Defer-to-Review tasks are tasks you merely want to put off for a while. You are doing this primarily because you have too much on your plate right now and want to get these out of sight. As discussed before, it is important that you reduce your Opportunity Now list to fewer than 20 items. For various reasons, you cannot or will not do, delete, or delegate these excess tasks, so tossing them out of sight is your best solution. For Defer-to-Review tasks, you have no specific day in mind on which you intend to do them, so you are simply deferring them to a future weekly review. In that review you will reassess their urgency.

There are two ways to create a Defer-to-Review task. The first way is what you've seen so far: placing all Defer-to-Review tasks on a single page called Over-the-Horizon tasks. This is what I recommend you start with, and what you should use for a month or two after starting to use the system.

But eventually this approach will stop working. Why? Because the Over-the-Horizon page will get so many tasks on it that you will not want to review it. Let me explain.

Have you ever used a system that included a single Master Tasks list? That's essentially what the Over-the-Horizon page is. It's one long list of all your excess tasks. In my first version of the system I also used a Master Tasks list, but I abandoned it for a newer approach, which I'll show you in a moment.

Why did I abandon the Master Tasks list? Because I found that most people did not succeed with a scheduled review of a very large Master Tasks list. If you put an appointment on your calendar to review your Master Tasks and you're a very busy person, you'll skip that review meeting every time.

Why? Two reasons. First, the list gets too big too quickly, so it becomes discouraging to review. Second, most of the items you review each week do not in fact need a review every week and you intuitively feel the time is wasted, and you start to skip the reviews.

Once users start skipping those reviews, I find they are reluctant to place tasks on the Master Tasks list at all (for fear they will lose sight of them), and instead leave them on their main task list (usually the Opportunity Now list), overloading it. The Opportunity Now task list then becomes unusable.

## Using Extended Review Cycles: Level 3 of the To-Do List

So at that point you should switch to the better way of doing Defer-to-Review, where you add the concept of "extended review cycles." Remember above I said that in a Master Tasks list approach, some items needed to be reviewed every week, but most did not? The extended review cycle method of Defer-to-Review takes this into account and simply asks you to think about a natural review period of a task before you toss it over the horizon, and set that date in the deferred task.

For example, I may have a task, "Redesign my Filing System." This is a very slow burn task, something I have mused about on and off, and I wrote it down at an inspired moment. I do not need to reconsider that task every week. In fact, reconsidering it once every three months will be just fine. So I set the review cycle to three months. Let me show you how you can do this.

If you are using Outlook, you would set the *start date* for the task to a date three months out. Using my Outlook configurations, this hides the task till then; when that date arrives, it pops into the Low priority section of my main task list, telling me it is time to review it and reconsider it.

Using paper is different. With the Workday Mastery To-Do List, the way to implement this is to create several additional Over-the-Horizon pages. Adding these pages then brings you to Level 3 of the Workday Mastery To-Do List. Here is how you do it.

Title the top of the first page, "Over the Horizon, Review Weekly." That's essentially the same as the one page you were using before.

You then extend the review cycle by adding subsequent pages, each with longer cycles. For example, the next Over-the-Horizon page is created by inserting a title like this: "Over the Horizon, Review Monthly; Next Review Date = _____ " and placing a date there approximately one month away (see second page from top of stack in Figure 6.6). I recommend you make that date the first Monday of the next month, and I recommend that you write it in pencil so you can refresh it. To ensure you actually do that review, place an entry on your calendar for that date stating, "Monthly Over-the-Horizon Review."

On subsequent Over-the-Horizon pages, use the same labeling at various intervals. Which interval to use I leave to you to decide, but you might consider 3 months, 6 months, 9 months, and 12 months (the rest of Figure 6.6 uses that sequence). Templates for this sequence are on my website, MasterYourWorkday. com. Look for Workday Mastery To-Do List, Level 3.

Be sure to establish the review date for each of these, write them at the top of each page, and then enter them on your calendar as meetings with yourself.

You should have four or five of these pages, all stacked behind your main Now Tasks page as in Figure 6.6.

In practice, the way you use this is easy. Simply stop for a moment before you toss a task "over the horizon" and ask yourself approximately when you might next need to check in again on this task—then enter the task on the corresponding Over-the-Horizon page.

**Figure 6.6**   Over-the-Horizon pages: Extended Review Cycle (Level 3).

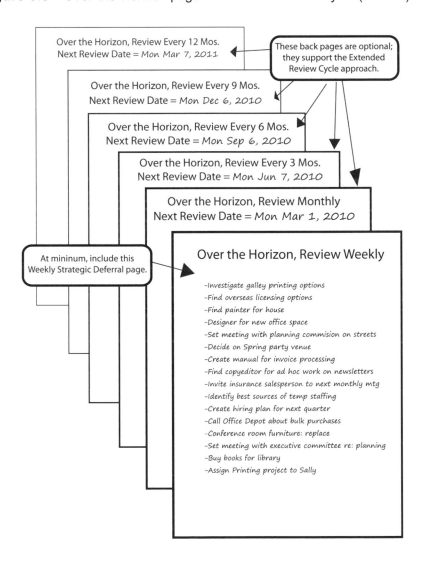

Over the Horizon, Review Every 12 Mos.
Next Review Date = Mon Mar 7, 2011

These back pages are optional; they support the Extended Review Cycle approach.

Over the Horizon, Review Every 9 Mos.
Next Review Date = Mon Dec 6, 2010

Over the Horizon, Review Every 6 Mos.
Next Review Date = Mon Sep 6, 2010

Over the Horizon, Review Every 3 Mos.
Next Review Date = Mon Jun 7, 2010

Over the Horizon, Review Monthly
Next Review Date = Mon Mar 1, 2010

At mininum, include this Weekly Strategic Deferral page.

Over the Horizon, Review Weekly

-Investigate galley printing options
-Find overseas licensing options
-Find painter for house
-Designer for new office space
-Set meeting with planning commision on streets
-Decide on Spring party venue
-Create manual for invoice processing
-Find copyeditor for ad hoc work on newsletters
-Invite insurance salesperson to next monthly mtg
-Identify best sources of temp staffing
-Create hiring plan for next quarter
-Call Office Depot about bulk purchases
-Conference room furniture: replace
-Set meeting with executive committee re: planning
-Buy books for library
-Assign Printing project to Sally

Whether using Outlook or a paper list, the benefit of this Defer-to-Review approach is huge. The weekly task review becomes much smaller and more digestible. It also ensures a higher-value list to review each week by removing the less important or less time-sensitive tasks—you do not repeatedly see tasks each week that are of little interest to you.

I cannot emphasize enough the practicality of this Defer-to-Review process. I have received countless e-mails from users saying this process has saved their lives from an otherwise out-of-control task system. Level 3 Workday Mastery To-Do List templates are also available on my website.

## The Review Steps

Once a week you should review your Over-the-Horizon weekly page and any other Over-the-Horizon page whose cycle date has arrived. The process is simple. When you look at a task, if you think the task needs to be done soon (in the next week or so), simply move it back to the Now Tasks page—either into Critical Now or Opportunity Now. If the task does not need to be done soon, leave it on the page for the next cycle's review. If you feel the task is losing importance quickly, you may want to move it to one of the lower-cycle pages. I find that 90 percent of my deferred tasks can be deferred continually just this way. Eventually those tasks can be deleted, especially if I've reviewed them several times in the past and finally decided that action just isn't warranted.

### *The Short Life of Tasks*

The fact that we can delete many tasks proves that most tasks we write down have a very short half-life—their importance decays quickly. This is absolutely true; most tasks, while seemingly very important when we first write them down, very quickly become less and less important. Granted, a few actually get more important or urgent, which is why I recommend doing the periodic reviews of tasks described above. But most lose importance and never regain that importance. The only reason we hold on to them is because they left an impression at the time we wrote them down, and so for a while we still hold the thought, "I *do* want to do this." But eventually a point is reached where it just doesn't make sense to keep reviewing the task, and we will delete it.

The reason most tasks lose importance over time is that personal and company priorities change quickly. The current hot project or problem dies quickly; new projects or problems suddenly get management attention.

At first it was amazing to me how many tasks I wrote down that actually became subject to deferral or deletion relatively quickly. It often made me think, "Why did I write these tasks down in the first place?"

There is in fact a mental model answer to that. It's that we all tend to overreact to tasks when we first see them. British author Mark Forster wrote a book about this called *Do It Tomorrow,* in which he describes what he calls the Reactive Mind. The Reactive Mind is part of the mental model we all hold about current events. The Reactive Mind tends to overreact and assign unwarranted levels of importance to things merely because they are in front of the mind now. The Reactive Mind tends to want to act now.

Forster's solution to the Reactive Mind is to "do it tomorrow," and thus the title of his book. He says we should never do a task the moment that it appears to us, but rather put it on a list for tomorrow and reconsider it then. His observation is that most tasks do not need to be done once they're rethought the next day.

While I cannot subscribe 100 percent to this theory, I do support it in general. The reason I do not completely agree is that there are many things I do instantly, on impulse, and do not regret; the timing turns out to be perfect.

That said, it is absolutely true that many of the things most people do instantly really just don't warrant ever being done, especially when compared to other things already on their list. The seeming high importance of many new tasks can be completely illusionary. The key is to be very discerning about when you opt for immediate action.

The hours many of us waste on low-value e-mail is a prime example. We read it, get excited about it, and spend hours on various replies each day. But in the long run, there are far more important things to do with our time.

## Why We Tend to Work on Low-Priority Tasks First

Why does this happen, why do we pounce on low-priority tasks? Two reasons. One is emotion. We tend to internalize a need the moment it is presented to us and that spins up our emotions, often leading to unneeded action.

The other reason is that we all have a need to complete some "quick hits" each day. A quick hit is a task that you can complete quickly. We all like to see at least a few things get resolved quickly each day. Quick hits feel good. They engender a sense of accomplishment, of moving forward. Unfortunately, much of the higher-priority core work we are assigned has longer time frames, with long waits before success is seen. So, while pining for quick success, we take on many low-priority tasks that appear to be doable quickly, hoping for the quick-hit high. Again, e-mail often leads to this, and I will talk about that in Chapter 8.

So yes, the urgency of many small tasks is simply illusionary; we do them primarily for the satisfaction of completing them, or out of emotion. But determining whether the need for the task is illusionary or not is often impossible at the time of first seeing the task; our emotions cloud our judgment.

### FRESH Prioritization

By the way, there is an optional process in my paper system that recognizes this natural decay of tasks. When you write tasks on a new Opportunity Now list, consider writing the first ones at the bottom of that section. Then, as you identify newer tasks in the days after that, write them above the ones you wrote before; in other words, populate the Opportunity Now list from the bottom up. Why do this? When you review your list, you will likely put your focus first on newer tasks at the top of the list. Those tasks, because they are newer, will tend to be more relevant, more energetic.

In the Outlook system I call this FRESH prioritization, where the acronym FRESH stands for Fresh Requests Earn Sorting Higher. This is an integral part of that system since computer lists can get very big very fast, and I want the oldest tasks scrolling out of sight only if the list is not kept clean.

I consider it optional in the paper system because with one page you can easily see the whole Opportunity Now section all at once. But again, consider writing tasks from the bottom of the section up, to see if it improves your usage of the task system.

So Mark Forster's assertion to write most tasks down instead of doing them makes sense. That can avoid a lot of wasted activity.

In fact, that principle is an integral part of the Workday Now solution in this book and my previous books. My rule of thumb is, if a task will take longer than a minute or two to do, don't do it now unless it's authentically urgent. Instead, add it to your task list and consider it later, along with everything else already on your prioritized list. Postponing allows the natural importance decay to reveal itself, and that decreases the number of low-value tasks we end up doing. This in turn creates more free time in our workday. This is particularly effective for tasks you can place directly in the Over-the-Horizon section. Using Strategic Deferrals shrewdly will make your workday much more manageable.

## Summary

In this chapter we focused on the details of managing the various urgency zones of the Workday Mastery To-Do List. Let me review the major points covered in this chapter.

It's important to be mindful of what tasks you put on your Critical Now list, keeping that list to a very few truly urgent, must-do-today tasks.

The optional Target Now urgency zone (Level 2) is a way to indicate which of your Opportunity Now tasks you most want to do today. You can either put those at the top of the Opportunity Now section of your page 1 tasks, or you can add them to the daily pages of a calendar planner system.

Most tasks do not have deadlines. For those that do, the deadline annotation is to label your task as follows: "DUE Apr 4: Submit Sales Report." Then, when that day arrives, move the task up to the Critical Now section. Or use a daily planner and place them in the Critical Now section of the deadline day. Check my website for preprinted planner pages for sale to simplify labeling your own.

Keep your Opportunity Now list to fewer than 20 items. The best way to do that is to use the Strategic Deferral process of moving the lowest-priority tasks to the Over-the-Horizon sections.

There are two types of Strategic Deferral approaches. The first is simply to place all excess tasks on one Over-the-Horizon page, as described in the Quick Start of Chapter 2. The better solution, though, is to note the natural review cycle of the task before you toss it over the horizon. Then place the task on one of four or five additional Over-the-Horizon pages (provided on the Level 3 templates), each with progressively longer review cycles, up to 12 months in length. Then review those pages on their stated cycle dates, and reassess the tasks then.

Due to rapidly changing business conditions, the importance of most tasks tends to decay rapidly. You will find that once you defer a task over the horizon, it is likely that it will stay there and you can eventually delete it.

In the next chapter, we look at task management in more detail, covering additional points that I think you will find provide even greater success on your road to Workday Mastery.

CHAPTER **7**

# Task Management at the Next Level

Prior to having an effective task management system in place, many people try to use their calendars to record and track tasks. However, most who try this usually experience problems.

For instance, I have a friend who put all her tasks on her paper calendar, right in the day, along with her appointments. I asked her what she did if she did not complete the task. She said she moved it to the next day, or she tried to remember to glance back at previous days when working tasks. She said she sometimes goofed and completely lost several of her tasks, which led to angry clients. But she had never learned a good task list approach, so this was all she had.

I have another friend who did the same, and actually *scheduled time* for each task in his day on his hourly calendar. I asked him if he really worked them at each scheduled time and he said no, usually not, he ended up skipping a lot of them. But he had always heard he should set aside time for each task, and did not know a better way to do it.

These two people were not using a single *list* for their tasks; they were using their calendars, and not very effectively. I find calendars can be useful at times for tasks, but a to-do list is usually much more flexible. It allows us to easily prioritize across all tasks, and it lessens the risk of losing track of tasks.

You may be tempted to use the calendar a lot too. Once you start getting serious about using an effective task list, you too are going to start wondering if there are exceptions to using the Workday Mastery To-Do List versus a calendar or something else.

You will also likely wonder where to list other task-like things. For example goals—should you put them on your task list? What about projects? How about very large tasks?

To help answer questions like these, study this chapter. Here I cover some obvious and less-than-obvious characteristics of tasks that will help you gain even better control of your workday.

To that end, I first want to talk about various types of tasks, starting with the important topic of *next actions*. You will see that using them will help simplify your tasks list, and make it more usable.

## Next Action Tasks

I highly recommend you learn the "next action" concept because it helps ensure that your tasks actually get done. There is nothing worse than having a task list full of items that sit there without completion. Using this technique helps you avoid that.

I first saw this concept in the book *To Do... Doing... Done!*, by G. Lynne Snead and Joyce Wycoff. They describe a system of top-down task creation where a small project is planned out as a whole, and then periodically the next action for each project is "time activated" and moved out to the daily tasks list or appointment calendar.

### David Allen's Approach to Next Actions

I have adopted David Allen's particular "next action" approach from his book *Getting Things Done* in my Workday Now solution. Allen challenges users to examine tasks they have on their to-do list and to ask themselves, "What is the very next physical action I need to do to accomplish this task?" The goal is to identify the most discrete and significant next action possible, and write that down on the task list. This stimulates action more effectively and clears tasks that tend to remain uncompleted. Once again proving that many good task management practices have been around for a while, David Allen attributes the idea to one of his mentors from 20 years back, Dean Acheson (no relation to the former U.S. Secretary of State).

Here are some examples of well-written next-action tasks:

- Call Fred and ask for new meeting date

- Mail James about IBM proposal

- Edit Chicago sales meeting summary notes

Note that each of the examples above has a verb in it; you really want to identify the action. Specifically, you want to identify the very next action needed to achieve an outcome—each of these represents a next step, not a broader topic.

So I suggest you write all your Now Tasks as next actions. That means they should not consist of generic nouns, such as "James's proposal" or "Summary notes," because these general descriptions leave you, on cursory review, uncertain of what to do. And even when using clear verbs, avoid using broad terms like "Process accounting." Instead keep the next action *specific*—"Collect bills for accounting input." Otherwise, when you encounter a poorly written task in the middle of a busy day, it will take you a minute or two to decide what the action really is—and how to get started—and that delay can prevent you from acting on the task.

Also, for a given larger outcome, only put the very next action task on your list; don't enter as tasks *all* sequential steps to a goal. Remember, your Now Tasks list shows only things eligible to do now. So if you list future dependent steps, you will clutter your list with unusable tasks.

## Appointments vs. Tasks

A question I often get is, "Should I enter an action as an appointment on my calendar or as an item on my task list, and if I put it on my calendar, is it still a task?" To answer that, let's start by defining *appointments*.

Appointments are time-defined events, usually meetings, which have distinct stop and start times. To most, this is obvious: you should manage appointments by placing them on your calendar. My Outlook-based system uses calendar appointments occasionally as a technique to complete tasks, but appointments are only a peripheral focus of that system; virtually all tasks go into Outlook's *task* system. I recommend the same for the paper system. If there is a specific time of day that a particular task must be done, yes, make it an appointment on your calendar. Otherwise favor the task list.

Tasks, then, are activities that do not need a specific time of day identified. They are the types of things you would normally write on a to-do list. They may have a deadline of a specific *day,* but as long as they are not time-specific, in general keep them on your task list. There *are* times I move a task to the calendar, for example, if a deadline is coming up and I want to delineate some specific time to work on it. But that is the exception rather than the rule.

### Ad Hoc Tasks vs. Operational Tasks

The distinction between ad hoc tasks and operational tasks can be important. All of the tasks we've been talking about so far are ad hoc tasks. On the other hand, a lot of companies have stable operational environments with daily repeated tasks and work steps that are best managed by dedicated workflow systems, either manual or automated. For example, if you process a hundred invoices a day, I hope you are using an invoice management system (a specialized application to process invoices). I do not want you to think I am recommending a paper- or Outlook-based task system for high-volume work processes like this, for which better, automated systems are available. The best way to gain control in those environments is to invest in one of those systems.

Note, though, that you might be assigned a related task outside such a system. For example, let's say you are a manager and do not routinely use the invoice management system. But say occasionally you are sent invoice-approval e-mails generated by that system. In that case, the ad hoc system described in this book can be useful for you, to track these one-off requests as tasks.

## Goals and Project Tasks

Do you need to identify your goals first before identifying tasks? Nearly all teachings on time and task management start with a discussion of goals. The general line of thought is this: how can you work on any tasks unless you know what your own goals are? The message is usually that you should not focus on tasks unless you have first mapped out your personal mission, vision, and goals and have ensured that your tasks link to those goals through planning.

This is sage advice. However, as I discussed in the introduction to this book, my experience is this: most people cannot get even their minimal daily tasks off their plate effectively enough to have time to focus on visualizing and planning any tasks based on their goals. They have no system for creating time to focus on higher-level goals. In the heat of the business day, inspired goals are usually the first things they abandon as they scramble to stay ahead of the freight train of work. There is nothing more frustrating than seeing your favorite goals crushed under the wheels of an out-of-control workday.

In the best of worlds, your goals and your work tasks would overlap. Many sales positions base their incentive system on that, as do some management positions. However, unless you are in sales, are self-employed, or are at a senior level in your organization, it is unlikely that all or even most of your daily tasks will map directly to your own goals. If you work in a hierarchical organization, your boss is much more interested in having you spend the majority of your time on tasks that map to the goals of the organization and to his or her department. If you work in a team environment, most of your tasks will be to support team activities. You need to add personal goal–inspired tasks on top of these.

As I stated early in this book, you should first perfect this system of tracking and working tasks, because tasks are how you take action. You need to get very good at managing and working tasks so their volume is less overwhelming; your use of this system should be nearly second nature. Once tasks are under control per this system, *then* you can work on ways to inject your goals into your task stream.

The next question I get is, "If I do identify my goals, should I place them on my task list?" For instance, should I put the statement, "Lose weight" or "Increase sales" on my task list? The answer is no; this is too broad a statement to put on your to-do list. There are practical reasons not to.

First of all, when you see a goal statement on your list in the heat of the business day, you will skip right over it—it is too big to do. You see, goal management needs a much different mindset than task management; busy task time is not the time to try to manage goals. Instead, what you should put on your Now Tasks list is some next step or action that you intend to take to reach that goal, for instance, "Make appointment with Jake the personal trainer," or "Register for Sales 101 class."

I discuss goals extensively in Part II. Once you read that, you will be clear about how to treat goals.

Similar to the question about whether goals should be listed on the Now Task list, you might ask if projects should be listed there. For instance, should you make an entry like "Rebuild garage" on this list? As before with goals, the answer is no, because this is too broad a task to place on your Now Tasks list; you will skip over a task like this in the heat of a busy day. Rather, once again, any next steps due against a project can and should be listed on your Now Tasks list. For example, "Call Jim for an estimate on garage" is a good task to put on your Now Tasks list. Also, see my section later in this chapter called Significant Outcomes. You will see some ideas there on how to handle larger, almost-project-sized tasks.

## All Tasks in One Place

So we've described what sorts of tasks *not* to put on your Now Tasks list. All other types of tasks *are* candidates: all ad hoc tasks, all next steps on projects and goals, actions from e-mails, actions from meetings, and actions from phone calls. All of these should go on your tasks list.

In fact, the very first and most important thing you can do to get ahead of your workday is to track *all* these ad hoc tasks in your one Workday Mastery To-Do List location (either the paper systems or in Outlook, if you're using my Outlook book). What you should not do is continue to use other formal or informal ad hoc task tracking systems such as separate paper to-do lists, yellow sticky notes on your computer monitor, journals, and so on.

Note: If you have a separate system to track operational tasks, such as those described above in the "Ad Hoc Tasks vs. Operational Tasks" section, or if you have a system to plan and manage future project tasks (like Microsoft Office Project), continue to use those. I am only referring here to multiple ways to track ad hoc tasks, daily to-do's, or current next steps on projects.

Why is having one place for all tasks so important? If you don't have one place to look, you will have to spend time checking and reevaluating your various tracking systems (sticky notes, to-do lists, etc.) to determine your next-highest-priority task. You will not get the benefits of being able, at a glance, to know what is on your list for today (and what isn't). More important, at the end of the day, you won't have a clear picture of whether all your critical tasks are done and whether you can leave the office in comfort. By having one and only one task list that you get in the habit of using, you will gain a huge sense of relief. Recall the image of the trained pedigree dogs versus the unruly sharks from Chapter 5? The neat line of trained dogs is the goal you are seeking—you want to clearly see what's left to do.

There are a couple of rather subtle traps to watch out for. For instance, something we all tend to do is leave important messages in our e-mail in-box with the intention of returning to them later to act upon them. By doing this, however, you have created a second home for storing your to-do's, and thus you are inviting a shark attack. Similarly, we all tend to leave important voice mails in our voice mailbox with the intention of following up later on them as well. More sharks.

It is very liberating to get into the habit of immediately transferring both explicit and implied tasks into the task system as soon as you receive them. The reduction in workday tension when you do is palpable.

## Keeping Tasks Out of Your Head

One more place you should not store tasks: your head! All good task management experts recommend getting out of the habit of trying to rely on your memory for tracking to-do's. This was a personal epiphany for me when I finally accepted this lesson years ago.

I thought I had a good memory, and I did, but that was not the point. The point was that until I spread my task list out in front of me visually, it was impossible to adequately prioritize, filter, defer, or dismiss tasks that were bouncing around in my mind all day. I would let emotion rule which tasks I did next, not priority. Or worse, I would act on whatever task happened to pop into my mind next. And the stress of trying to recall *all* my tasks often became intense. I kept feeling I was missing something.

You should use your mental energy for strategic thinking, planning, analysis, appreciating life, and so on, not for constantly tracking and revisiting responsibilities. And if you are currently experiencing any anxiety about the number of tasks you seem to have on your plate, storing them only in your mind will exacerbate that anxiety.

It's the tasks you cannot remember but you know are there that have the most destructive effect. Long-standing research shows that the human mind cannot clearly remember a list of more than six or seven items at once. Beyond that, items become a blur, and it's this blur that increases mental stress. The nagging feeling that you are ignoring important responsibilities has a negative effect on your attitude, your sense of well-being, and your self-esteem. For some, it can be hard to relax on the weekend or in the evening after work when they sense that they have much work left undone. What a tremendous relief my clients report when they finally get all of their to-do's out of their heads and into one visible location.

If you adopt and maintain this approach—recording to-do's immediately in one location as they come up, rather than holding them in your head or on multiple notes scattered about—you will be amazed at the sense of freedom it provides.

### Physical Piles

One of the common sources of tasks is stacks of paper on your physical desktop, bookshelf, or cabinet, or in a desk drawer. A primary benefit of implementing an effective task management system is no longer feeling haunted by piles of paper with work in them. You know that sinking feeling you have when you look at a foot-tall stack of old paperwork and think to yourself, "I know I have things in there I need to act on."

So from now on, as you receive physical documents that you know require action, rather than using a pile as a to-do system, immediately enter the required action on your task list, before you drop the item on your desk. Then when your system tells you the time is right to work it, go find the item as required.

If you find you are currently overwhelmed by an out-of-control pile of materials on your desk or an overflowing physical in-basket, David Allen, in his book *Getting Things Done*, has some great techniques to get you past that (see Chapters 5 and 6 of his book). He describes a system that will get rid of your piles and create very simply organized and highly usable file cabinets. His techniques will help you to get those tasks out of your piles, dovetailing nicely with transferring them into the task system taught here.

# Time Management

When people say they need to learn time management, I find they usually need to learn *task* management. You can meet most of your time management needs by following the task management principles you have learned so far. You will use your time much more efficiently and effectively. Most users of this system say they gain back at least 25 percent of their workweek; many say much more.

Beyond the task management principles taught in this book, however, a few simple time management techniques are, in fact, part of this system.

For example, just as important as deciding what tasks to do is ensuring that you have time to do them. Your task list is useless if you have no time to work the list. Everyone's work patterns are different. Some of you have endless meetings all day long. Others of you may sit at your desk working assignments most of the day. Or you may have operational responsibilities scheduled throughout the day. Some of you may travel extensively. And I'm sure there is everything in between. So you will need to design an approach to making time for working tasks that is appropriate for your workday.

## Setting General Tasks Appointments

My typical day is mixed. I am often 50 to 60 percent booked with meetings, so I usually have time between those meetings for working tasks. During busy weeks, when meetings are more prevalent, I need to schedule blocks of time for working tasks in general, and I have no problem doing so if I plan ahead of time. When needed, I place one- to two-hour appointments on my calendar labeled simply "Tasks." During those appointments, I work down my Now Tasks list, trying to complete as many tasks on my list as possible.

If you have trouble finding time to work your tasks, do the same: schedule a one- to two-hour appointment block on your calendar every day of the week, well ahead of time, to prevent the open slots from being claimed by appointment seekers. It is something you should strongly consider because it prevents your only available task time from being after hours. Many of the meetings that subsequently cannot be scheduled probably were not critical anyway.

### Declining Low-Value Meetings

In fact, something that many workers in large companies discover, often too late in their careers, is this: you do not have to attend all meetings you get invited to! This can be a psychologically difficult idea to accept since we feel obligated to respond positively to all work requests. But recall my harsh reality #1 from Chapter 4:

*As a busy professional, you cannot possibly get it all done. You will think of, and be handed, way more tasks, meetings, and e-mail than you can possibly act on fully.*

Notice this rule includes meetings too; you can't do them all. When I finally accepted this, it freed up an immense amount of time on my schedule, and I started using that time for more important activities. When you decline, ask that any generated meeting notes be sent to you and promise to respond to any issues you see in them.

### Setting Appointments for Individual Tasks

In a previous discussion, I mentioned that my rule of thumb was to leave tasks on the Now Tasks list as much as possible and not make calendar appointments out of them. And I said I occasionally did schedule tasks if deadlines were imminent. Let me elaborate on that.

Only if a long-duration task (two hours or more) is coming due soon do I actually block time on my appointment calendar, and that is only if I feel I may have trouble clearing time to do it. Why not block time for most individual tasks right on your calendar? You might think this would prevent the accidental overbooking with meetings described above. You might think it would ensure task completion. "What gets scheduled gets done," right?

There are three reasons not to do this. First, since these are self-appointments, usually based on nearly random decisions of when to work a given task, you are almost certain to ignore or change the task in that slot due to other priorities and inspirations arising at that time. You know how that goes—you are on the phone with a client and your calendar says you should be working on a specific task; you aren't going to hang up on the client for that.

That means you'll need to reschedule your task, and such constant rescheduling is cumbersome. There is too much overhead associated with making and moving calendar entries, so you will quickly start to ignore the appointed tasks, and possibly drop them.

Second, since you are working with next actions, they tend to be small tasks. Small tasks are more efficiently worked off a list than as individual appointments because our duration estimates for small tasks are usually off. This leads to inefficient completion, as you will fill the allotted time even if less time is really needed. It is much more efficient to march down a list of small tasks and attempt to get as many done as possible within a large block of general task time.

Third, the best time to attack a given task may vary and present itself naturally to you when you least expect it. You will find opportunities to work tasks synergistically with others. You will find that throughout the day priorities change, and that you postpone tasks you thought you were going to do that day and reprioritize other tasks first. Trying to keep track of that with individual appointments on your calendar would be nearly impossible.

However, there are exceptions to that rule. Occasionally you will come across a task that is accurately recorded on your Now Tasks list as a next action, and yet it is clear that it will take several hours or more to accomplish. An example might be writing a report, or reviewing a large document. Or perhaps you have a task that has a hard deadline that you need to ensure gets done. In cases such as these, rather than counting on your prescheduled general "task time" to cover them, it is better to add the specific task by name on your calendar as well. It is a good way to make sure these large or deadline-driven tasks have task time set aside for them. It also highlights the importance of a task. However, please do this rarely; I still recommend you rely on the Now Tasks lists and general task time for most of your tasks.

### Going Mobile

A lot of people try to use handheld devices as a way to make use of wasted time, such as when riding a bus or waiting for an elevator. You can see your tasks on most of these. BlackBerry® devices, iPhones®, Windows Mobile® handhelds, and Palm® devices—all these handhelds come with applications to handle to-do's. Should you use them?

The best way to use them is if you can synchronize them easily with Outlook and you are using the Outlook system in my Outlook book. The best synchronization setup is that available in many corporate settings, where the handheld synchronizes e-mail, tasks, and contacts wirelessly with your corporate Outlook system every few minutes (or seconds). Not all devices listed above can be configured to use my Outlook system, however, so be sure to study my Outlook book and website for more details.

If you are using another e-mail and PC-based task system, investigate if there is a way to synchronize your handheld with it. And then try to arrange tasks in a similar fashion as in the paper system in this book.

Some people have success using their handhelds alone as their sole task system. By all means, if you can enter text quickly into your handheld, give that a try. Just see if you can set up the handheld task list to mimic the paper system in this book.

## Follow-Up Tasks and Delegation

This technique can protect you from fire drills caused by colleagues or staff who don't deliver. How often in your organization does someone promise to deliver something but never follows through? Perhaps you're in a meeting and a promise is made to fix something. Or you direct someone who works for you to complete some work by a certain date. The trouble is you usually forget that the promise was made until well after the item is due. Then you kick yourself for not doing something earlier to usher the task along.

Whether this is a formal delegation or simply a promise made in a meeting, if you want to make sure it gets done, you need to follow up with the person who promised it at some point before the deadline, to encourage them on. Sometimes people say they will do something and really intend to, but just forget. Other times they say they will do it only to get you off their backs.

Wouldn't it be nice if you had an automatic way to remind yourself to check in with these people to make sure the promised activity was being done?

Many task management systems use a "waiting-for" list to track items like this. It is one long list of all the things that you are waiting on others to get to you. The idea is to check that list every day or so and then follow up with those items that seem urgent.

I don't like using a waiting-for list. The problem with this approach is that there is no way to tell by examining the list which waiting-for items need urgent follow-up and which can wait. You need to think about each item, consider when you last checked on it, decide if now is a good time to do another follow-up, and then move to the next item. I find this way too much work to do every day on a long list. Plus, keeping a separate list to check is one more process you need to remember to do each day.

### Create the Follow-Up Task

Instead, my recommended approach to items that you are waiting on is to create dated follow-up tasks in your task system for each item at the time the promise is made, and then take action when the date arrives. Here's how: as soon as someone promises you something, at that point decide when an appropriate date to follow up would be. Then create a task on your own list as a Defer-to-Do task, dated as appropriate for your follow-up date (see the Defer-to-Do section in Chapter 6). When you write down the task, put an "F:" (for "follow-up") in front of the subject line and perhaps the name of the responsible person, for example, "F:Tom–Send me Planning Dept. file." Then, on the date that task moves to your Critical Now on your task list, do the follow-up; call the person or write them an e-mail. This is much better than a waiting-for list because follow-up tasks appear right in the same task list you use every day, so you are more likely to do the follow-up.

### Task Assignment

Here's another way to use follow-up tasks that will help you track the full cycle of a task you delegate to others.

Often you decide you want to assign a task to someone well before your next meeting with that person. In-person meetings are the best times to delegate task assignments, as the face time is important for creating buy-in. So while waiting for that meeting, create a task in your Opportunity Now section with the word "Assign:", the person's name or initials at the front of the task name, and the task description. For example, "Assign:Jim-Plan sales meeting." That way, the next time you are ready to meet with your staff, you can just scan for the word *Assign* in your list.

When you meet and assign the task, negotiate a reasonable follow-up date, and then immediately convert the task into the follow-up task as described above—just replace the word "Assign" with "F" and date it per the Defer-to-Do section in Chapter 6.

If you use Outlook, I describe a much more complete system of delegation in my Outlook book, based on this same approach.

# Significant Outcomes (SOCs)

You may recall that I recommended you place only next-action tasks on your Now Tasks lists—don't place larger items like goals or projects there. That recommendation may lead to the following question: "How do I show bigger things I am working on?"

I call these larger items "Significant Outcomes," or "SOCs" for short. These are usually the bigger deliverables you want to create (for example, a large report) and you are actively working on, in between meetings and other ad hoc tasks. They might also be a less tangible accomplishment (a cleaned-up and organized office, for example) that you would like to get done as soon as possible.

You often have no specific time you intend to work on them. Rather, you intend to fit some work on them into your schedule when you can. Or you may have smaller tasks on your Now Tasks list that are leading toward the larger outcome, and you want to track that overall outcome.

## SOCs Are Smaller than Goals or Projects

SOCs are not significant enough to be called goals—*goals* implies something beyond the task level and I cover the subtleties of goals in Part II. I do not like calling them projects either—the word *project* implies a much bigger activity, often employing formal project management methodologies.

SOCs are just very large tasks, and as with most tasks, typically you focus on these when you have time and it feels right. For example, you may decide, "During this week my major effort between meetings will be to get the quarterly report done." Or you may think, "This week I want to make major progress on designing my new filing system."

It is especially satisfying to complete a few important SOCs each week, as it leads to a significant sense of forward momentum. I call this "knocking your SOCs off." So I encourage you to list a few each week and track them.

Deciding how to record SOCs in your task system can be a quandary. Just listing them as Opportunity Now tasks seems too small because they may get lost; you want them in your awareness all week. And they are not Critical Now tasks for any given day, so putting them there does not make sense either. Scheduling specific time for them on your calendar may not feel right either, as you may not be sure when during the week you want to work on them; this is often a background activity.

So you need a way to give these Significant Outcomes a general focus—to keep your attention on doing them during a given week or two.

## How to Show SOCs

I recommend two ways to indicate SOCs in the Controlling Your Workday Now solution.

First, if you use a monthly or weekly calendar, you can place them as a banner appointment across a period of time, such as a week, or even longer. In Outlook, that means creating a nonblocking banner appointment on the Outlook calendar for the week, and then listing one or more SOCs in that banner appointment. Figure 7.1 is an example of how this might look in the

**Figure 7.1**   Significant Outcomes (SOCs) in Outlook.

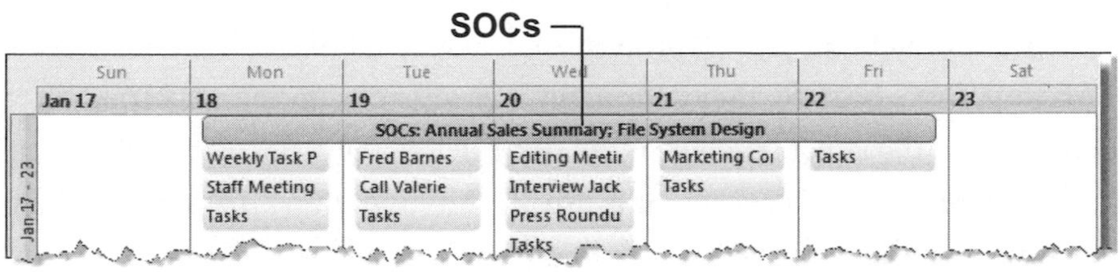

monthly view (in Outlook 2007). If you are using a paper monthly or weekly calendar, you can do the same by hand.

Another way to do this in the paper system is to add a new section to the Now Tasks page of your weekly paper system, and write SOCs in there. Put that section above the Critical Now section. See Figure 7.2 for how this looks in a revised Now Tasks list. I prefer this approach over the calendar approach since it integrates well with the task system. The Level 3 templates include this.

Don't forget to also put any appropriate next action tasks for these SOCs right in your Opportunity Now list as well.

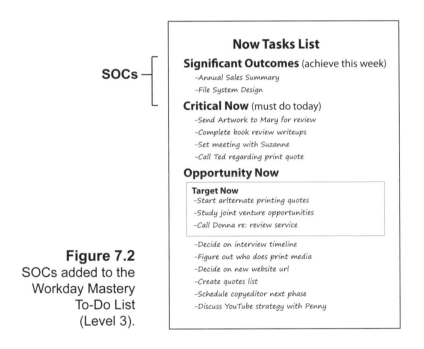

**Figure 7.2**
SOCs added to the
Workday Mastery
To-Do List
(Level 3).

## SOCs are Excellent for Deadlines

SOCs are excellent items to put deadlines on. Do you recall how I said that I rarely put deadlines on the typical small next-action tasks I place on my Now Tasks list? That's because they are usually smaller steps on the road to a larger outcome, and the larger outcome is the thing that usually has the deadline. Well, a SOC is perfect for this because it is usually the larger thing that I am working toward—it is exactly the right place to put the deadline.

How should you indicate the deadline? The best way is to write that deadline date directly on the SOC subject line, either in the paper item or within Outlook. For example, "DUE Fri Mar 7, Quarterly Report." This is the same way I showed you how to indicate deadlines for tasks, so it should look familiar.

Or you can use a bit more complicated approach—a SOC Milestone— which I cover in the accompanying inset of the same name.

---

**SOC Milestones**

SOC Milestones are single-day entries you make on your calendar to indicate an important upcoming date for the larger Significant Outcome. For example, you might have a SOC called "Write Training Manual" and it might have a few deadlines associated with it, the main one being the day you have to turn in the finished manual. So on a paper calendar that final deadline might simply be entered on the due date as "Turn in Training Manual."

Rather than using a paper calendar, though, I recommend you put these on your *computer* calendar, since nearly all computerized calendars allow you to create an alarm against that date. In Outlook that alarm is called a Reminder. You can usually set that alarm many days ahead of the event if you like, and that will give you fair warning of an upcoming deadline. You may recognize this as being the same as the deadline calendar entries I described in the previous chapter for tasks; with larger SOCs you may want to set the Reminder farther in advance, so you have time to get them done.

I recommend you use these SOC Milestones in addition to the week-long SOC Outlook entry I described above. Here is a fine point. You might wonder, "Why not just use the Outlook Reminder on the SOC banner entry itself?" Well, unfortunately, that does not usually work as well. That's because, in Outlook, that reminder is always set against the *start* of the date range, not the end, where the deadline usually lies. That said, you could still set the Reminder on the banner entry, get the notification at the start, and then "snooze" the Reminder to a more appropriate day—that could work well for you. If you do this, just make sure you write the deadline in the Subject line of the SOC banner

*(continued next page)*

*(SOC Milestones, continued)*

entry—that way, you see the deadline in the Reminder dialog box when it is triggered. Other calendar systems may have other ways to do this.

The other reason to use a SOC Milestone in Outlook separate from the SOC week entry is that a given SOC might have *multiple* milestones. You might have an intermediate deadline halfway through the SOC and then a final one at the end; for example, the one in the middle might be, "Turn in outline of training manual." So using a separate entry allows you to create as many of those as you want. Multiple milestones can be useful—however, the trouble with using a lot of milestones per SOC is that if the whole SOC effort slides to a later time frame, you may need to search for each milestone and move it the same amount—and that can get messy. So do this sparingly.

If for whatever reason you don't use a computer calendar, you can give yourself advance notice of upcoming deadlines by placing "advance notice" milestones on your paper calendar. That means making an entry on your calendar a "safe" number of days before the deadline, such as, "Manual due in 4 days."

## SOC Milestones and Project Management

If you do have quite a few milestones for a SOC, your SOC is starting to sound like a *project,* and it is probably time to use project management tools. If you have studied project management methodologies before, you will recognize SOC Milestones as being identical to project milestones used in project management tools. However, those tools have much better facilities for handling them—linking of multiple milestones and tasks is the main useful feature that comes with those tools. So if your SOCs get really big, it's time to switch to a project management tool like Microsoft Project, or a simpler tool like JCVGantt. JCVGantt is especially useful since it links in with the powerful brainstorming tool MindManager. Since brainstorming tasks is often the first step of laying out a project, tying the tools together is quite useful. I discuss that more in Chapter 13.

## Summary

In this chapter we covered more advanced strategies for working with tasks on a daily basis. Here are some highlights.

It is best to put nearly all tasks on your Workday Mastery To-Do List, not to try to schedule them individually on your calendar. That said, you do want to schedule general task time on your calendar to ensure you have time to work down your tasks list. And creating occasional deadline-driven task appointments makes sense.

The power of putting all tasks on one list was pointed out; doing so greatly reduces the risk of overlooking tasks, makes prioritization much easier, and clearly indicates when your day is done.

The usefulness of next actions was emphasized—they help you get tasks moving by identifying small chunks of work that are easy to do in one quick sitting.

I recommended that you not list your goals and projects on your task list. But you do want to list any next actions for these on your list.

I mentioned the power of creating follow-up tasks, and how they can be used to track delegations.

And finally, I discussed how to show Significant Outcomes, or "SOCs," on your Workday Mastery To-Do List, or on your calendar. That way, you can keep an eye on the broad accomplishments you are aiming for in a given week.

Next I am going to switch gears and discuss a topic that will be quite helpful to many of you: how to get your e-mail under control.

CHAPTER **8**

# E-mail Mastery

## The Trouble with E-mail

I have coined a term: *in-box stress.* That's that sinking feeling you have when you glance at an overwhelmed in-box. It's the scary knowledge that there are too many unread e-mails and too many incomplete actions waiting in there. Guess what—in-box stress can be cured.

Learning how to use e-mail efficiently is essential to succeeding in the modern work environment. Why? Because e-mail, which was supposed to improve work, actually makes us work harder. And I am not referring to just the time it takes to read or respond to e-mail. Rather, the real reason e-mail makes us work harder is that e-mail leads to many more business interactions per day than we would have with only live phone calls or in-person meetings. Both of those were limited by the hours in the day, but the e-mail in-box knows no such limits.

Business interactions almost always lead to required action. Think about it. If someone sends you a business e-mail these days—Tag, you're it. "I sent you an e-mail on this. Didn't you read it?" You are now on notice, either to process the info or, more commonly, to take some additional action. You can get hundreds of these per day.

And while more business interactions per day can multiply our business success (more sales, more clients, and so on—the upside of e-mail), the added actions represent added work. So yes, we are busier at work, due to e-mail, than ever before. Using e-mail in a smart way and managing it efficiently is essential to succeeding in the modern work environment.

People have tried lots of strategies to get around the e-mail problem and optimize its use. For example, some people suggest you control when you read e-mail so as to decrease its impact on your workday. There is even a book titled *Never Check E-mail in the Morning* (by Julie Morgenstern). And some well-known personalities have posted "e-mail bankruptcy," declaring null and void all old e-mail.

I agree we should batch up our reading of e-mail, and not read messages as they come in. Research shows it takes several minutes to recover from a work interruption, and that's what e-mail is. I recommend you turn off your e-mail notification, if needed, to prevent the constant interruptions, and then check mail, say, once an hour.

But beyond that, the real problem is not with reading e-mail but rather with *doing* e-mail. It is not reading spam or unneeded cc'd mail (colleague spam) that bogs down our ability to get through the in-box. In fact, it is the *relevant* e-mail that bogs us down. It is reacting to *meaningful* e-mail, e-mail with potential actions for us to do, that makes us skid off track. It's mail with actions that kills a huge chunk of our day. The trouble is, we do not have a natural way to prioritize our reactions to mail like this, so our in-box and workday spin out of control.

## The Solution

The solution is to use the following core principle of my training and this book:

*Unless it is time-urgent, don't take significant actions on e-mails when you first read them. Instead, quickly place a corresponding action entry in your task system, and continue to read or scan all your new mail to the bottom of your in-box. Then file that mail out of the in-box, and work tasks off your Now Tasks list.*

This is an important, powerful, and simple-to-implement rule. Here's why it's important. Many of us try to work action requests as they arrive in the in-box, thinking we are being proactive. But the trouble is we all get too much e-mail these days—way too much to act on everything each day. If we attempt to act on every e-mail as we get it, we miss other important work. And in acting on mail as it comes in, we are likely working our lowest-priority tasks first. No wonder our important work is not complete at the end of the day. And we'll never get to the bottom of our in-box that way.

Or some of us completely skip over most e-mail action requests and then spend hours, later, trying to find the important items in our in-box to get caught up on it. What a mess and unnecessary churn this creates.

Instead, if you follow the principle above, you will speed through your mail by spending only a few seconds converting such action e-mails into prioritized tasks in the task system—without taking action first—and moving on. You will then work these tasks later along with your other work, in priority order, using the task system. As a result, you will end up purposely deferring or later deleting many e-mail actions that do not make the priority cut, and that is a good thing in today's overloaded work and e-mail environment. Only the important items get first action.

If you are using my Outlook task system, there are easy shortcuts for converting e-mail into tasks. When using those, all text and attachments are transferred to the new task, so you do not need to find the e-mail later. Please see my Outlook book for instructions.

Unfortunately, if you are using a paper system as suggested in this book, automatically converting e-mails to tasks is not possible. And not having a link to the e-mail contents is especially inconvenient.

### How Paper System Users Turn E-mail Into Tasks

Therefore I recommend the following approach for paper users. In your mail system, create a new mail folder, or category, or tag, and call it Task Mail. Then, when you get an e-mail with a task, *copy* the e-mail into that folder (or set the category or tag) and *attach to it a sequential task number* (you can easily see the next number by glancing at previous assignments). Hopefully you can put that number right at the front of the subject line of the e-mail copy in the folder (you can do that in Outlook if you open the message and click inside the subject line; it does not appear editable, but it is). But if the e-mail subject line is not editable in your system, then try to find some field you can expose in the e-mail list view into which you can type a task number. In either case, when you write the task subject down on your paper task list, put the number with an E in front of it—e.g., E121—right in the task name or label. That way when you work the task later, you can easily find and refer to the e-mail in that folder for details.

---

**If You Cannot Enter a Number**

If you are using an e-mail system like Gmail, where you cannot record any numbers at all within existing mail, here are two options. One is to reply to the e-mail, sending it back to yourself; as you create the reply, edit the subject line, adding the task number there. Then apply the Task Mail label or tag (or copy that e-mail into the Task Mail folder if your system uses folders). O,r as a last resort, write the date and time of the e-mail somewhere on the paper task label like this: E2010-12-16-2:40PM, or maybe like this: using military time E2010-12-16-14:40. Clearly you will want to write small. But again, do that so you can find the e-mail later when you act on the task. And if the e-mail is extremely important—say, it contains details you will need on the road—in those rare cases, you might consider printing it out to carry with you.

---

Finally, if the e-mail is truly urgent and you can do the task in a minute or less, just do it instead of converting it to a task. But be careful, because those supposedly quick tasks can easily get out of hand and eat up time. That is particularly true with e-mail replies, which I cover next.

## *Flag Mail if Simply Replying Later*

If the action needed for an e-mail is simply to reply to it, but you know you don't have time to do it quickly in the moment (say, because it will take more than a minute or two to compose a reply), it would be silly to convert it to a task in your task system (paper or computer). Rather, I recommend you flag this message somehow in your in-box, for later reply. Outlook has a small red flag called the Follow Up flag that is useful for this; Gmail uses a gold star. I'll bet your e-mail system has something similar that you can activate by clicking on it.

You should then make a commitment to yourself to return to and reply to those messages before the end of the day or early the next. I try to reply to all mail within 24 hours; your organization may want to set a standard for maximum reply times.

That said, I consider delaying long replies and batching them all to do at the end of the day to be a workday best practice. That's because end-of-day replies tend to go faster—you are trying to wrap up the day, so you tend to be more succinct than you might be in the morning, which is a good thing. Also, many issues delivered by e-mail resolve themselves by day's end, making the reply unnecessary. Recall the discussion earlier about the short half-life of a task? This applies to e-mail as well, so delaying a reply can work wonders in clearing unnecessary work.

## Filing E-mail

I am a strong proponent of emptying the e-mail in-box every day. The e-mail in-box was designed to play the role of receiving e-mail, not the role of a bulk filing system, and not the role of a task management system.

If you do not keep it clean, the in-box becomes hopelessly cluttered. A cluttered in-box represents a congestion of unattended responsibilities. Emptying the in-box every day relieves that congestion in a very noticeable way. It also makes you more efficient, because without clearing your in-box, you'll be constantly glancing through old mail in search of passed over to-do's and unfiled information. It saves you time because it allows you to clearly delineate between the mail that needs further processing and mail that you no longer need to read. Once you start extracting tasks from the e-mail in your in-box, daily filing becomes much easier. The mail is no longer "locked" by the presence of tasks.

Filing approaches vary greatly, depending on which e-mail system you are using. In my Outlook book, I describe a number of filing approaches suitable for that technology. If you use Outlook, check out Lessons 5 and 8 of the Outlook book (2nd ed). Even if you do not use Microsoft Outlook as your mail system, you can probably get some ideas from that book applicable to your system.

For now, though, let me go over here, independent of your e-mail application, what the main filing approaches are and why you might want to use them.

First of all, there are two reasons for filing. One is to empty your in-box so that it is not cluttered, with the possible side benefit of making space in a limited in-box storage area. The other reason is so that you can find mail easily later. Whatever method you use for filing, you will want it to be fast and easy, so that you can achieve the first goal—an emptied in-box—quickly and often. Yet the method needs to be comprehensive enough so that you can achieve the second goal—mail that's easy to find when needed.

## Types of E-mail Filing

Of all the ways to file e-mail, the most common one is filing by topic into topic-named "folders." This is what nearly all people who file mail use; if your mail application provides user-defined folders, I'll bet this is what you use.

Next is filing in bulk (for example, into one folder or storage space) and perhaps using some sort of tagging mechanism to indicate topics. Google's Gmail uses a tagging approach called Labels. Outlook uses tags called Outlook Categories. Once tagged, you can show folder-like groups of e-mail, but still view all mail chronologically, or by sender; this flexibility in viewing provides a very nice way to visually search for mail.

Another way to file e-mail is to file all mail in bulk and not apply any kind of topic designation; instead you will just use a full-text indexed search engine when you need to find your mail. This is what I mainly use, and I assert that most people can get by with this. It saves lots of time that we would normally spend on filing. When using a high-quality indexed full-text search engine (as built into most webmail like Gmail, and built into later versions of Outlook), I can normally find mail within a few keyword attempts. Due to the indexing, the searches are blindingly fast, and so I can cycle through a number of different search terms quite quickly. I have never needed to spend more than a minute or so searching for mail this way, and usually I find the item in just a matter of seconds.

There are some industries or professions, however, that need topic-based filing. Legal firms, for example, often need a way to definitively show the entire collection of e-mail associated with a given client or case, and so a simple search may not be the way to go; they need the assurances of a topic-based filing system.

### Rule of Thumb

This leads me to a rule of thumb on when I feel topic-based filing is required, versus when a full-text search approach on bulk mail is adequate. Perhaps this rule will help you. If you ever feel you'll need to retrieve and display *exhaustively* all e-mail associated with a given topic, then use a topic approach. You might need to do this, say, to transfer a collection of mail to someone else or to another server. However, if your intention is just to be able to find individual e-mails or related e-mails, then I recommend you do not waste the time it takes to folder-file or apply tags to e-mail when filing; I'd rather see you save that time, file quickly in bulk, and rely on the full-text search at search time. You can gain quite a bit of time back in your workday this way, with no loss of control.

Filing unnecessarily by topic is one case where I feel the cost of organization outweighs the benefits. Unless you are in a profession that requires topic filing, you probably cannot justify the time it takes to do topic filing; it just does not make sense. And since filing in bulk is so speedy, it means you are more likely to empty your in-box frequently, perhaps every day, which can lead to a large improvement in your workday efficiency, as discussed at the start of this e-mail section. As long as you are extracting tasks before you file, you should be able to file in bulk.

## Curing E-mail Addiction

Even once you start extracting tasks from e-mail and managing those tasks well in a task system, and even once you are filing daily, you may remain addicted to e-mail, and you may still be wasting a lot of time on it. What I am referring to here is the number of times you elect to check and read your e-mail, and the huge amount of time you spend in your e-mail system reading and writing messages. E-mail addiction is a huge problem these days. Just watch how many office workers are spending over half their day processing e-mails, and note how many BlackBerry users are zoned out in their meetings as they feed their fix.

Being an e-mail addict is a bad thing. Studies show that individual productivity is dropping as a result. People are losing much of the time they would normally be doing more productive work.

How do you know if you are an e-mail junkie? If you stop what you are working on over 20 times per day to attend to e-mail, then you are probably an e-mail junkie, and you are interrupting your workday way too much. If you cannot get through a business meeting without checking your BlackBerry much of the time, you are probably an e-mail junkie, and missing the flow and value of the meeting. If you spend over 30 to 40 percent of your day reading and writing e-mails, you are probably over the top. In all these cases, you are greatly degrading your productivity at work, because, face it—most of the time that is spent on e-mail is of very low value and priority compared with what you are leaving undone on your plate.

This assessment is of course job-role dependent. If you are a help-desk staffer whose job role is to respond to help requests by e-mail, well, then, that's your job; same with some sales and customer service roles. But for most of us, there is no justification, and we are wasting lots of valuable work time.

So how do you get unhooked? You do not need to completely give up e-mail; there is no need to go "off the grid." Rather you just need to reduce the number of times you check it, and the amount of time you spend on it. How to do that depends on the underlying problem, which I recommend you try to find. My advice is to use a little self-reflection and ask yourself, "What am I looking for when I consistently go to my e-mail? What am I seeking?" In the answer to that question, the solution can be found.

## Why We Check E-mail Too Often

I have found that most e-mail junkies are looking for one or more of the following three things when they jump to the in-box at every opportunity. They are usually looking for

A. New bits of information to noodle on from friends, colleagues, or news sources;

B. Small, quick requests they can effectively act on now (satisfying quick hits); or

C. Urgent issues that have recently come up that they may need to solve quickly.

None of these needs are good reasons to obsess on e-mail. There are other, less disruptive, ways to fill each need. So if you can break the requirement to do these obsessively in e-mail, you can break the e-mail addiction, and gain a huge share of your time at work back. Let's talk about each of these and the corresponding solutions.

## A. Information Noodling

The first is the need to look for new bits of information to noodle on. If this is your need, chances are you are bored with whatever you are working on. You are probably looking for a change in focus or pace to freshen your perspective, and checking the in-box for new mail provides that instantly.

Or you may be looking to "stay in the loop" at the office, to have your finger on the pulse. Information can be power, and to know the latest status of unfolding events can sometimes make you think you are staying ahead of them. It may help you feel a sense of control to consistently monitor e-mail. At least, that is what you may be thinking. Or you may just want to stay connected to friends, colleagues, or the outside world.

In all these cases, you are engaging in these purposeful distractions at great expense to your productivity. The solution? You need to break that e-mail information-noodling habit and use other, healthier ways to get the same result. First, you can decide to no longer use frequent reading of e-mail as a way to change the pace; there are other and better ways to do that. Second, you can easily stay in the loop by checking e-mail only a few times a day; events rarely unfold more quickly than that (but if they do in your e-mail, see the section below about urgent e-mail).

To help with both of these, as a first step, turn off e-mail notification, so the notices don't pop in your face every few seconds as new mail comes in. Outlook's is particularly invasive, as it shows just enough of the message to pull you into the mail system. See my Outlook book for instructions to turn that off for Outlook, or go to *www.michaellinenberger.com* and find the same instructions linked to the Outlook book support page. Other e-mail systems have similar controls. This is a hugely important first step for all e-mail addiction solutions.

Next, if boredom with current tasks is your reason for drifting to e-mail too often, instead of using e-mail (or, even worse, surfing the Web) to change pace, find something interesting to study within the work currently at hand. Look at the project you are currently doing and see if something stimulating can be found within its domain. You may be stalling out on the current task, but earlier you may have put off other project tasks that now might feel right to do. So scan your project task list and look for something interesting. Or examine your general to-do list and see if something there grabs your fancy. Chances are, something within your current priorities is interesting and will in fact give you the change of pace you need.

The problem with looking in e-mail for interesting diversions is that items there are probably the least important things you can study, and they rarely advance your current priorities. Once you enter the in-box, you will tend to get lost in the myriad of low-priority messages that gush into the box, minute by minute. As a result, if you do go to the in-box for a quick diversion, you will likely get stuck there and, before you know it, you will have lost a large chunk of your day. So again, use other real work items as your way to change your pace. And commit to checking e-mail only once every two or three hours, or even less often. Check it only on a schedule, and do this away from meetings, where your full presence is needed—no more casual BlackBerry reading in your meetings. Handhelds are fine if you are waiting for an elevator or on a bus, but not in meetings, where your attention is most likely expected.

## B. Quick Accomplishments

The second big reason many of us keep turning to e-mail is that we are looking for small, quick action-needs we can respond to meaningfully, and that's why we gaze toward the in-box several times an hour. When we look for these, we are looking for opportunities to make small chunks of progress, because we all like the feeling of constant progress. I call these quick hits, and I mentioned them earlier in the book.

Why do we like these quick hits? The current task we are working on may have a longer burn to a tangible outcome, so having small successes by acting on e-mail requests makes us feel good, useful, and important in the interim. That's not a bad thing; you really do have good intentions on this. The problem with this habit, however, is that these small chunks add up and rob you of time, and they are likely your least important activities of the day. It is not that you should not do any of these tasks; it is just that you should not do them the moment they arrive in your in-box. And certainly don't look for quick hits all day. Instead, during scheduled e-mail reading times, convert these to prioritized tasks (following instructions at the beginning of this chapter), and do them later, in priority order, only when you work your prioritized tasks. And, as with avoiding e-mail noodling, only check your mail once every two to three hours to look for quick hits, no more. Spend the rest of your day on your high-priority activities.

But some of you may object that many of these incoming e-mail requests might be urgent, and waiting two to three hours to check your mail is too long, that you will miss an urgent e-mail.

## C. Urgent E-mail

This brings me to the third and final excuse for obsessing on our in-box: the need to monitor urgent events through e-mail. Watching for urgent mail is the excuse most people give for constantly reading e-mail. In some offices, e-mail has become the mode of all urgent notices, the place to find things that need attention right away. It is the place to check to see if your boss needs something now; the place to find an announcement of a short-notice mandatory meeting, or to see the cancellation of meetings. So checking e-mail often feels proactive, like you are doing your job correctly.

However, I think the policy of using e-mail for urgent requests is wrong, since it makes us unproductive slaves to our in-box. The fact is, very few people work in a job role where they should need to constantly monitor e-mail for urgent requests. Again, if you work on an internal help desk, then yes, maybe you can and should do that; that may be part of your job. Or if you are in a sales or service organization and need to respond to client requests quickly, then consistently monitoring e-mail may make sense. But most of us do not have that sort of job role. For most of us, e-mail should not be an instant response medium. The problem with people in your organization, especially supervisors, sending e-mails they expect urgent responses to is that it gets all staff in the habit of watching all incoming e-mail all the time, and that is way too distracting.

But what if you typically *do* get time-urgent requests by e-mail? Well, if the e-mail system in your office has become a required instant-response medium, then have a meeting with your boss and/or workgroup and get that changed. In my opinion, e-mail should only be used for things that can be ignored for up to 24 hours, or even longer. As the e-mail sender, you should expect that many people may read mail as rarely as once a day, and you should not rely on it for making requests that require quicker response than this. Doing otherwise, especially if you are the boss, creates a workforce addicted to e-mail, and a nonproductive work environment is the result.

So what if you do have a time-urgent item for someone? How should you notify them, if not by e-mail? Here are a few ideas.

If you are in the same building, make it part of the culture to walk over to someone's desk and talk to them live about an urgent matter. Or start to use the phone again. A March 2008 article in the *New York Times* commented that in many offices the phones never ring anymore; everyone is using e-mail instead. Some phone reduction is good, but not using the phone at all anymore—I think that's a shame. If you make it a policy to use the phone, instead of e-mail, for the occasional urgent communication, then you can solve one source of work productivity problems.

You may ask, "What about group urgencies?" or "What if there are details or attachments best delivered by e-mail?"

For group urgencies, consider using Instant Messaging (IM) if your organization has IM activated and has training on it. You can use group distributions in most IM systems, and the way IM pops up on the screen is a good indicator of urgency. Just reserve it only for urgent communications.

Or if the urgent communication is best delivered with longer details or attachments, send the e-mail and then call the person, saying you just sent something that is urgent and ask them to please look at it.

If e-mail really is the only way to go (say you are sending an attachment or long text to a group), consider using the High Importance flag if your e-mail system has that (Outlook does), and configure the e-mail systems for your group so that only such flagged mail raises a received-mail notification. You will need to create and promulgate a workplace policy around that, and it is worth it. See instructions on how to make that setting change for Outlook in my Outlook book (Lesson 11 in the 2nd ed.), or see the Outlook book support page on my website *www.michaellinenberger.com*. You can use those same instructions to raise a received-mail notification only for mail from certain people or distribution lists. I am sure other e-mail systems have the same settings.

There may be other creative ways to replace e-mail in your office, such as a phone tree. The point is, you need to remove any office cultural expectations that cause people to check their mail every few minutes for urgent e-mail. This is a large source of wasted productivity, and one you can fix.

## Summary

Learning how to use e-mail efficiently is essential to succeeding in the modern work environment; otherwise, e-mail can easily distract us away from more important work.

E-mail that contains actions for us to do bogs us down the most. If we try to do the actions right away, we are usually doing low-priority tasks at the expense of core work (and likely leaving much mail unread). Or if we leave uncompleted action mail in the in-box to come back to later, we are trying to use the in-box as a task manager, and it does not have the tools to do that effectively. In either case, we end up with a stressful and overflowing jumble of mail in the in-box.

So the number one best practice you can implement to solve this is to not act on most e-mail actions as they come in, but rather, create tasks in your task system stating the actions needed. Then empty your in-box by filing mail away—you can then work your tasks off your task list in priority order. With this approach, low-priority action mail does not sabotage your more-important daily work.

However if the action needed in a new e-mail is simply to write a long reply, rather than converting it to a task, simply flag such mail and respond to all flagged mail at the end of the day.

Using both of these best practices can keep your workday much freer of e-mail churn and enable you to accomplish your core work.

Filing is important because an overflowing in-box leads to rehashing of old mail and a sense of incompletion of old work. My recommended best practice for filing is, after extracting tasks, to file all mail in bulk in one folder, and then use a full-text indexed search engine when you need to find an item.

Most people try to file into many individual topic-named folders (or perhaps to tag all mail on individual topics). However, very few professions can justify the time it takes to do that. Only people who absolutely need to see an exhaustive list of all similar mail should do this, and I assert that few of us do; full-text searches can nearly always find the mail we need.

Even with these best practices, e-mail can still be addictive—we can linger way too long in our in-box or BlackBerry. My first recommended solution is to turn off notifications and only check mail on a reduced schedule. Next, try to agree with all in your work environment that e-mail will not be used for urgent communications; use other means for that. And finally, if you need a diversion from current work focus, don't use the in-box for that, as it tends to lock us into low-priority actions. Instead, attend to other important tasks on your task list—that way, you are moving forward with your priorities.

PART I CONCLUSION

# Summarizing the Control-Level Solution

Let's wrap up Part I before moving on to the next section of the book. The Controlling Your Workday Now solution presented in Part I is all about controlling urgency in the workplace. The Workday Now model states that nearly all your workday attention is placed on a time period from now to about 1.5 weeks out. Stress and anxiety in the workplace almost always stem from too many urgent tasks coming due within that period, which can make your entire job feel as if it is out of control. The Workday Now solution addresses urgency overload directly with a system that, using that time frame, sorts tasks into four urgency zones—stipulating *appropriate* levels of focus for each zone. This approach greatly reduces your workday stress, and ensures that your highest-priority work is addressed first. It is the first step on your path to Workday Mastery.

Once your urgent tasks are well managed, you can then start thinking about goal-oriented tasks, and even do some career planning, using the new approaches that are presented in the next two parts of this book. But please do take some time now to get your urgent tasks under control; that way, you can relax enough to start thinking at a higher level about your work.

Let's summarize the task (and e-mail) management system you've learned in this part of the book.

# A Simple Two-Page System

First of all, the Workday Mastery To-Do List is a simple two-page-plus system, with the first page devoted to tasks you want to consider working today or in the next week or so (your Now Tasks), and the second page devoted to tasks you want to keep out of mind for now. Level 3 of the Workday Mastery To-Do List includes optional pages showing tasks with extended review cycles.

The Now Tasks are divided into three urgency zones: Critical Now tasks, which must be done today; Opportunity Now tasks, which you will work today if you have the opportunity, but which you probably will not get to till later this week or next; and the optional Target Now tasks (used in Level 2 and 3 templates), which are your most important Opportunity Now tasks, tasks you would very much like to do today (see sample on next page).

### Use Strategic Deferrals to Keep the List to 20 Items

The Opportunity Now list should be kept to fewer than 20 items, to keep it readable and well managed. Move lower-priority items to the Over-the-Horizon list—the second page and optional subsequent pages—using a process called Strategic Deferral. You will review these tasks once a week, or even less often, depending on the review cycle you set for them. Strategic deferrals are a fantastic way to keep your daily task list short and well managed, yet still retain a way to check in on the deferred tasks.

Another type of Strategic Deferral is called a Defer-to-Do task. These are tasks you assign to a specific future date with the intention of doing them that day; essentially, these are scheduled tasks.

### Significant Outcomes

At the top of the Now Tasks page, you can optionally list Significant Outcomes you are working on this week (shown in the Level 3 templates). This is useful when you want to focus on an overall outcome during the week, one that is not indicated clearly as a next-action task. Think of these as the major accomplishments or deliverables you'd like to work on this week.

## Level 3 Workday Mastery To-Do List

The two-page system, including Significant Outcomes and the optional Target Now section, is displayed below. Also shown are the additional pages you may have if using the extended review-cycle method of Strategic Deferrals.

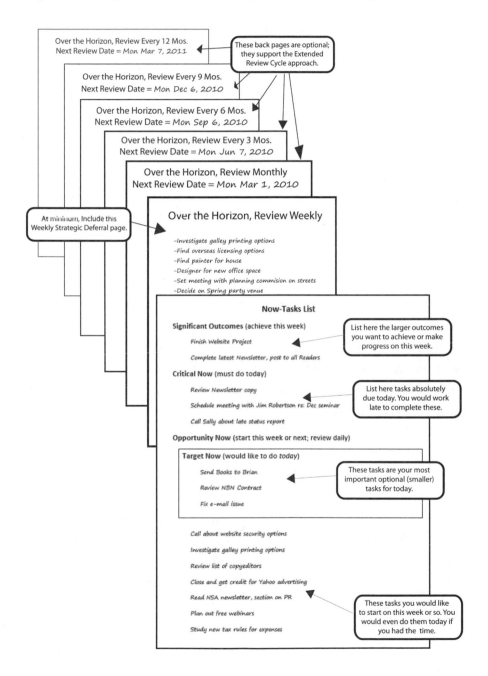

### Free Templates

Free templates for all these pages can be found at the book website, *MasterYourWorkday.com*. Preprinted paper sets and binders should also be available for *purchase* by press time; check the website for more information.

### Add to a Larger Planner if You Like

You can insert this two-page-plus system into the front of an existing planner that has daily pages if you like, and use the planner's daily pages primarily to handle Defer-to-Do tasks, per Chapter 6. However, I recommend starting with the two-page-plus system by itself, due to its simplicity; daily pages can complicate management.

### E-mail Management

To manage e-mail, the most important thing you can do is make entires on your task list for requests you get via e-mail; treat these like any other prioritized tasks. This removes the tension from the in-box, allowing you to file all mail nearly immediately. I recommend you file in bulk and use a full-text search engine to find your mail; use topic filing with folders or tags only if absolutely necessary. I also recommend you turn off e-mail notifications and then check e-mail no more frequently than every two to three hours; avoid getting trapped in e-mail all day. Also, try to convince your team or organization to avoid using e-mail for urgent notifications; use other methods instead—otherwise, you will be checking e-mail way too often. Batch all your replies to do at the end of the day using the e-mail flag tool.

# In Conclusion

I think you'll find this Workday Now–based task system to be much more usable than any other task management system you have used before. It is lightweight, it matches workplace reality, and it just feels right for most people who try it. The system gives you a way to handle and control urgent tasks, and it gives you a way to manage less-urgent tasks, so that you don't lose them. It gives you confidence that all your tasks are under control, which is ultimately the goal of the system.

The feeling of being in control is probably the most important outcome. This frees up your mind and emotional energy for more important things, such as setting and achieving your goals and developing your career. The first of those, setting and achieving goals, is covered in the next part of this book, "Part II: Creating Your Workday Now."

# PART II

# Creating Your
# Workday Now

The Workday Mastery Pyramid

CHAPTER **9**

# Rising Above Control

After applying the principles in Part I, I'll bet that your workday is starting to come under control and is becoming more productive. Now is the time to take work to the next layer of the Workday Mastery Pyramid. The next layer is typically seen as a more advanced level of your career. It is when you become less reactive, more proactive. For example, at the Control layer you may be merely responding to requests from your boss or clients. At the Create layer you will start to formulate those requests for yourself and others.

This is when you become a creator of outcomes. Your productivity is built around accomplishing things of significance. You start to formulate tasks that have longer-term impacts, you face and overcome bigger obstacles, and you use more original thought. You start thinking about self-inspired goals at work and how to achieve them.

Recall that in Part I of this book I said that work was largely a mental game. I then showed how to use the Workday Now mental model to gain control at work.

In Part II we will discuss another Workday Now mental model approach, one that helps create your larger outcomes and goals. In the chapters ahead, I will lay out a new, 4-step process for setting and reaching your larger outcomes and goals. I call goals created this way *Now Goals,* and I will explain why ahead. It is a simple and quick technique for building goals that work. Each chapter in Part II will build on that 4-step Now Goal process. You will find this to be a new and powerful way to make major progress in your career and life.

## Creating Outcomes

As I said, this section is all about how to create outcomes. Using the word *create* may sound odd in the workplace, but it is not. Whenever we use our brains for higher thinking, we are using the creative process. Whether it's solving a problem for a client, writing a proposal for a sale, or meeting with the boss to plan an event, all of these are creative processes.

In contrast, I would not call doing very simple tasks a creative process. For example, using long-established steps for processing an invoice or filing a document doesn't qualify. But for most knowledge workers, much of what we do *does* require some, or a lot of, creative thought.

Creating requires a different energy than controlling. Creating goes beyond rote execution of small tasks—but the distinction goes beyond task size. It has to do with *approach.* Even with a larger, more difficult item, if it is accomplished by just doing a series of straightforward, sequential step-by-step tasks, then that is just outcome *execution.* Outcome *creation* implies more.

For example, compare the phrase "assemble new table" to the phrase "conceive, design, and build a new table." The first is following established steps and controlling the process. The second requires creative insight. Some element of original or added thought needed to reach the endpoint is usually part of the creative process. At work it could be at either the management level or the individual contributor level—it does not matter.

In creating an outcome, there is a sense of seeing it through to a larger end; a sense of using some extra creative effort. Creating usually requires seeing the bigger picture, perhaps more strategically than tactically. Inspiration is often involved, and there is a sense of seeking more than you had before.

Control-layer activity, in contrast, is usually more focused on stopping and preventing, or limiting. For example, if you have a number of steps to do to complete a straightforward task, your energy may be devoted to preventing distractions and interruptions, controlling small obstacles, and so on. At its best, controlling also includes directing, which may sound like it is at a higher level. But simple directing is usually separate from creating the decision of what to do. Someone else can create a new idea, but you might still direct and control its execution.

Even project management, which many consider a higher skill, is a mixed bag. The design of the project plan is certainly a Create-layer activity; but once the design is complete, most project management discipline focuses on controlling the project, keeping it on track.

Creation is associated with positive interest and forward movement; control is associated with holding back chaos and adding discipline. Part I, the Control Your Workday Now section, was all about keeping tasks managed to a reasonable level and controlling which ones you focused on at any given time. That is an extremely valuable skill, but a much different skill than the creative process we will talk about here in Part II of the book.

So that is the focus of this section. It is on Create-layer tools to help you achieve outcomes. Creating outcomes can be very satisfying; by creating outcomes you thrive in an improved situation. You often gain self-confidence in your ability to make a larger difference at work.

## Goals Lead to Your Most Significant Outcomes

Probably the best and most classic example of creating outcomes at work is making and achieving *goals.* The word *goal* is usually associated with larger outcomes. The word itself implies going beyond the easy level. It usually implies a sense of achievement. The phrase, "That person has goals" implies a person with drive, energy, and direction.

Goals are usually achieved using a creative process, not a control process. For example, you do not normally think of people *controlling* their way to the top of a mountain; instead they *motivate* or *inspire* themselves to the top. Since controlling implies holding back, it is not normally a skill that is associated with striving for goals. Rather, for goals you think in terms of finding solutions, seeking inspiration, and motivating your way forward.

So by definition, we are not merely talking about large tasks when we mention goals. Many people do use the word *goal* when referring to a large task. For example, someone might say, "My goal for today is to write my status report." But I don't consider that to be a goal. If it is something they've done before, and can easily do, given the time, then that's not really a goal; in reality, that's just a large task.

You see, goals are usually associated with a larger outcome where a stretch is required. Often it is something that may take days or weeks or months to do, and may represent an increase in a person's accomplishment level. We are almost always talking about some sort of self-improvement or challenge to overcome.

## A New Approach to Goals

The concept of goals has been tossed around the workplace for decades. It is common in management training, common in management speak, and often used in setting performance standards.

It is also used a lot at the personal level, the idea being to set your personal goals and achieve them. However, many people moan when they think about setting their goals. Why? I think it's because they are so often let down. I think it's because chasing goals hasn't worked for most people. And that's because most people approach goals the wrong way.

Many people think of goal accomplishment as merely a process of willpower, hard work, and diligent execution. But those terms refer to Control-layer activities. What seems to be left out is a Create-layer approach. So I say we need another approach to setting and working goals, to achieving larger outcomes— one that includes more creative energy, which represents how goals differ from tasks. The Workday Now approach provides a structure within which to find that better goal approach.

First of all, recall the Workday Now mental model, which is copied in the figure on the next page. In that model, you have the immediate now, and you have the Now Horizon, which is about a week or two out from today. And you have the time period between today and the Now Horizon, which is your Workday Now, and represents the time in which nearly all your active interests reside. Beyond the Now Horizon are tasks and activities you are not currently attending to or very concerned about—they are in the Over-the-Horizon zone.

Where do goals fit in this model? For most of us, goals sit beyond the Now Horizon. We set them and forget them. We set them because we feel we are supposed to, but then they don't occupy our active interest.

Granted, we might set tasks to achieve those goals, and the Control-layer Workday Now management practices can help us accomplish those tasks. That is how most people who do in fact work toward goals proceed; they identify the goal, and then identify actions to help achieve it, and then try to do those

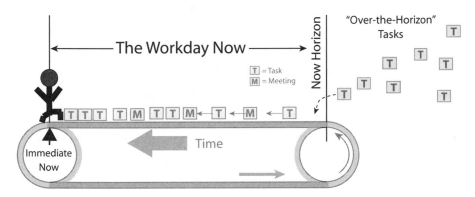

actions. But if the goal is challenging, as most goals are, they often fail at that because there is a creative process there that is still not identified.

Recall that one premise of this book is that if we can understand typical mental models at work, we can use that understanding to get ahead at work. We will use the same approach here in the Create layer. The solution has to do with the very left edge of the Workday Now conveyor-belt model, the Now. By "Now," I do not just mean today, I actually mean right now, *this instant*. I call that the Immediate Now, or "I-Now" for short.

The Immediate Now, or I-Now, provides a powerful tool for creating outcomes and goals.

## Creating Your Goals: The 4-Step Approach

So you will see that Part II is all about a new and more powerful way of setting and accomplishing your goals. Let me summarize how the chapters ahead lay out the 4-step Now Goal process that I mentioned at the start of this chapter.

Step 1 is in Chapter 10. There I discuss how *vision* is the usual component missing from our workplace goals and how by creating *Vision Goals* we can make our goals more powerful.

Step 2 is in Chapter 11, where I introduce the concept of *Target Goals*, goals that usually focus on measures. I will explain how merging Vision Goals and Target Goals leads to the Now Goals—complete goals ready to be activated.

Step 3 is in Chapter 12. There I discuss the very important concept of *activating* your goals. That discussion shows how the I-Now of the Workday Now model, described above, helps you achieve your goals; you will see how Step 3 is the "secret sauce" of this Create-layer solution.

Step 4 is in Chapter 13, where I add the fourth step, *Taking First Action.* That concludes the complete 4-step Now Goal creation process to construct, activate, and achieve your goals.

Chapter 14 then goes beyond these four steps and covers how to tackle your tougher goals. It shows you some new approaches to take for goals that you may not believe you are able to accomplish.

## Summary

The Control-level tools of Part I are about discipline—they are about limiting and holding back chaos, and they are appropriate for organizing and accomplishing tasks. But once you start setting your sights on more significant outcomes, Create-layer tools become the source of necessary additional skills. Goals are the best example of this; they represent larger aspirations, a stretch or leap in skills, and they perhaps even require a little magic to accomplish.

Part II is about using Create-layer tools to set and fulfill your goals, and it introduces the 4-step Now Goal creation process, incorporating a new goal-creation approach. I lay out these steps in a clear and logical way—one that you should find very easy to apply to your own goals. For perhaps the first time ever, you will have a logical and powerful way to attain the larger outcomes you seek.

CHAPTER **10**

# Step 1, Vision–
# The Missing Component
# of Workplace Goals

I feel that the process for an individual to set and achieve goals in the workplace is fundamentally broken these days. To me, goals are supposed to be a source of inspiration, of rising above, of inner drive. Yet most workplace goals are anything but that.

Instead, workplace goals these days are set for what seem like entirely wrong reasons. Often they are set because a required performance review process involves some blanks to fill in on a form. Or they are created by leadership as a nearly cynical measure to prod employees to be more productive. To call such measures "goals" is, in my mind, an abuse of the original concept of the word. Goals should be a self-envisioned aspiration to excel, not a stick to prod people with.

Still, most other managers and I feel there *is* a place for measure-driven targets; we do often need to set numerical objectives when we strive for our goals. But due to this conflict of intention, many people feel goals don't make sense anymore; the concept of goals seems to be muddled.

Furthermore, goals are hard to achieve. Even with goals we set ourselves and strongly believe in—whether workplace or personal—most of us still have trouble achieving them. Even with the best intentions and a strong commitment, we often flounder.

In this chapter I will make sense of goals. I will do that partly by identifying the missing component of the goal-setting and achievement process—*vision.* Incorporating vision into your goals reenergizes lifeless "paper goals"—goals you write down but never get anywhere with—and it serves as the basis for the next steps to achieving all your goals. Incorporating vision represents Step 1 in the 4-step Now Goal creation process.

To start this story, let's look at why we usually fail at goals, and then some ways to fix that.

# Why We Fail at Workplace Goals

As I said earlier, most people moan if you mention the topic of goals and goal setting. One reason is that they have often been disappointed by previous efforts at achieving their challenging goals. There are other problems as well.

## It Takes More than Just Setting Goals

Part of the problem is that the power of merely *setting* goals has been oversold. For example, it is a commonly quoted statement that a low percentage of the workforce set formal career goals, perhaps only 1 or 2 percent. That statement is often followed by the invitation to "join the 1 percent club," urging you to set your own goals. The unfortunate aspect of that statement is the implication that just setting a goal is the biggest part of creating it. But for any of you who have set goals in the past, you know that is not true.

It is true that not enough people set goals. But just setting a goal is such a small part of the goal achievement equation, it is almost not worth mentioning. In fact, mentioning it may be worse, because to imply that setting the goal is nearly all that is needed, you then create expectations that will be broken, and then setting goals can fall out of favor completely.

## Goals Are Too Often Set by Others for You

But even if you are diligent in taking actions toward your goals, you probably still feel disappointed. Goals unfortunately are not that easy to achieve. If they were easy, they'd simply be tasks. It often feels as though achieving goals requires some bit of magic or extra effort.

Probably the biggest problem with goals is lack of ownership of the goals by the people who have them. Peter M. Senge, in his book *The Fifth Discipline*, states that for goals to work you must passionately "want" the goal. However, too many goals are set by *other* people on your behalf, and you accept them to please the true goal owner. From your parents you often accept career goals and family goals they want you to achieve. From your boss you accept performance goals. From your spouse you accept a variety of goals that you may only give a nod to in order to keep peace at home. However, if your heart is not really in these goals from other people, you cannot get excited by them and pursue them passionately.

Let's take goals introduced in the workplace. In some organizations, your goal is set by your boss. For example, you may have a performance milestone that your boss assigns you. Say you work for a sales manager who says this month your goal is $40,000 in sales, and if you do not make it, you are penalized in some way. I think goals like this are not really "goals." Goals such as this are usually used as a stick, as a way to persuade. They are more like threats than inspired goals, and are clearly Control-layer activities being applied at the goal level. They fail not only because you do not really own them, but also because they are fear-based.

But even goals that you *do* buy into and *own,* and perhaps even set yourself—even these goals are often based on fears or on "shoulds" established by comparing yourself to other people. For example, "I should make a lot of money (so I am as good as my peers)," or "I should lose weight (so I don't compare poorly with others)," or "I should be a doctor or a lawyer (to impress my parents)."

All of these are formulated in negative ways. They lack an inner positive inspiration, and, as you will see, are often doomed from the start; fear-based goals usually fail.

### The Approach Most Use for Achieving Goals Is Wrong

Let's raise this one more level. You probably do have some goals you set for yourself, that you *do* buy into, and that are *not* based on fear—but they are still not getting achieved. Let's say you truly do want to increase sales 20 percent, but you just cannot do it. Why are such goals often so hard? The other core problem is that the approach most of us use for achieving even positive goals is wrong.

The commonly taught method to achieve goals is to identify a metric or some other measure to make sure the goal is being reached, and then just work until the metric is reached. If the metric is not reached, you are to scold yourself, and then try again harder; then keep repeating as needed. This is an accountability approach to goals, and one that has, at best, mixed results.

Granted, using a measure is an effective way to check to see if the goal is done, and a good way to track its progress. And granted, this kind of discipline could be what some people need to get things done, particularly for moderately easy goals that are just being procrastinated on. But again, all of these are Control-layer techniques. They are not bad, and they are necessary in some cases, but they are just *not sufficient* in most cases, because they ignore Create-layer tools.

You can raise the bar on this significantly by using a more pull-based approach. This is what incentive or bonus structures are based on. "If you meet your goal, you will get a bonus." It is the carrot side of the carrot-and-stick approach. If it is a real bonus (and not just a threat to lose pay), this approach can get closer to the creative side of goal achievement because it stimulates positive inspiration and often ingenuity of thought on how to achieve an outcome. One reason capitalism works so well is that the profit motive stimulates creativity and action, as do similar internal corporate bonus structures.

But over the vast domain of business and personal goals, surprisingly few goals are applicable to such bonus structures; and even for those that are, we have all seen how these approaches often fail. If over time the bonus becomes expected, then it becomes a fear-based goal: the pull is lost.

If the goal is a difficult goal, incentives alone may not be sufficient anyway. That's because with really tough goals, we may just run out of steam and give up on the bonus structure.

Some goals are hard because they require an approach that goes well beyond fear or incentives. Think how hard it can be to lose weight, for example, even with the angst of being overweight and even if we set rewards for ourselves.

And some goals seem beyond our power to achieve because they rely on influencing or changing other people, and so seem completely beyond our control. For example, take the goal of convincing a difficult sales prospect who has already made up his or her mind not in your favor; or increasing sales in a down economy.

Finally, sometimes we fail at workplace goals because we just do not really "get" the goal. Often we are assigned intermediate steps to larger outcomes, and because we do not hold the larger picture, our steps do not succeed. That might be because we do not understand our role in the larger picture, or because we have trouble getting excited or motivated about our small part of it.

## Adding Vision to Your Goals: The Create-Layer Solution

This leads me to what I feel is the main missing component of most goals, which is the *vision* the goal is trying to achieve. Vision implies a big picture. My definition of vision includes an appreciation of the reasons for the goal, the Why of the goal. Vision, to me, implies a depth of purpose associated with the goal. It provides a positive overlay to the activities taken to reach the goal.

Without such vision, goals lack substance and then merely become chores to pursue. The lack of the vision component is probably the biggest reason goals fail.

You will see in the pages ahead that identifying and using a goal's vision component is one very important key to achieving the goal's outcome. Vision is the missing Create-layer component of goals. With a vision in place, if it is strong enough, goals can be achieved much more easily.

I suspect you intuitively know this is true. You can feel it when there is a strong vision behind a project or a goal, and you can feel it when there is not. Visions move people; they motivate based on their intrinsic value, not on some outside or artificial motivation.

They also add character to people who hold them. Managers often notice and recognize staff members whose goals are based on vision. Leaders are often hired for their sense of vision. And even romantic relationships are sealed by one person recognizing the vision in the other.

Adding vision "correctly" is the secret Create-layer tool to achieving your goal.

### Why Vision Is Usually Lacking

If this is so obvious, why don't we add vision automatically to our goals—why is it so often missing?

It depends. If the vision is set by others for us, the vision is often not conveyed to us at the time the goal is assigned. Rather, just the action or measure is conveyed. When this happens, we could try to add vision ourselves. However, we usually do not think to do that because the goal as conveyed doesn't connect with us internally; we are usually not motivated to find a vision.

In contrast, if we are the ones setting the goal, we all usually *do* start with a vision, whether we realize it or not—it's just that in this case we usually lose the vision quickly. Why? This is because the typical focus on action and measures can actually work against us if we are not careful. In our hard work to achieve the goal, we focus so much on how to do it and on measuring our progress, that we lose sight of the compelling positive reason we wanted the goal in the first place. We get caught up in the implementation and associated problems. Put very simply, we lose the spark behind the goal. Keeping the vision in sight through all steps of execution can solve this.

### Understanding What Vision Is

But there is confusion about the word *vision* too, and that leads to people not even trying to create or maintain a goal's vision.

For example, most people think that vision should be used only at the highest level of an organization—that it should be used only at the senior level of the organization chart, or only for the largest goals. Few people consider emphasizing vision down at the worker-bee level.

Confusion also reigns on the definition of vision—what it means, what it should be, and how to create it. There are endless arguments about the difference between vision and mission. Consultants make tens of thousands of dollars helping organizations to identify their vision and mission, and to create a compelling statement for each.

## Vision Is Simple

First of all, let me say that nearly all this confusion is based on a lack of understanding of what vision is. Vision is actually much simpler than most of us think.

What does the word *vision* mean? It does not need to mean Corporate Purpose, as is so often assumed. It does not need to be a complicated statement created only through hours of analysis.

Rather, the definition can be as simple as "how I see it, how I picture this thing." Most often it is a little more elaborate than that, but not much more. It is usually a simple description of an outcome that includes a sense of going beyond, and a sense of purpose and inspiration.

My definition includes but goes beyond merely "how I see it." My definition is much closer to the more elaborate version. *Vision to me is a description of an outcome that conveys a sense of how the new outcome transcends the status quo—in a way that engenders inspiration for action.* And to that I add a sensory description of an outcome, so that a mental picture can emerge, one that captures the emotional impact of the new outcome.

So vision, at its simplest, is a passionate image of an outcome. At its best, it is a multisensory image of an inspired outcome. It is a mental image usually mixed with a personal emotional connection to the outcome. The emotion is usually

---

**Varied Vision Definitions**

The common definition for *vision* varies in the business world. One standard definition is that vision is the What of a goal—that it simply describes the thing being sought—and that the term *purpose* or *mission* is used to describe the Why—the reason, the passion—of the thing. However, I merge all of this into the one word, *vision*. Vision needs to describe both the What and the Why. Vision especially needs to capture and convey the passion behind the goal. I feel that most people equate vision with passion, and that all the best visions reflect passion.

---

a strong positive desire for its creation, a passion to see it done, but it may be one or more of a number of positive emotions like enthusiasm, faith, hope, or belief, among others.

On a more subtle level, note that in that definition, the multisensory image gives the vision its form, and the emotion gives it its power. Form and power together are what lead to creation of the vision's goal. In fact, once you learn how those elements of vision can lead to a goal's achievement, you will no longer be confused by how to define a vision. The components of successful visions end up defining the thing for you. We'll talk more about that in Chapter 12.

## Vision Can Be Created at Any Level

Notice there is no scale of size or importance stated here; vision can be applied at any level of an organization or activity. You may think that my definition of vision—a multisensory image of an inspired outcome—might take so much work to create that only large goals qualify. But in reality we create visions all the time, every time we become passionate about an outcome.

For example, your vision could be as small as finding and purchasing a high-quality stapler for your desk. In this case, if you have a strong desire for finally getting a stapler that really works and you can start to picture and describe it—you have just created an authentic vision.

Or it could be as large as developing a new life-changing product for the world. Visions truly can be created at any level.

### A New Term: Vision Goal

A correctly identified vision is the component that is usually missing when goals are set, even though it is the most powerful element of a goal. To emphasize this component, I am going to coin a new term—Vision Goal. A Vision Goal is a goal that is written in such a way as to emphasize the vision. It does so in a way that describes the outcome, conveys a sense of how the new outcome transcends the status quo, and engenders inspiration for action. In other words, it allows you to picture the goal and get excited about it. Creating a Vision Goal is Step 1 of the 4-step Now Goal creation process highlighted in this part of the book.

How do you create one? The key to creating Vision Goals is to focus on the *reason* for the desired outcome. Write text that captures the Why of the goal, as opposed to the How or merely the What. Try to represent the excitement, the inspiration, the passion of the goal in that text. It's easy to do, and I have a simple formula for writing Vision Goals.

### Formula for a Well-Written Vision Goal

When creating the Vision Goal, Step 1 of the Now Goal process, you want to create a very emotive statement. That's because an emotive statement is required for goal *activation,* as I will describe in Chapter 12. So here is the formula to do that: just make sure to include all the following qualities—they are ones that help elicit an emotional experience during goal activation. Those qualities are:

A) Appropriate length

B) Descriptive text

C) Emotive text

D) Always positive

E) Written in the present tense

Let's go over each of these qualities, with examples.

A) Appropriate length: The length needs to be long enough to capture the other four qualities, but short enough to be easy to review quickly every day. Just because there are five qualities doesn't mean your vision statement needs to be long. If your goal is modest, you can even fit all qualities into one short sentence:

*I am achieving a healthy optimal weight that looks great and feels vibrant.*

This is a personal example, but the concept is equally applicable to workplace goals. You will see, as you work through each quality below, that the sentence above has all five qualities.

If your goal is larger or more complex, you do want to use more detail. And as you will see in Part III, life's-work goals can occupy nearly a full page.

B) Descriptive: Describe how things will look once the goal is complete. It can be short, but you want enough description that you can picture it in your imagination. Again, the short Now Goal statement above is quite descriptive for the topic it is addressing. However, if you were describing a new house, for example, the description might take several sentences to capture all the features. You might want to describe the style and color of the house, the type of location it is in, any particular features that are important to you, and so on—all in a way that builds a clear mental picture.

C) Emotive: Include in that descriptive write-up some colorful and passionate text that provides an indication of your feelings and emotions about the achievement. The activation process coming in Chapter 12 has you reviewing this write-up one or more times per day, so think in terms of how this will feel and motivate you the next time you study this statement. If a goal write-up seems dry, one way to find emotive text is to ask yourself, "Why do I want this thing?" Search for the positive reasons behind wanting this goal. Focus on the Why. In the example above, the words and phrases "healthy," "optimal," "looks great and feels vibrant" are all emotive expressions.

D) Always Positive: This is extremely important. Always describe the goal in positive language. You want to be sure you are spinning up the positive outcome, not reinforcing the negative present state. For example, if you want a job with more autonomy, describe the new freedom you will feel. Do not write, "I don't want to have an overly pushy boss anymore." That statement focuses on something you do not want and your subconscious may focus on it. Instead, describe what you *do* want: "I have a job with great autonomy and freedom of direction." In the example above, note that I did not say, "I want to lose weight." That may seem positive at first, but it is emphasizing a negative—too much weight. As you can see, creating truly positive statements can sometimes be tricky.

E) Present Tense: In your text, you should always write as if the goal were already achieved and present now, so use present tense language. Instead of "I will get the department head job," write, "I have the department head job." When you read this goal later, the intent is to feel as though the goal were already there.

The reasons for including elements C, D, and E (Emotive, Always Positive, and Present Tense) will become clear in Chapter 12.

Adopting all these elements, here is another Vision Goal example. It is also short, but you will see that it has them all.

*My family is greatly enjoying the additional purchasing power we now have due to the increase in pay I just received; we are sprucing up the house just the way we want, and we have scheduled a dream vacation in Hawaii this year.*

And for a business example:

*My sales have increased substantially. It feels great to be exceeding my monthly targets. I can now relax and enjoy the conversations I have with my clients, knowing I am set and every sale I make is extra. What a fantastic experience it is to be ahead of the game, month after month!*

## Summary

You can and should write a Vision Goal for *every* goal you create. This Create-layer tool is a major element missing from how the world approaches goals. A strong Vision Goal can make your goals, even small goals, successful.

The reasons we usually fail at workplace goals are as follows:

- Merely listing a goal will not make it happen.

- Goals are often set by others; as a result, you do not buy into them.

- Goals are often based on "shoulds" or fears, and so lack positive conviction.

- Goals go beyond large tasks, so simply identifying action steps and measures, while *needed,* is usually not *sufficient.*

- Even incentive-based goals often fail because we try to use Control-layer tools to achieve them.

Vision is the missing Create-layer element that can solve these problems. Adding vision in the form of a Vision Goal represents Step 1 of the 4-step Now Goal creation process. Here are some additional aspects of vision:

- At its simplest, vision is a passionate image of an outcome.

- Visions are not just for large goals or businesses—they can be created at any level and should be for all your goals.

- Vision is usually lacking either because we are handed a goal without the vision, or because in the complexities of working our goals we allow the vision to fade.

- The new term *Vision Goal* signifies a goal that has been written to include a well-articulated vision.

- There is a simple formula for creating Vision Goals, one you should use for all your goals. The elements of this formula are as follows: appropriate length, descriptive and emotive text, always positive, and present tense.

Next, let's see another element of goals that needs also to be present for success. It is something many in the business world are familiar with, but probably have not thought through enough—something I call Target Goals.

CHAPTER **11**

# Step 2, Merging Vision Goals and Target Goals to Create "Now Goals"

I want to tell you a secret that will clear up a huge amount of confusion about goals. You will not see this explained anywhere else, as these terms are newly introduced in this book. Here's the secret: there are really two main kinds of goals, Vision Goals (which you learned about in the previous chapter) and Target Goals, which I discuss in this chapter. Once you understand Target Goals and how they differ from Vision Goals, you will understand how and when to use each of them. I feel that will clear up much of what I call "goal confusion."

In this chapter you will also learn that for nearly all goals you create, you really need to include both—the Vision Goal component and the Target Goal component. Together, these two elements combine to form what I call Now Goals. As you will see, Now Goals are complete goals, ready to be activated. Adding Target Goals to your vision is Step 2 of the 4-step Now Goal creation process.

Since we just discussed Vision Goals, let's talk about Target Goals and their important role in creating your goals. Then we'll cover how to create a Now Goal by merging the two.

# Target Goals Provide Focus for Action

To clearly distinguish the vision portion of a goal from the measurable, or executable, portion of a goal, I have created a new term: *Target Goal.* Target Goals are an important component of all your goals. As I describe them, they will probably look familiar to you—elements of them are already in consistent use in many companies.

In fact, most of the things we refer to in the corporate environment as "goals" are really Target Goals. Target Goals are usually tactically oriented. They are measurable elements of a larger outcome, and as such they are usually numeric goals. For example, when you receive a sales goal—a dollar amount in sales that you are supposed to reach—that is a Target Goal. If your goal is to meet a certain number of satisfied customers, that's a Target Goal. In fact, if you set any number to reach and it measures any aspect of your performance, that's a Target Goal. In general, Target Goals are established for planning, for accountability, to track progress, and to add focus.

Target Goals don't have to be numeric per se; they should just be very specific. For example, if you create a list of cities to start new branches of your business in, you are creating a target list for a larger vision of expanding your business. That list is a Target Goal.

Target Goals often describe the How component of the goal. They answer questions such as, "How will we know we've reached our goal?" To a lesser extent, they may also answer "How can I clarify the goal?"

While Vision Goals may sound more exciting than Target Goals, Target Goals are clearly very important. They provide the focus for action. They provide the structure around which visions are executed.

And while Vision Goals work at the Create layer, Target Goals, as you will see, work at the Control layer. Since Target Goals are usually the measure against which success is determined, they are the core measure in incentive plans and the accountability element when tracking the progress of goals.

When people do not deliver what is expected of them, Target Goals are sometimes the missing element. They provide the specificity needed to focus performance. Target Goals often hold enough specificity to define a set of steps for their achievement, so much so that they can be the main elements of a project plan.

## Is Vision or Target More Important?

Should you focus more on the Vision Goal or the Target Goal? As I emphasized in Chapter 10, the concept of vision is unfortunately rarely discussed at the goal level, particularly when creating goals for employees; that discussion is rare even for personal goals. Rather, vision is almost always discussed at the corporate level, with the question usually asked on a senior management retreat, :"What is the vision for our company?"

Even at the corporate level, however, the pendulum has swung both ways on where management attention should be placed—whether on vision, or on targets and execution. A decade or two ago, vision was all the rage, and consultants were making good money helping companies establish their vision statements. Targets and Target Goals, which are usually associated with the more sober execution stage of outcome creation, were much less sexy to discuss.

But in recent years, *execution excellence* (and the role that metrics play) has gotten more attention. The focus is now more on accountability in management, a trend highlighted by the success of the 2002 business book *Execution: The Discipline of Getting Things Done* by Larry Bossidy, Ram Charan, and Charles Burck.

I don't lament the swing at the upper levels; execution *is* very important. But even though a balance of vision and execution is still important at the upper levels, I think the low-hanging fruit of how goal setting can help workplace productivity is best reached at the middle or lower levels, or even at the personal level. You see, at the lower levels of an organization the focus has *always* been on execution. For decades, upper management has decided the vision, and then ordered the middle and lower levels to implement actions to achieve it, to execute it.

But as middle and lower level management focus on execution, they usually ignore vision. Usually only Target Goals get distributed down to the lower levels from upper management, and lower level managers are neither trained nor encouraged to create or share vision on their own. So the Vision Goal element is nearly entirely absent at the levels where the work is done, and this is the gap to be filled in most cases.

In essence though, we all need *both* elements in the goals we create. We need a Vision Goal as the passionate description of the primary thing we are reaching for, and we need a Target Goal to add structure and definition to our actions. While vision should always be primary, to achieve balance the pendulum should rest squarely in the middle, emphasizing both.

## Advancing Beyond SMART Goals

And that brings us to SMART goals. If you have been in the business world long, or read any goal-setting books, I'll bet you have learned how to set goals by using SMART goals. The use of SMART goals has become widespread—they have caught on in the management world.

What is a SMART goal? A SMART goal is a goal that is written in such a way that makes the goal more specific. That is done by identifying five particular elements of the goal. To make that easy, a template is usually provided that lists those elements and provides a place to write them. The five elements that line up with the letters in the word SMART are usually these (there are variations):

S = Specific, M = Measurable, A = Attainable, R = Realistic, T = Timely

The SMART goal template is taught in most management training curriculums that cover goal setting; it is the most widely used method of defining business goals.

While there are various reasons for applying the template, SMART goals are usually suggested in order to establish realistic and accountable goals. They are often used as a set of criteria when a company implements an MBO (Management by Objectives) process for performance improvement.

My observation about MBO, and SMART goals, is that they almost always result in Target Goals—sets of measures against which the company and employees are evaluated. The common rallying cry is "What gets measured gets done."

While I applaud the focus on measures (it is often absent), I think the concept of SMART goals is dated—it's time to evolve beyond them. Why?

First of all, none of the elements in the SMART list emphasizes *vision*. The listed elements cover the How, but not the Why, of the goal. This reinforces once again my point from Chapter 10, that vision is the element most often lacking from business goal setting—and that it is a key missing ingredient of goal success.

Next, the SMART template doesn't discuss how to work or manage the goal other than simply chasing the measure. As you will see ahead, when you work and manage your goals, you need to implement some key activities that go beyond dinging people for missed targets.

In general, while the focus on targets is admirable, I think SMART goals emphasize the target element of goals way too much.

## A New Term: *Now Goals*

So a better new framework for creating business goals is to focus on goals that balance vision and target, and to incorporate more effective goal management activities. The framework of Now Goals does this. Now Goals should be the next evolution of goal setting for individuals and for companies.

Now Goals are goals that take advantage of the Workday Now concept to strike an optimal balance between Vision Goals and Target Goals. To create a Now Goal, just make sure that both elements are adequately present and that both are well articulated.

Since, as I said in Chapter 10, the Vision Goal portion of a goal is usually the missing element, adding or improving that comes first. In a Now Goal there is always one Vision Goal—it represents the overarching thing to achieve, and it represents the feeling behind the achievement.

Keep in mind, though, that Now Goals don't have *only* the vision element. The Target Goal element is still required. It's just that Now Goals have the right balance between vision and target, and since vision is usually what is lacking, it is the thing that probably needs to be added.

However, in some cases a goal needs to be improved by adding a missing or improved *target* element. That usually means adding a specific measure to the goal statement, but it could be more. Let's talk about the role of Target Goals in Now Goals.

## How to Identify the Target Goal for a Now Goal

Target Goals provide the detail behind the Vision Goal. They can help focus the vision by providing an unambiguous measure of achievement. They also help add clarity to the vision.

Typically, a Target Goal is added to or extracted from a Vision Goal by asking the question, "How can I measure this outcome?" So, for example, if your goal is to increase sales, you want to identify the new sales number you wish to achieve. The idea of adding a measure is fairly simple, and is a common recommendation by nearly all goal management writers.

But try to do this only to the extent that it helps to find a feeling and clarify the picture. For example, if your goal is to increase sales, it certainly makes sense to include the target percentage, so that the magnitude of the increase is included in your description. The feeling around increasing sales 5 percent is much different than the feeling around creating a jump in sales of 25 percent or more.

On the other hand, many goals, particularly intangible ones, don't lend themselves to targets. For instance, it would be silly to state a goal like this: "I feel 25 percent more confident in my job." So don't think you *always* need to include a Target Goal. Add them only if doing so clarifies the goal.

Targets usually improve vision-only goals. For example, the sample Vision Goal in Chapter 10 for a raise had no target, and can be improved by adding a target number of $20,000 as shown below.

*My family is greatly enjoying the additional purchasing power we now have due to the **$20,000** increase in pay I just received; we are sprucing up the house just the way we want, and we have scheduled a dream vacation in Hawaii this year.*

Beyond just adding a measure, Target Goals may also be created by asking the question, "How can I clarify the goal?" This question isn't always asked at goal-setting time, but it can be important. You see, for some goals it can be useful to add multiple targets, or even mention the strategy to get there. This usually can be done by adding just a few words to the Now Goal statement that refine the target, as shown in Example 3, below. However, again, only do this if it's needed to clarify the goal—generally you will want to save the action details for later planning.

# Putting It All Together: Examples of Creating Now Goals

As I said, Now Goals are complete goals that have both a Vision Goal and a Target Goal in the goal statement. When you write out a Now Goal with both components, I call that a Now Goal statement.

Here are some examples of Now Goal statements (both personal and business). These examples, when originally written, were not very powerful because they started primarily as Target Goals only—a fairly typical problem with goals—and as such they were out of balance. In these cases I've added a Vision Goal to create the full Now Goal statement. In Example 3 I've also improved a Target Goal.

## Example 1, Losing Weight

Weight loss is a classic example of a difficult-to-achieve personal goal. Often what someone will say as the goal is, "I want to lose 20 pounds." That simple statement leaves too many options open and does not cover any of the positive reasons or emotions behind the new outcome. It lacks the positive vision component. We saw the Vision Goal in Chapter 10, and here a target is added to create a Now Goal statement (this statement assumes you currently weigh 180 pounds):

*I am achieving a healthy optimal weight that looks good and feels vibrant. To do that, I easily reach a comfortable weight of 160 pounds.*

So you see the vision component is now the main part of the statement, and the Target Goal of 160 pounds is thrown in to add clarity. Also note that positive words are used, and instead of saying *lose* 20 pounds, the target weight is articulated. As I mentioned in Chapter 10, a focus on *losing* something is usually counterproductive since it puts the attention on the thing you want to get rid of and the associated negative emotions. Better is to describe what you want to achieve, along with the feelings of being there, all in positive emotive language.

## Example 2, Increasing Pay

In this next example we will look at a goal to make a higher salary. In the original goal, the individual simply states, "I want to increase my pay by 25 percent While positive, this is a typical example of a money goal that focuses too much on the financial target alone. I would counsel this person to examine why they want the increase in pay. I would ask them to come up with more positive statements that describe the improved state the extra pay will make possible, and then emphasize those in the Vision Goal. But I would still have them include the Target Goal for clarity. What should be written is of course dependent upon the person's needs and motives, but here's one possible version:

*I just received a fantastic raise of 25 percent. That means I can now buy that convertible I have been longing for—I can see myself now, driving down the coast, the sun on my face, the wind in my hair. What a sweet experience this is! I am also going out to dinner every weekend—I love great food.*

### Example 3, Increased Corporate Sales

Next is another numeric Target Goal that not only lacks vision, and therefore any passion around it, but has a poorly defined and ambiguous Target Goal as well. The original goal, set by the CEO of a company, is "Our company will increase sales by 15 percent." To start on making this better, the Target Goal portion of the goal needs to be rewritten somewhat:

*While increasing our number of satisfied customers, we are lifting sales by 15 percent and maintaining our profit margins.*

So we added "increasing our numbers of satisfied customers" and "maintaining our profit margins." Granted, this expands on the first goal, but in a way that's needed. It is needed because there are so many ways a simple increase of 15 percent could in fact go wrong for the company; you could increase sales by slashing prices—but you might then lose profitability. Or you might reach profitable lower prices by cutting quality, but lose customer satisfaction in the process. So the added Target Goal statements clarify that by answering the optional second fundamental Target Goal question, "How can I clarify the goal?"

Let's now add a bit more vision to this goal, and even more target specificity. Here is a more complete version of this Now Goal using more descriptive and emotive language, and more cohesive targets:

*We are transforming our company to be a healthier, stronger, and profitable company in a way that increases shareholder value, all the while expanding the number of customers that can enjoy our products. To do this, we anticipate a 15 percent sales increase, maintenance of profit margins, and stable or better measures of quality and customer satisfaction. Analysts applaud the strategies, shareholders are delighted, and the board recognizes management for their superior work.*

There is a lot of passion (and specificity) in that statement. It has both strong vision elements and strong target elements; it is a statement worthy of a motivational and successful CEO.

## Rules and Suggestions for Tweaking Target and Now Goals

I gave you the formula for creating Vision Goals in Chapter 10, so let's now look at some rules and suggestions for creating Target Goals. There are a number of things to keep in mind that will help you succeed with creating your Now Goals.

### Keep Target Goals Flexible

Target Goals add focus and specificity. Yet you need to balance the focus and specificity a Target Goal brings with the potential for frustration if it is not reached. I don't want you to make the Target Goals so imperative that they are crushing if they're not achievable. Don't let managing the measure overshadow the vision.

Instead, make them flexible and see them for what they are: specific targets to help you focus on your desired achievement—not a stick to beat yourself up with if you don't obtain them. Keep them flexible, both in your written goal statement and in your opinion about them.

Granted, in the business world, you may have more rigid stakeholders that want hard targets, but try to work with your stakeholders as best you can to share and pursue the *vision* at least as much as, if not more than, the target.

The reason I emphasize this is that sometimes events unfold such that earlier-set Target Goals cannot be met even though the vision can be. We sometimes get so hung up on the target that we lose sight of the vision. So don't allow target difficulties to discourage your continued pursuit of the vision.

To use an extreme example, it's said that Edison created 700 light bulb failures before he got one to work correctly. If he had quit the first or second or even the hundredth time that one of his Target Goals was missed, where would he be? He held onto the vision. Mistakes and missed targets are signposts for how to improve your route to the vision. So perhaps use ranges in your numeric Target Goals, or just be sure to keep a flexible attitude about them. Don't overly obsess about the target; obsess about the vision.

## Target Goals Should Fit You

Target Goals need to be a fit for you; they need to be believable to you. In fact, when writing down a target number, if you feel in your body a sense of tightness or even fear because you know that it will be hard to achieve and probably disappointing when you don't achieve it, then scale back the number to a number you're more comfortable with (this assumes you are setting the goal yourself). Doing that will help greatly; you can always up the number on the next round.

However, if scaling back the number for round one leaves you with little additional achievement to enjoy, if it generates very little excitement, then this goal is one that you will want to advance to Chapter 14, "Stretch Your Now Goals." In that chapter I talk about changing your beliefs so that you can accept the larger goals that you set.

Sometimes Target Goals are given to you by someone else and you do not have the flexibility to change them. If that is the case for a given Target Goal—e.g., "You must sell $40K in product this month"—you will either need to find a way to get truly passionate about it, or just know that it is not a real Now Goal. In the first case—if you can get passionate about the target—then add a Vision Goal that you truly believe and want. That transforms a weak Target Goal into a true Now Goal, one you can activate.

However, if the latter case is true—you've been assigned a target you can't get passionate about and don't believe in—then don't try building a fake Vision Goal around it; that will only fail. Rather, just treat the assigned target like a Control-layer task and use a pure action approach—create tasks on your Now

Tasks list to work on it. This is the old way to work goals, and is less effective than creating a true Now Goal (because Step 3—Goal Activation—cannot be applied), but this is all you can do for a Target Goal you do not own yourself. If the target is not too challenging, such action alone may be sufficient.

### Ignore Detailed "How" Statements

Even though Target Goals help define the How of the goal, try to avoid any detailed How statements when you write up the Now Goal. What I mean by that is, don't try to describe in your Now Goal statement the details of how your vision will be achieved. Don't list action steps there. Don't describe a path to reach your goal (unless the path is a goal itself). The point is to focus on the outcome, not to focus on the way to get there.

For example, I would not create a goal that says this:

*I will start going to the gym and join the aerobics class so that I can reach a weight of 160 pounds.*

There may be many different ways to attain your weight goal—so unless you have absolutely decided an aerobics class at the gym is the only way, putting that specific action in the goal statement restricts your options too much and may distract your subconscious mind from finding even better solutions. Instead, write the goal more generally, and then in any action planning you do (Chapter 13), identify detailed action paths you might take toward the goal—that's where you would list joining the aerobics class.

### Put Dates in Action Steps, Not in the Now Goal Statement

You may think you should include a firm due date within your Now Goal statement. And in fact, most goal writers throw in a due date as one of the required elements of a goal—the T for "timely" in SMART usually implies including a date.

But I rarely put firm due dates on my Now Goals; rather I put due dates on action steps and milestones I am setting in my plan to reach the goal (I discuss action steps in Chapter 13, and I discuss putting deadlines on Significant Outcome Milestones in Chapter 7). Due dates help drive action on large *tasks*, but larger goals often rise above a firm date.

Why? Recall that goals are different from tasks, and their achievement is usually not assured by merely taking a specific set of steps. You certainly need action steps with goals—it's just that when working with goals it is rare that you can sequence such steps all the way to a firm achievement date. If you set a firm due date anyway, what can you do if the date is missed (as often happens with goals)? Usually you just feel helpless and disappointed. Instead, set the firm due dates on the action milestones, not the goal. Then complete all those steps by their deadlines, and reassess the goal status periodically to see if other action is needed for the goal.

That said, *general* time frames for goals do make sense. For example, for small- or medium-sized personal goals I often list a set of goals against a *season* of the year. That's because some goals often match naturally to a season (sports goals or outdoor projects, for example), and if you do not reach them, those goals are moot. Also, the length and "feeling" of a season often align naturally

**Figure 11.1**   Now Goals list.

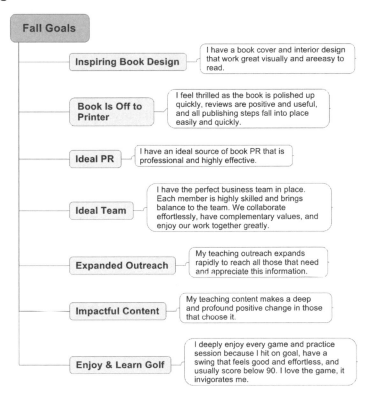

with the forward motion of a goal. Furthermore, as a season starts to come to a close I have a quite natural timeline to track the goal achievement against, but no hard date to beat myself up with.

With this in mind, I will often collect a set of smaller Now Goal statements on one page, marked at the top with the current season (e.g., Fall Goals), and review the current set together in each daily goal activation session. I call such a list a Now Goals list (see Figure 11.1).

## Using Money as a Target Goal

Money is a wonderful Target Goal as it causes you to focus on what it is you really want. You can learn a lot about yourself as you start to set a money Target Goal, and that can lead to better-articulated goals. However, let me caution you about how you use money as a Target Goal.

Sometimes people write down money as a target, assuming that if they obtain a certain large amount of money, then all their other goals will be possible. They may do that if they are lacking money and are just thinking, "I need money," or perhaps if they have read success books that encourage focusing on money.

Here's the problem with doing that: instead of focusing on the substance of their goals, they try to focus on the single money target itself as if it were a vision. Money numbers, like any other Target Goals, are never visions in themselves. Money is a means to obtain many of the things you want in your life, and those things are themselves the core of the vision. So when you write your Now Goal statement, if you include money as a Target Goal, make sure the money figure really is just a way to enhance your description of the vision, and that it is not the vision itself.

Instead, describe the vision of the specific things you want with the money (like a new house, car, and so on); describe how they will look and how having them will feel. If you need to create a number of separate goals to do that, that's okay.

For example, I would not write as a Now Goal "I want to make a million dollars." It is weak and lacks vision (and it may be beyond your current beliefs). Writing "I want to be a millionaire" is slightly better if you believe it is possible, since the word *millionaire* for some people implies a certain lifestyle—one that can be visualized. But I still counsel you to describe, in your goal description, some details of lifestyle changes you want. Ask, "How does life look with my new money goal in place?" Also ask, "What new things are in my life that I will see and feel?"; especially ask, "How do I feel?" Remember, you want your Vision Goal to be emotive. This leads me to my next point about *intangible* goals.

### Using Money for Intangible Goals

Money is often desired for *intangible* goals, and a little introspection about this can greatly help you simplify, focus, and better articulate your goals. For example, let's say that after a bit of thought you realize one reason you feel the need for a certain amount of money is that you sense it will allow you to feel safe and secure, able to pay all your living expenses and a bit more. To that end then, you should focus on that statement about security, and add the dollar target amount at the end for specificity.

For example, your Now Goal statement could be something like this:

*I feel safe and secure. I know that all my living expenses are easily paid and I can enjoy a few nice things in life like going out to dinner often, a nice vacation a few times a year, and buying gifts for my family. A dollar amount of $80,000 per year should meet those intentions just fine.*

In this example, the central element of the vision is what you're getting from the money, not the money itself. And the emphasis at the start is on the *feeling* the money brings. That is the right way to approach money in your Now Goal statement.

There are other examples of intangible qualities people are pursuing when they ask for money. Here are some typical intangible areas that money brings to people that you should consider as you add money to a Now Goal.

Security: as already mentioned above, no longer worrying about having enough money is important, so describe the feeling of always having enough money such as (from above):

*I feel secure in my finances; I know that all my living expenses are easily paid.*

Freedom: freedom to do what you want, to work in the activity you want, and to take time off when you want can be key. If freedom is your goal, make sure you include qualities of freedom in your Now Goal statement, such as the following:

*I have a life with great autonomy and freedom of direction, I have exactly the work activity I enjoy, and I work only with the clients I like. My time is my own and I can easily batch my work so that taking time off is simple to do.*

Simplicity: many people feel that life becomes too complex as they try to do everything for themselves and their families. If simplicity is what you are hoping money will bring, be sure to include statements that paint a picture of simplicity, such as this:

*I have a simple and refreshing lifestyle. I can focus entirely on my family and my creative work. For nearly all complex areas of my business and life, I find excellent people who handle them for me, and they handle them well.*

Variety: abundant money can enable a constant string of new experiences, whether new places to travel to, new material items to buy, or even new people to meet. You can list ways to experience variety in your life that may or may not require large sums of money. For example:

*I have an exciting and varied lifestyle. I enjoy consistent changes in projects that send me to interesting and exotic locations. I enjoy meeting new and stimulating people nearly every day.*

There are even more intangibles: self-respect, personal power, confidence, courage, inner peace, happiness, maybe even love. Sometimes money can help us achieve a few or all of these indirectly. However, as you start to target money to achieve qualities like this, stop for a moment. Stop and examine your Vision Goal statement, and your soul, and consider what you really want. Ask yourself if money is really what you are seeking after all. The qualities listed above do not *require* money to achieve them, and so you may be able to get them without chasing large sums of money. By using money as a proxy for these things, you are dictating the How, the way you will get them, and that is usually not the role of a Now Goal statement.

Consider instead describing these qualities in your vision *without* attaching money; consider them in their pure form. For example, you can create a vision of being happy, secure, and confident, without ever mentioning money. It might make that intangible goal easier to achieve and could make the vision statement feel much more honest to you, much more believable. All these qualities can come in various ways, and money is not the only way, so don't feel you have to emphasize money if it does not feel right to do so. In general, if you do not believe or connect well with your vision statement, then the activation step won't work, so be genuine.

In fact, any time you find yourself focusing obsessively on money as what you need in life, do the above exercise. I think you will find a feeling of peace once you realize the things you think you want money for may be achievable in simpler ways, and that you can pursue those simpler ways with less effort. If you are using money unnecessarily as a How for your goal, you may be making the goal harder.

## Summary

To summarize, Target Goals are numeric or specific measures and statements that help give focus and clarity to a vision. They typically answer the question, "How can I measure this outcome?" Target Goals often also answer the question, "How can I clarify this outcome?" Adding Target Goals to a Vision Goal, to create a Now Goal, is Step 2 of the full 4-step Now Goal creation process. Now Goals are goals that are written in such a way that they include a powerful Vision Goal and include applicable Target Goals that help clarify the vision. Now Goals are the next evolution of personal and workplace goal setting, improving greatly on the previous standard of SMART goals.

By the way, you may wonder why I use the word *Now* in the name *Now Goal*. I do that because such goals are *doable* now, and are kept "active in your now." By *doable,* I mean they are complete goals that have all the components needed to take them to the action phase. What I mean by "kept active in your now" is that you will take steps to activate these goals, as discussed next.

# CHAPTER 12

# Step 3, Activating Now Goals—The Key to Goal Success

Okay, so I implied if you clearly articulated the Vision Goal, and used Target Goals in a way that added clarity to your Vision Goals, you were mostly ready to start working your goals. You might say, "Okay, can I get to work?" Most goal experts at this point would say, "Yes, just do it!" They would urge you to define the goal and just take action. And yes, you do need to take action. But first there is one more step, probably the most important step. You need to *activate* your goal. Activating your goals is Step 3 of the 4-step Now Goal creation process.

## What Is Goal Activation?

Activation is simply taking a few steps each day to embrace and internalize the vision portion of your goal. It is very easy and surprisingly powerful.

What does it mean to embrace and internalize your goals? For goal activation, after you clearly write up your Now Goal statement, I am going to define a few steps for you to take to practice "spinning" your Now Goal statement briefly each day.

I use the word *spinning* here with good reason. Let me explain.

Have you ever had a day where a song gets "stuck" in your head? It seems to spin over and over again, often in the background of your mind. You may have noticed that happening with a thought too—often a bad one. For example, imagine you are running late to an important meeting. Because of that, you are under stress; perhaps you cannot call the person, or even if you did it would not help. When that happens to me, during the last part of the drive or walk to the meeting (the part where I should actually be in the meeting room), I am thinking over and over, "Darn, I am late. Shoot, I should have left earlier. Why didn't I get out the door sooner," and so on. I am spinning the same thoughts over and over again in my mind.

This happens in much less urgent situations as well—perhaps even all the time. We all get minor thoughts spinning over and over again in our heads. In most cases they seem completely out of the blue—random firing of brain cells, so to speak, triggered by events or things around us in the moment. But in other cases they follow trends or even logic. It can be a repeated thought about an upcoming or past work event, a conversation we just had, or something at home. Perhaps we keep reviewing an ongoing issue, or maybe we have background thoughts on the next project we are about to start, or the next person we are going to meet.

Often such thoughts are spinning in your subconscious mind, just below the surface level. Sometimes they pop to the surface and you even stop and consider them. In either case, most of you also know how strongly such background thoughts—self-talk—can influence your attitudes and your success at work, especially when a thought spins consistently.

If we have negative self-talk about our work, it affects our outcomes; we've all seen that. If our self-talk is positive and we feel good, it helps. Like the small cloud of dust that followed Pig-Pen around in the old  *Peanuts* cartoon by Charles M. Schulz, the cloud of surface and below-surface thoughts that spin inside us all day long often defines us, and sets the stage for how we approach work and life.

What I propose is that you will actually "seed" those spinning thoughts with a short segment of purposeful focus on your goals each day. In general it means reviewing—reading and picturing—your Now Goal statement each day, and getting your vision of the goal activated in your subconscious mind. By doing this, your habits of background thought start to be more and more in support of your goals. You may find opportunities to take action on your goals more readily. And you may find yourself more motivated to act on your goals.

Now, I admit this positive effect on goals may seem far-fetched, so I don't expect you to buy into this based on the short explanation above. Also, this may sound similar to things you may have seen and dismissed in the past—positive thinking or positive affirmations, perhaps. But goal spinning is different from these, and it is much more, as you will see.

To clarify this interesting topic, in the rest of this chapter I provide the details of this process I call goal activation. I explain some theories of why it works so well, including another perspective on the word *spinning* that I think makes this even more intuitive. I also describe examples of how goal activation works, other situations in which it is used successfully, some subtleties to it, and more.

And I propose that you start doing this for all your goals. It does take some technique to do it right, which I describe, and it takes some discipline to do it every day. I cover all those details in the pages ahead.

## Why Activation?

Why do we need to activate our goals? Because it makes achieving them much easier—and I assert that you will never achieve some of your harder goals without it.

There are many benefits to activating your goals in this way. First of all, activation often solves procrastination issues because it puts the goal in sight every day, with positive energy. Activation also makes things possible that do not seem possible; it does this by activating the power of your subconscious mind to find solutions that may not be obvious. It puts the goal into "pull" mode, where effective actions toward the goal come more automatically.

The main reason you need to do this is that goals need a little magic to achieve. You see, if goals were easy, they would not be goals; they'd just be large tasks. As I said in the introduction to Part II, goals represent going beyond a simple set of steps. Using the common example of losing weight, if that were just a set of steps, it would not be a $40 billion industry. The steps are easy to list: eat less, exercise more. But why do so few of us succeed? Clearly there is more to success with goals, and this is what separates *goals* from merely lengthy tasks.

Beyond adding vision, you might think *willpower* is the main additional piece needed for goals. But is the key to accomplishing goals simply applying willpower? That's what most people say,: "Define the goal and steps to get there, and apply willpower as needed to keep doing that work." That is certainly the implication with losing weight. People say it takes willpower to stick with a decision to eat less, and it takes willpower to keep up a discipline of exercise. The subtext is that if you cannot do those things, your willpower is weak. The same assumption is made with many work goals.

While some willpower is certainly necessary, I say the magic of getting goals completed goes well beyond the application of willpower. *Activating* the goal can provide that missing element.

## How to Activate Your Goals

Activation should be applied to the vision portion of the Now Goal because the subconscious reacts best to emotions and feelings, not numbers; you cannot activate the goal without the Vision Goal in place. This is one reason the Vision Goal component of a goal is so important, and why I spent so much time describing it in Chapter 10. It provides the core material from which you'll activate the goal; it provides the thing for the subconscious mind to hold onto.

So the first step is to create that Vision Goal portion of the Now Goal statement. You want it written with vivid sensory description and emotive language, according to the formula in Chapter 10. It should be a goal you truly want, not one you have begrudgingly accepted from someone else. If all that is true, you are ready.

### *Reading and Picturing the Now Goal Statement*

Once you have created the Now Goal statement, one containing a strong Vision Goal, you will then "spin it up" daily by reading it. This is fast; it should take a minute or less for small goals, and just a bit more for larger ones. But you should read it in a particular way.

While reading, you will picture the Vision Goal outcome using your imagination. You want to get, even if only for a brief moment, a clear and passionate picture of the outcome.

And there is a key "trick" to this. You should picture the goal *as if it were already accomplished* and already active in your Workday Now (your immediate now, and a few weeks out). Try to experience, in your imagination, the positive *feeling* of the goal already being accomplished. Just for a moment, live it, breathe it, and feel it. See it as being established in your work life, both right now and in the week or two ahead from now.

This is where the Workday Now model comes in. During this short daily review, you are actively imagining how the period of your Workday Now would be different if the goal were done. Again, the Workday Now is the time span we usually attend to mentally on the job, so it makes sense that this time period is what we want to visualize as being different in the new goal. It gives life, right now, to the new outcome.

And there is good reason to visualize the goal in your Workday Now *as if it were already accomplished.* Jack Canfield, in his book *The Success Principles*, explains it well in his Principle #12, which he calls "Act As If." On page 90 of his book he describes it as follows:

*Acting as if sends powerful commands to your subconscious mind to find creative ways to achieve your goals. It programs the reticular activating system (RAS) in your brain to start noticing anything that will help you succeed, and it sends strong messages to the universe that this end goal is something you really want.*

So while reading your goal during goal activation, mentally put yourself in your new reality. Doing so will have a profound effect later in helping you achieve your goal.

## Visualize Using Focused Attention

Also recall from the Workday Now model shown in Chapter 9 the concept of the Immediate Now, or I-Now for short (see Figure 12.1 below). Specifically, the I-Now refers to your mental attention and how you are applying it right now, either in the form of focused point attention, or background dispersed

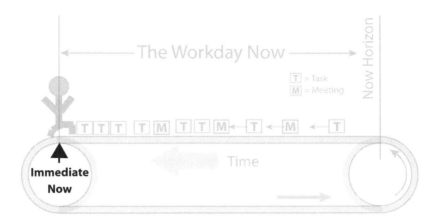

**Figure 12.1**    The Immediate Now, or I-Now for short.

attention. We are going to use it, and its relation to the Workday Now, as a tool to accomplish goals.

You see, normally your focused attention is on action at work—getting tasks done, communicating with people, or studying material needed for a task or project. And your background attention might be on secondary matters related to the task. It might be on small observations about the person you are talking to. It might be on fear of not getting a task done right or getting it done in time, and so on.

To activate a goal, we are interested in using the focused attention element of the I-Now, and we want to apply it to your Vision Goal. Visualization is always done in your I-Now, your focused now, meaning you are using high-quality attention, and being fully present during that process. If there is ever a time to focus on something, this is it. Don't just read the statement in a rote manner, or memorize the statement; instead, review it with full attention. Apply your imagination so that you "live" the statement as you read it.

This is the essence of visualization. If you study visualization as applied to sports, health, or many other things, you will see nearly this exact process described again and again, the process of picturing in your mind's eye the result you want, as if you were there. It has been an accepted process for decades in sports, but somewhat less talked about for work-related goals.

For most day-to-day goals, if the Now Goal statement is well written and passionate, you may be able to activate the goal in your subconscious mind over time just by reading and envisioning that short statement once or twice every day, for even a minute or less each time. If the statement is positive, emotive, and captures the passion and the experience, that may be enough.

For larger or more difficult goals, though, you may need to spend more time on visualization. And you may also need to "adjust your beliefs" about the goal. I will cover that in the "Stretch Your Now Goals" chapter, later in this part of the book. And for life-sized goals, like creating a new career, study Part III of the book—extra tools are provided there.

## The Power of Human Attention

You may be wondering at this point, before committing to a new routine each day, "Does activation really work? Is it proven? Why does it work?" Let's start with why activation works, and then discuss the abundant evidence that it does.

### Why Activation Works

Human attention is a very powerful thing. Advertisers are well aware of this. That is why when we watch TV, they bombard our attention with their TV ads, trying to get us to buy their products when we are shopping later.

Notice the key word "later" here. If you watch an advertisement on TV, most advertisers do not expect you to jump up out of your chair that moment to buy (ignore for now the late-night "call now" ads). Rather, they are making an impression on your attention for later reference. It may seem obvious, but it is important to know that what we put our attention on *now* influences strongly our action *later.*

When we put our focused attention on something in the manner we do with TV commercials, it activates the brain in several ways. TV commercials are designed to make a multisensory impression. They mix visual cues with voice and music, and they tell a story designed to elicit our emotions. Due to that multipronged method, the impression gets stored in various memory locations in the brain all at once, and because of that a TV commercial can be quite effective at making a lasting mark. So the act of putting our focused, multisensory, and emotional attention on something can influence us strongly later.

This is not just true of TV commercials, but of many things in our lives. If we get excited about something we see, especially repeatedly, it makes a big impression that can influence us afterward.

For example, you've seen this in action when you are thinking about the latest purchase you want to make (e.g., car, camera, or clothing). You probably notice that once you start to focus on the item, studying pictures and articles about it in magazines or reading about it online, you later start to notice the item much more. If it is a specific model of a new car, then when driving down the road it seems as if every 5 or 10 minutes you see that same model of car—it suddenly appears to be everywhere. The mind becomes enthralled with your repeated intense focus and emotional attention, and then later your mind starts drawing your attention to peripheral observations, ones that you would not have noticed otherwise.

That same mechanism can be used to help achieve our goals. By focusing on our goals in a similar way, we can activate the mind to help us achieve our goals. It does this in obvious and not so obvious ways.

First, just as with the car, our peripheral observation starts to notice things related to the goal, and that helps direct us to work on it. We may even subconsciously look for things to help us achieve the goal. We may start to lean toward decisions that lead us to the goal, even without realizing it.

A bit less obvious, we may start to experience newfound energy and momentum that helps us achieve the goal. The goal can then be achieved with much less effort.

## Creating Your Own TV Commercial

I find most people accept the truth in the statement, "What you put your attention on grows." Just as a carefully constructed TV ad can dramatically influence our purchasing decisions, I consistently see evidence that using short periods of focused attention on my goals works amazingly well at helping me achieve them. I see it in my life and in others' lives. I see it too often to dispute it.

For the goal spinning exercise I described at the beginning of this chapter, what I essentially had you do was to create the equivalent of a TV commercial, but one for your goal instead of a product. I then asked you to "watch" it repeatedly. In this case it was not a video; rather, it was your written Now Goal statement, enhanced as much as possible to make it colorful, positive, and emotive.

I asked you to spend a few minutes each day reading and visioning it, thereby creating a clear mental picture of your goal on a repeated basis, as if you were watching a commercial over and over again. And then throughout the day you will pursue your goal as you normally would, using whatever action is planned or seems appropriate—nothing else. It may seem hard to believe, but this simple extra "activation" step has a remarkable influence on making your goals more achievable. People who do this report that their goals become easier to fulfill, and that action toward them becomes much more effective.

## Theories on the Power of Human Attention

How does this work? Again, it works largely by "predisposing future attention," the way TV commercials seem to work. (Remember the car you suddenly start noticing everywhere?) You start to notice opportunities to act effectively on your goals—ones you might not have noticed otherwise.

But the power of attention also seems to go beyond just that. There are so many examples of people using positive visualization, which is essentially what I am teaching, to win at sports, to overcome mental and physical handicaps, and more. People who repeatedly visualize a particular outcome even describe "coincidental" meetings that end up getting them closer to that outcome. The power of attention to help you achieve goals often seems to go well beyond what logically makes sense. It does seem to work in an almost magical and unseen way.

Why does it work? Since it usually happens in an unseen way, people are prone to find widely varied and sometimes challenging explanations, and which explanation you accept depends largely on your worldview.

Some say that God is answering prayer; others say that our attention and thoughts attract the object of our attention to us because of the vibrational nature of the universe. But I think the best worldview for the business world is psychology: attention works by the power of the subconscious mind. The subconscious mind, as I am sure you have read and possibly experienced, is an amazingly powerful thing. It can allow us to do things we never thought possible. For example, under hypnosis, due to the power of the subconscious mind, relatively weak people can lift amazing weights, shy people overcome inhibitions, smokers quit smoking, and so on.

I feel that we are essentially programming the subconscious mind when we repeatedly put our conscious attention on the desired outcome of our goals, and so activating our goals in this way will help us achieve them. Yes, the power of the subconscious mind can explain this seemingly amazing phenomenon, and I am going to use this as the explanation in this book.

Of course, the topic of the subconscious mind is a deep and complicated subject in itself. So rather than try to explain it medically or by using psychological theory, I am going to use a new physical analogy in a way that I think will help you get a feel for what is going on and why it works as a means to achieve your Now Goals more easily. It is an analogy that I will use repeatedly through the rest of this book, and is in fact one I have already referred to—spinning. But now I extend my analogy to the spinning of a physical wheel.

### Spinning Wheel Analogy

One very effective way to see how using the power of your attention to spin up thoughts in your subconscious can strongly influence outcomes is to use the analogy of a spinning wheel. It provides a good model that makes intuitive sense. Many people I describe this to say to me, "Oh, now I see how activating goals works!"

### Maintaining Your Direction

Have you ever put a bicycle upside down and spun the front wheel up to a rapid speed? If you have, you may have noticed that if you try to change the orientation of the quickly spinning wheel by moving the handlebars, the front wheel quickly reorients itself back to its original spinning direction. I suggest you try this sometime; it is remarkable how much force "pushes back" and keeps the wheel directed in its original spinning direction.

In fact, when riding a moving bicycle, this aspect of the two quickly spinning bicycle wheels is what helps keep the bicycle upright and pointed straight. It is why you can take your hands off the handlebars of a quickly moving bike and the bike will still go straight and not fall over, or veer off to one side. So the spinning wheels on a bicycle resist redirection and, absent a determined force to turn, those spinning wheels keep you upright and oriented toward your target.

This is called the gyroscope effect; perhaps you have seen the small toy gyroscopes that you can balance on a tiny point—even if that point is sitting off center? It maintains its balance due to the rapidly spinning wheel inside it. Likewise, spinning toy tops do not topple. This is all due to the stability-inducing power of spinning wheels.

In fact, this ability to maintain direction is what keeps the compasses in airplanes and ships pointed to true north. Many people do not realize this, but these high-end compasses are not magnetic—rather they all contain small spinning gyroscopes inside. I used to fly a private airplane, and one of the first things every small-plane pilot knows to do when they start the plane is to make sure the gyroscope in the instrument panel is turned on and spun up (you can hear it), and is then aligned to true north. Once it is, it keeps its directional accuracy nearly indefinitely (at least until you turn the plane off).

So a quickly spinning wheel can provide a consistent direction—it can act like a compass. Are you seeing the connection to goals? Can you see how a consistently spinning thought about your goal in your subconscious mind may guide you in the direction of your goals? Let me take this one step further.

## Great Power and Momentum

Not only do the spinning wheels retain direction toward a target, but a spinning whccl also stores great energy or power within it. In physics, the energy of a spinning mass is called angular momentum, and the force stored within can be quite substantial. If the spinning wheel is heavy and has lots of mass, it's called a flywheel, and can be used to power a machine.

For example, in the 1950s in Switzerland, very heavy spinning flywheels inside some experimental city buses powered them across town with no other motors; other such vehicles were tested in the United States.

And today, giant building-sized flywheels—simple spinning wheels with great mass—are coming online in the U.S. to store energy on our nation's electrical power grid during off-peak generation. This is to increase grid capacity during peak demand. Here's how that works: the flywheels are spun up with huge electric motors late at night when energy demand and costs are low, and then those same spinning wheels are used to turn electric generators during the day, when demand is high. The energy stored in spinning wheels can potentially power a whole city.

So a quickly spinning wheel with large mass can hold quite a bit of energy. I am going to call this ability to hold power in a spinning wheel *the flywheel effect.*

The important take-away from this entire discussion is that a spinning object gives you both firm *guidance* to keep you pointed in an intended direction (gyroscope effect), and great *power and momentum* to get you there (flywheel effect).

And this can be compared to thoughts spinning in the subconscious.

## Goal Spinning Works in a Similar Way

Your habits of thought in your subconscious are like these spinning wheels. Once you get a consistent habit of thought going in the subconscious, it will give direction and power to your thinking, and keep you in a somewhat consistent stance, thought- and attitude-wise. Like the spinning wheel on a bicycle or gyroscope, this will keep your related thinking oriented in the same direction.

This can be good if the habit of thought is a good one. For example, if the thoughts spinning in your subconscious are ones of self-confidence, then many of your subsequent thoughts and actions are guided by that spinning; they tend to be ones of confidence even in the face of an unstable outer world.

They can be specific too. If your positive spinning thought-habit established over the years is "I will be a fireman, just like my dad," then your spinning thoughts will predispose you toward activity that helps you reach that goal. The momentum of those background thoughts (the flywheel effect) can give you the energy and drive to help you get there.

Once you get a thought spinning deeply in your subconscious, it takes on a life of its own, and directs your future thoughts and actions, often in an unseen

way and as an unseen force. This explains many habits of behavior you see in other people and yourself, both positive and negative.

So naturally, you want the ideas spinning in your subconscious to be ones that support your positive work goals, goals such as getting the raise, making the promotion, creating the new product, reaching high sales numbers, and so on.

This is where goal activation comes in. Getting a habit of thought "spun up" in the subconscious that supports your goals, especially new goals, is important to their success. As described at the start of this chapter, goal activation means taking brief daily sessions of "spinning" up your goals, and envisioning the outcome.

## Abundant Evidence That It Works

At this point you might be on the fence, not knowing whether to believe me about this or not. In case you doubt that goal activation can work, let me just say this: there is abundant evidence that it does.

As I have said, what I am proposing you do is really just another form of visualization, like that often used in sports training. You have probably heard about visualization in sports—that if you clearly picture a performance in your mind first, it then becomes easier to do it physically. This has become such an integral part of serious sports training that there is now no question as to its benefits. And a quick search on Amazon for books on sports visualization yields dozens of titles describing success stories from its use.

For example, Jack Nicklaus and many other famous golfers have reported the very powerful effects of visualizing the outcome of a golf swing before actually taking it. They describe seeing in their mind's eye the golf ball flying through the air and landing where they want it to land. And they almost universally credit visualization with helping them achieve success.

Many other famous athletes have described the same for other sports. They describe how doing visualization either immediately before the sports activity, or in mental training weeks before, leads to a successful outcome.

The important point here is that visualization works just as well on non-sports activities.

### Psycho-Cybernetics Book

I have a favorite book on this topic of visualization; it is called *The New Psycho-Cybernetics* by Maxwell Maltz, and I encourage you to look at it. It was written decades ago, has sold millions of copies, and still inspires readers everywhere. Maltz calls the results of visualization the "automatic success mechanism." The *Cybernetics* portion of the title of the book is a reference to mechanical servo mechanisms used in many industrial and military devices that automatically steer their way to a target.

Maltz's point is that once you visualize a goal over and over again, your subconscious will automatically steer you to it. He feels this automatic success mechanism is already built into the subconscious mind; we just need to exercise it. His main tool for exercising it is using imagination to visualize the outcomes that you desire, much as I have described earlier. Just like in sports visualization, he suggests that you see in your mind's eye the successful outcome you want to live, for any goal.

Hypnosis is an accepted and widely utilized therapy for overcoming mental blocks, whether they are fears, bad habits, or mistaken beliefs. This success of hypnosis tells us that the mind is capable of making changes based merely on the power of subconscious suggestion. Maltz, in his book, explains how during visualization, we're making a repetitive suggestion to the subconscious mind that is not too different from hypnosis, so that the subconscious mind begins to believe the visualization is true, and starts to act like it is. The subconscious mind then starts to encourage decisions that support the new understanding of reality. Maltz provides many examples of this working in business.

For instance, Maltz describes how salespeople often do role-playing to practice and visualize the intended outcome during a sales meeting. By repeating over and over again the way the salesperson wants the client activity in the meeting to go, the sales are more successful. This can be done live or mentally; it is shown to work both ways. It's the same with goals; by repeatedly visualizing the outcome of the goal, you can help make it happen.

There is a range of other examples in the Psycho-Cybernetic book about how mental visualizing can improve performance. There are examples of how people use it to get a better job; a concert pianist who practices entirely in his head without touching the keyboard; sports instructors who have the student practice the performance *only* mentally; and visualization to help cure injuries or slow the aging process. I encourage you to read that book if you want to see the many examples of how this can work, and to see further explanations for why it works.

Maltz's main technique for visualization described in his book is what he calls the Theater of Your Mind. You write a script of how you will see yourself performing once your goal is achieved. Then you close your eyes and run through the script mentally, once each day. During that time you mentally visualize yourself succeeding at your goal. Maltz says that after 21 days you will see remarkable results.

### Activation Is a Common Element of Success

This visualization method of helping achieve goals has been recognized for decades. It is a common element of many widely known and reputable success and management books.

The earliest well-known proponents of this were Wallace D. Wattles in his book *The Science of Getting Rich*, and Napoleon Hill in his book *Think and Grow Rich*. This latter book was a best seller for many decades, starting back in the 1930s, and it still sells well now. In it, he describes the same phenomenon I discuss above. In that book, Napoleon Hill has you write a statement describing the success you want, and asks you to read that statement every day—the same formula I just presented.

## Recent Coverage

The same approach has been revived by various recent authors. In Stephen R. Covey's book *The 7 Habits of Highly Effective People*, Habit 2 is called Begin with the End in Mind. In discussing that "habit" he describes how all things are "created twice." There is what he calls a mental or first creation, and then what he calls the physical or second creation. The idea is that you should visualize the outcome you want before you attempt to achieve it.

In Stephen R. Covey's other well-known book, *First Things First*, he goes into more detail on this. He describes many times using a visualization technique he calls *creative imagination.* He says that just as visualization can be used to improve athletics, it can be used to improve your quality of life. He encourages you to set aside some time each day alone to close your eyes and visualize yourself acting out what you want to achieve. He also encourages you to write a mission statement and then use your creative imagination to visualize yourself living it. He insightfully notes that "we can live out of our imagination instead of our memory."

Success writer Brian Tracy, who has created over 50 books and audio CDs on success, goals, and related topics, and who lectures extensively throughout corporate America, refers often to the power of attention. He repeatedly says in his books that managing our attention is a key to achieving goals, that what we put our attention on in life grows. In his book called *Goals!* he talks about using visualization to change your mental picture of yourself. He describes a four-part visualization exercise where you hold a mental picture of what you want—it helps you achieve it.

The recent book called *The Answer* by John Assaraf and Murray Smith describes a process similar to Napoleon Hill's. The authors also add practical ways to merge the process into your business activities.

## The Law of Attraction Approach

Recently this theory has been elaborated on in a different way. The term used most often to describe a similar phenomenon these days is the Law of

Attraction, and it is core to the teachings of Jerry and Esther Hicks, who have been the main voice for it since the late 1980s. The theory basically says that since like attracts like, by visualizing our goals we can attract their creation. The DVD and book *The Secret* by Rhonda Byrne, released in 2006, caused a lot more recent interest in the concept of the Law of Attraction. That DVD sold millions of copies and stimulated the realization by viewers that the power of our attention may be quite profound.

While the emphasis is different, I think the Law of Attraction is describing basically the same phenomenon I have described in this chapter. However, for many readers, it seems to overly simplify how they can obtain their goals. And recently, too many get-rich-quick books are starting to use the Law of Attraction as their central argument, and praise its practice as a foolproof way to make millions, which it will not be for most of us.

Instead, my focus is simply on the value of human attention. As I said earlier, I find most people accept the truth in the statement, "What you put your attention on grows." That, combined with recognizing the power of the subconscious mind, as demonstrated in the field of psychology, is the core of my goal activation approach.

### Hundreds of Other Books

There have been hundreds of other success books over the past several decades that discuss this as well, and thousands of testimonials from people who say it works. Over and over again, people have said that what you put your attention on grows in your life, so one way to help achieve goals is to focus your attention (in certain ways) on your goals.

So as you can see, the principles I outline in this book are time-tested and heavily supported, and perhaps you have even seen or tried them before. I just hope that my particular presentation here provides you with a fresh and positive look at the topic.

You see, I have found that many of the past and current books on this topic unfortunately get a little carried away on a message of how miraculous this can be, and I suspect that scares many businesspeople away from doing it, or makes it sound too unbelievable for them to even try. I feel my concept of goal activation and goal spinning is a much better image of how these principles work and that it will help you picture this in practice.

And that is a key point. Goal activation is really just another management technique; you should manage your goal's *visions* just like you manage your goal's *actions*. In fact, the biggest payoff for reaching a goal may come from managing the vision rather than the action. Activating goals is a very important thing to do if you want to succeed at your goals. Think of it as another work activity, and one that you should do regularly. That's why it is a central element of this workday management book; this is management work, plain and simple.

## Is This Really Necessary?

Sometimes I get this question. If the concept of how to get your Now Goals activated is so simple, is it really necessary to do it on purpose? After all, many people achieve their goals without studying a goal statement every day. Don't we do it naturally anyway, when we work on and think about our goals?

That's partly true. In certain jobs, separate goal activation should not be necessary. Ideally, the goal is already the main thing you are focusing on at work, and your repeated focus on the vision as part of your job activates the goal for you.

For example, let's say you are a builder working from a set of architectural drawings. Every day while studying the details of the day's work, you cannot help but refer to the overall drawing of the building. Every day as you do this, you are reminded of the big picture and how it is all coming together. And if you are lucky, you have even met the future owner, have felt the owner's passion and excitement for the building, and are sharing that enthusiasm. Perhaps you even find the design something you like very much. Work like that is virtually the same thing as doing the goal spinning exercise I just described—or even better, because it is done all day long.

This kind of vision-oriented work, when applied positively, is why so many great and challenging goals in the business world are achieved, even without formal visualizing exercises. Many individuals just naturally activate their goals in a positive way, throughout their normal workday like this; it is part of their jobs.

This is the ideal case, where, in the course of your work, you are constantly reminded of the overarching vision and the positive passion behind it, and so are already spinning up the goal without extra effort. If you can arrange a job like that, you should.

Or maybe you are in a job where you participate in a daily "sales" or start-the-day meeting used to rally the troops, focusing on the positive vision of your group's activities. Or maybe your organization has frequent motivational meetings or management retreats that focus on the vision in a positive way.

### Most of Us Need to Purposely Do This

More likely, though, you are not in a job like that. For most of us, the positive vision is rarely in sight in our full-time work. Rather, most workers are assigned only a small piece of the action, and they rarely hear about the vision behind the assignment. Usually they only hear about the problems.

And even for those of us that are in a role that "should" be exposed to the vision daily (owners, executives, managers, and self-employed), we usually are not. What happens is we get so caught up in deadlines, issues, and fire drills that we very quickly lose sight of the positive vision that brought us to our daily routine.

Similarly, one-off motivational meetings may work for a few days, but seldom have a lasting effect.

You might think that project teams working full time to execute a vision would remain tuned into that vision and naturally activate the goals during their work. After all, they have studied the vision from every angle, they have created plans to execute the vision, and they review the plans daily.

However, even project teams often quickly lose sight of the vision. Just like management, the details of *execution* become so dominant in daily activity that the *vision* fades from sight. So working a plan is not enough; you need to constantly remind yourself of the vision you want to achieve, and do it in a positive and emotive way. Most workday activities just don't do that.

Finally, perhaps the Vision Goal you are pursuing has nothing to do with your full-time job; perhaps it is a personal vision that you do not have time to focus on in the course of the workday.

So in all of these cases, you will need to find time to activate the Now Goal every day yourself. I want you to make it a specific daily task, to ensure it gets done. You will probably be doing this as an individual; but if you are leading a team working toward a goal, you might find a way to have your team activate the Vision Goal each day together.

## Isn't This Just Positive Thinking?

You might be wondering at this point, "Haven't I seen this before—isn't this just positive thinking, or using positive affirmations?" Well, the fact that you said "just" means you probably have a bad impression of positive thinking, or feel that it is not very impressive. In fact, most people teaching visualization techniques similar to the goal spinning technique I just outlined try to distance themselves from positive thinking. Why?

Positive thinking has gotten a bum rap over the years. Many people have tried it and found it did not work. The reason I think it did not work for them is because most people are missing the visualization step. While positive thinking *could* include visualization, and in many books on the topic it *does,* most people just don't use visualization when they exercise positive thinking. And so it becomes a dispassionate exercise of repeating affirmations with no real impact.

So no, this is not positive thinking in the way that term is usually used these days.

## How Much Time Will This Take? How Quickly Will This Work?

The next questions I usually get at this point are, "How much time do I need to spend on this?" and then, "How quickly will it work?"

To answer the first, this is fast. You only have to write the Now Goal statement once. After that, it is simply reading the statement while building a mental and emotional image as you do. That might be 30 seconds to a couple minutes per goal—longer obviously for more elaborate Now Goal statements. And longer for a more powerful effect. But in general if you have a list of five average goals, you should be able to jump through them in 5 minutes or so.

To answer the second question—how quickly will it work—most references that talk about this or similar processes say you can start to see positive results in

20 to 30 days. I know that time frame is possible because I have seen it happen for me and others—but it can take longer. After all, there are no guarantees. I have been doing this or something like it for decades on various goals and have seen it work quickly, if the goal is reasonable and I keep up the habit. But there are so many variables, it is hard to predict. We will talk more about those variables ahead.

But I want to say something important right now. If the vision is positive, well written, and inspiring, you will enjoy this process greatly. It just feels good to focus on the best things possible for your work and life, and to pretend even for a moment each day that you have already achieved them. The attitude that I like to take about why I should do the exercise is this: even if this activity doesn't magically lead to my goal right away, the positive feelings I get from focusing on things I want most in life are worth the time.

In fact, that is the measure of a well-written Now Goal statement: does it generate overall positive feelings in you? If not, you may need to rework your Now Goal statement following the formula in Chapter 10. Or adjust the goal if the reason it does not feel good is it is not right for you or not believable. We will talk more about that in Chapter 14, "Stretching Your Now Goals," later in Part II.

Also, this needs to be *your* goal, one you own and really want yourself. If your boss hands you a Target Goal that your heart is not in, I doubt the spinning process is going to help much, even if you do wrap a half-hearted vision around it. Make an effort to find the vision in it that you are truly inspired by, or pick a different goal.

## The Importance of Positive Spinning

Even with all the writing and evidence of the power of goal activation, some of you may still think this is silly. You may think, "I know what my goal is. I know I want to make more money; I don't need to read this silly Now Goal statement every day. In fact, I'm shown every week that I do not have enough money in my paycheck. So I know what my goals are; I don't need a formal reminder."

Well, this is a perfect example where you *do* need to do goal activation. Here's why. In the activation process you are not just "reminding" yourself of the goal. You are using the power of your imagination to feed your subconscious the experience of *having* the goal. Almost nobody does that. We are taught to be so practical that imagination is never used. But using your imagination is the key.

And in fact, the statement above, "I'm shown every week that I do not have enough money in my paycheck," leads to another important topic that reinforces the need for goal spinning. That's the topic of how important it is to spin positively, covered next.

## Getting Beyond Issue Spinning

If you are wondering whether you want to bother with goal activation, note this: the principle of spinning up outcomes is working, whether you believe it or not. So unless you take positive, repeated management steps to focus on the outcomes you want, you may be inadvertently "negatively spinning." You see, all your thoughts contribute to spinning to some extent, whether you think them on purpose or not. In the absence of positive spinning, if you absently focus on the negative aspects of your job, project, or goal activities, you may in fact be spinning up more of the same stuck issues.

In the example above ("I'm shown every week that I do not have enough money"), the thought you are spinning is about lack of money; in essence, you are negatively goal spinning. You are repeatedly focusing on something, and that can cause it to occur more. You see, the subconscious mind doesn't care whether you are saying, "I want it" or "I don't want it." The subconscious mind only cares *what* you are focusing on, and tries to lead you to more experiences of it. So if your attention is consistently on passionate bad feelings about lack, then that is what you will get more of. I call this *issue spinning*.

In another example, on some work teams it often becomes fashionable to criticize the work, the project, the management, the company, and so on. Many of us may join in that conversation just to try to fit in. Do you see how this can have a strongly negative influence on obtaining the things you want from work? By doing this you are negatively goal spinning—you are issue spinning.

And even more practically, some people feel the way to best manage a project, after the plan is in place, is to attend mainly to all the things that might stop it; in other words, focus on and manage the negative issues, one at a time, as they come up. Just put out the fires.

Well, certainly you need to manage around roadblocks. But if you lose sight of the Vision Goal in the process and all you do is focus on roadblocks and issues, think about what you are doing. You may in fact be spinning up more negative issues and you may be making your project goal harder to reach.

Issue spinning during the day can even nullify your morning goal spinning. It can stop progress on your goals by creating opposing mental chatter. Picture, for example, an all-wheel drive car lifted above the ground by a small crane. The car has two wheels spinning forward (from morning goal spinning) but incorrectly has two wheels spinning backward (from issue spinning during the day). If the car is lowered to the ground and engaged with the road, it will thrash about but go nowhere. If, however, all four wheels are spinning in roughly the same direction, then the momentum forward will be significant once the car has engaged with the road. So support your specific goals with a positive general attitude during the day.

This works on a personal level too. Anytime you kick yourself after a mistake and say, "I always do this," you are negatively spinning. Think of what you just said: you said to yourself, with strong emotion, that you *always* do this bad thing. That's an affirmation; that's a statement that your subconscious may take literally. So the next time you see something in your action or behavior that you do not like, stop and picture what you *do* want. Put your attention on visualizing the outcome you would prefer. That way, you are spinning the outcomes you want.

## Getting Beyond Fear and Worry

One thing you absolutely need to do to move your goals forward is to get beyond fear in your workplace. This is another form of issue spinning. In fact, fear and worry are the worst forms of negative spinning you can do. If you're afraid of your boss, afraid that you're not meeting your work targets, afraid for your job, or focused on anything that causes fear in the workplace, that fear will have a negative effect on your ability to achieve your goals.

The key is whether you buy into the fears. The potential for fear-creating situations will always be there, so it's how you react to those fear-creating situations that is important. If you are able to rise above them with confidence, they'll have no effect on you and then you will be fine. If, however, you find yourself reacting negatively to them, buying into the fear, then negative spinning will occur. If you are in the latter situation, use one of the "adjusting beliefs" tools that I mention in Chapter 14 to flip fear to a positive stance.

*Worrying* is strong negative spinning too. Consider what worrying is; it is picturing in your mind unwanted outcomes, with great emotional energy. In other words, it is negative visualization. You may think you are being responsible by worrying about and planning for all the possible things that could go wrong on your journey to your goal. But in fact the opposite is true; if you spend too much time worrying about negative outcomes, you can in fact delay the achievement of your goal. If you notice such self-talk, use it as an opportunity to "flip the dialogue." That means, from the negative talk, identify what it is you *do* want, and create a statement that summarizes that. Then focus on that for a few seconds.

On large business projects, certainly you should do *some* planning for possible negative outcomes; that's called risk management. But I urge you to spend only a moment or two mentally on the negative outcome you are covering for, and then switch quickly into solution mode, spending most of your energy there. Focus mostly on what you *want* to have happen.

### Counterbalance Any Long-Term Negative Habits

Also consider this: you have been spinning goals and issues all your life. There are numerous predispositions already programmed into your subconscious that have been there for years. These spinning predispositions have lots of momentum built up from your childhood and later years. They can spin forever, like a satellite spinning in frictionless space. These momentums may be positive or negative. The positive ones obviously help us in our activities. But we all have many negative experiences from our past that hold us back. Negative childhood and adult experiences can create internal issues in your subconscious mind, and these spinning issues feed inhibitions and negative self-talk to your conscious mind. They will inhibit achievement of your goals, unless you do something about them.

Marci Shimoff, in her *New York Times* best-selling book *Happy for No Reason,* says that scientists tell us we have on, average, 60,000 thoughts per day, 95% of which are similar to, or the same as, our thoughts from the day before; and that 80 percent of our thoughts *are negative.* Think of the negative spinning we do every day without realizing it.

So it is your job to actively spin up counterbalancing positive predispositions that are beneficial to your goal at hand. If you do not, you may be left to the mercy of possibly decades of negative training. Doing nothing—not spinning up your goals—is not an option for anything but the easiest of goals.

In Chapter 14 I discuss approaches to move past long-standing self-limiting issues.

## Goal Activation in Daily Practice

Do this formal goal spinning every day. I have a routine of doing it every morning with my coffee. I take out my one-page list of Now Goal statements, and run through the whole thing in five or ten minutes. I like doing it. It feels good to remind myself of what is important in my life and work, and to get a bit jazzed each morning on why I go to work every day. If you create a similar one-page list of your goals (see the sample list in Chapter 11) and run through the whole list each day, I think you will like it too.

One caution is this: do not think that since you can at least remember the goal you can skip a formal review each day. This is an easy habit to fall into, and it's really a trap. Sure, you can recall what it is that you're trying to reach without reading the full vision statement, but that's not the point. You want to recreate each day the *full* picture of it. The problem with doing it from memory is your memory will miss elements of the vision statement, and then eventually the memory of the goal details will start to slip away from you. And furthermore, the detail of the vision statement is what elicits the emotional positive imagery that is so important for a complete activation. So do this full activation every day.

If you are part of a team working toward a goal, then consider doing this goal activation together. That's essentially what motivational meetings are, so, in a way, this is nothing new for many sales organizations. However, the frequency and detail of the spinning process described here probably is more than most do.

For individual goals, you might consider forming a group to activate those individual goals with others who know the process, particularly if the goals are somewhat related across the group; there is nothing like a scheduled group meeting to make sure the goal activation gets done. Also, Napoleon Hill, author of *Think and Grow Rich*, found that on related goals, such groups increased the power of the results by creating a larger attention power greater than the sum of its parts. He called such groups Master Mind groups.

If, as is more likely, you are doing this on your own, then to ensure that you *do* activate the goal every day, make a meeting with yourself to do it; schedule some time on your calendar for every morning.

Consider doing this twice a day. As I said, I activate all my goals in the morning while having my morning coffee, and often in the evening I activate my personal goals once again, right before bed.

Also, after a few weeks or months of goal spinning, you may want to rewrite the Now Goal statement for one or more of your goals. This is to freshen it up so you do not zone out while spinning it. This may also be needed if the underlying Vision Goal has changed over time and you want to revise the statement to match the new vision. And it will certainly be needed once you've attained your goal!

## Optional Daily Additional Attention

An optional part of the activation process, useful for important goals, is to pay more attention to your goal throughout the day too, in addition to the formal spinning process. When possible, lean toward positive consideration of your Now Goal in your daily self-talk—in your internal conversation. And certainly do the same in any conversations with others about the goal. In a sense, I want you to become somewhat obsessed with the goal. One way to look at this is that you should create a mini-PR campaign around your objective in your own head. In fact, one use of the word "spin" is to describe what media experts do to change the coverage of a news event to their liking; they create stories and interviews that present a particular point of view favorable to their ends. We have all seen how that can work, so for your important goals, do the same thing; in your thoughts and actions during your workday, spin everyday events so that you consistently see your goal in a favorable light.

One way to do this is by focusing on elements of your vision statement throughout the day, working them into everyday events and actions. For example, if the goal is to get the big promotion, and it is really important to you, then throughout the day perhaps imagine what you might be doing at any given time if you had the promotion. As e-mails come in, imagine how you would handle them if you were in the new position.

In fact, at Accenture, where I worked for years, when the management team I worked on was deciding whether to recommend junior staff for promotion to the manager level, our primary decision factor was this: was the employee *already acting like a manager,* well before the promotion? If the individual showed they had so thoroughly embraced their desire for the next level that they *acted* like they had it, they got the job. I recommend you do the same with your goals.

# Summary

A fundamental lesson in this chapter is that by applying the Immediate Now, or I-Now, portion of the Workday Now model, you can activate your goals. Let me talk a bit more about that.

### The Power of Now

You may be aware of a book called *The Power of Now* by Eckhart Tolle. In that book, Tolle talks about how important our Now is. He is referring to the same Now that I refer to in this chapter, the I-Now. Tolle's message is that your approach to your Now holds the secret to enjoying life now and in the future, as summed up in this quote from page 60 of that book:

*If it is the quality of your consciousness at this moment [the Now] that determines the future, then what is it that determines the quality of your consciousness? Your degree of presence.*

Tolle is saying that the way you are present in your I-Now influences your experience of life now, and in the future.

Well, I would like to extend that further. I assert that the most important outcome of exercising high-quality presence in your I-Now is the fact that doing so during *goal activation* creates your life. It is by maintaining a high-quality presence, focused on your goals, for a few minutes each day that you create your goals, your future, and your life. To me, goal activation is the true Power of Now.

## Goal Activation Recap

In this chapter I presented the very important topic of *activating* your goals to make them easier to achieve. Activating goals is Step 3 of the 4-step Now Goal creation process.

I described how to activate goals using the process of goal spinning; this is a process of reviewing and visualizing your goals for a few moments each day. The point is to get the goal "spinning" quietly in your subconscious mind so that you are more predisposed to choose action that favors and helps achieve your goals. With the goal active in your subconscious mind, you will often find solutions that may not be obvious.

Activation works because the human attention is a very powerful thing. It works in the same way TV commercials work—it activates our mind on the level of emotions and feelings, leading us toward actions that are in line with the topic we put our attention on.

Goal spinning can be compared to a compass because by spinning our goals, we point ourselves in the direction of our goals. We gain energy toward working on our goals. It puts the goal into "pull" mode, where actions in the right direction seem more obvious and automatic. As a result we find ourselves more successful at achieving our goals.

Goal activation is important to do because our background self-talk is a very powerful thing—we want to influence our self-talk to be more in line with the outcomes we want. If we do not, we may fall back to old default habits of thought that, without our realizing it, may be negative regarding the outcomes we want.

There are hundreds of success and management experts that have for years attested to the power of visualization, which is what goal activation essentially is. It is time-tested and well proven. My contribution to the field is to show you some intuitive ways to think about visualization, and provide detailed instructions on how to do it for work goals.

Goal activation is easy, quick, and even inspiring to do. It may take some discipline to ensure you do it every day, but the results are worth it.

In the next chapter I present Step 4 of the 4-step Now Goal creation process: Taking First Action on your goals.

CHAPTER **13**

# Step 4, Taking First Action on Your Now Goals

In this chapter we put the final step into what you have learned so far for creating your Now Goals. Up to this point in Part II, I have described the core material behind the first 3 steps of the 4-step Now Goal creation process. I call this fourth step Taking First Action on Your Now Goals. This is a short chapter, but an important one.

Taking First Action on your Now Goals is something you should do whether you are inspired to or not. You should jump into some action right away. To most, this may seem obvious; but to others, it may actually feel counterintuitive.

Why counterintuitive? If you carefully read the previous chapter on goal activation, you may have noticed I stated that once a Now Goal is activated, it will be put into "pull" mode, and it can pull you toward actions nearly automatically. So you may think you do not need to plan your actions or force any uninspired actions to get your goals moving. A natural response might be, "Hey, forcing an action is a Control-layer activity; I thought Part II was about the Create-layer!"

It is true that an uninspired action on a goal can be a waste of energy, as it often goes off track. But whether inspired action comes right away or not, I *do* want to make sure that you take some first action on this goal in its early stages.

Why the emphasis on jump-starting a first step? Well, there's a value to nudging the process a little, particularly at the start of engaging a particular goal. Action focuses thought and clarifies thinking; if nothing else, early action points out to you problems with your vision of the goal and causes you to do more thinking about the goal. You may even decide to rethink the goal and reword your Now Goal statement.

So use action as a seed, as a way to get various aspects of your mind wrapped around the goal. Ideally, use "forced action" only a few times. Use it at the very beginning, when first kicking off the goal, and perhaps occasionally later if the goal gets stuck—*inspired* action is still the better route, as it is much more productive.

Also, if your goal is for a team or an entire organization, first action is a remarkable way to drive support (or defiance) out of the team. You've probably seen this happen. If you merely propose a new goal for a team, everyone nods or moans, but nothing happens. However, once you or someone you assigned it to starts taking action toward the goal, and people see things that affect them beginning to happen, they finally start to engage with energy (positive or negative). Either they don't want to be left behind, or they fear the challenge to their status quo. Their reaction may lead you as a group to finally focus on the goal and gain clarity.

So take first action as soon as you can. If you cannot do something right away, pick a task and put it on your Now Tasks list for action soon.

How do you identify what action to take on a goal? Should you create a plan for the goal? Let's talk about that next.

## Brainstorm Action Steps

Brainstorming is my preferred way to come up with initial action plans. To do that, think about the end goal, identify smaller pieces of it or earlier states of it, and then think about what action might be needed to get there.

My favorite brainstorming process is mind mapping, a system of drawing and formulating ideas. You do it by writing the goal right in the middle of a page, and then brainstorming major topic areas around it. You then write subtopics next to each major topic, branching out in a radial fashion on the page—building a tree-like picture. The idea is to move quickly, recording inspired ideas as you get them. In my experience, the free-flowing format seems to stimulate ideas better than a linear list.

You can create these mind maps on paper, but one of my favorite software tools for doing that is MindManager by MindJet. This tool, which I have been using consistently since the early 1990s, automates the mind mapping process and makes mind maps that are easily modified and reorganized during brainstorming. You can collapse branches, move them easily, and add symbols.

For example, here is a mind map I created in MindManager for a goal to build a webinar capability, importing content from my speeches.

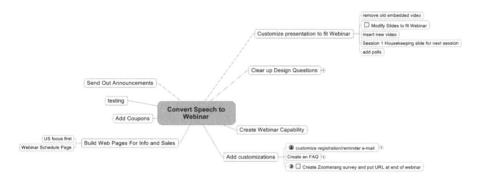

There are quite a few steps on this mind map (many are hidden in collapsed branches). I only do this extensive level of brainstorming if the goal leads to a fairly complex set of actions. In contrast, for most of my goals, I brainstorm a relatively small number of action steps. I place those right next to the goal statement on my Now Goals list—the one described in Chapter 11. The figure below is an example of how I did that on the Now Goals list I had already created; note the actions off to the right of one of my goals. This was also

created in MindManager, but you can of course do this using either a simple word processing program, a drawing program, Microsoft Excel. Or do it by hand on paper.

Even though brainstorming is a great tool, at the early stages of a new goal, I recommend you not get too carried away with this kind of planning. Rather, spend just a few minutes thinking through some possible action paths, record a number of steps perhaps, and then let it percolate for some days or even weeks and do it again, this time more seriously.

Why only a little planning at first? You see, after activating the goal every day for a few weeks, it is likely that a different set of steps will emerge as your subconscious mind looks for and finds a better action path. So be prepared to toss out the initial brainstorm as new inspirations emerge. When those new insights do emerge, as soon as possible after that, brainstorm the steps that match that strategy. Such insights are often accompanied by a burst of enthusiasm, which can help carry you through the action steps.

## Planning the Action

If there are a large number of steps, I might try to create an actual schedule of action steps with dated milestones. See the Significant Outcome Milestones discussion at the end of Chapter 7 for ways to do that on your Now Tasks list and on your calendar. For larger goals with lots of interdependent milestones, the MindManager software I mentioned above also has an optional integrated project management add-on module called JCVGantt. It picks up the brainstormed tasks from the mind map and turns them into a linked project timeline. This ability to link a plan to a mind map is nice—it saves time, and changes you make in the plan sync back to the high-level map view.

For example, in the figure at right I have a JCVGantt timeline for the Webinar project I described above.

Project plans like this are useful, mainly for tracking dependencies and associated dates. However, for your personal goals, I doubt you will create them that often—personal goals are often more general than that. And if you do create such a plan, don't be a slave to that plan; certainly use it as a guide, but always be open to inspired new directions and replan as needed. Goal activation can

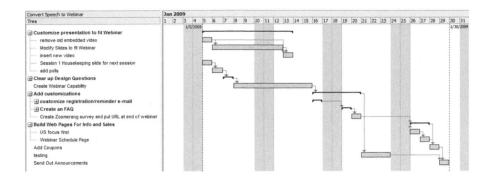

lead to new insights that take you in a totally new direction at a totally different pace, so be ready for that.

## If Managing a Goal for Others

If you are working for others and working on a goal that is very large—one with major deliverables that affect multiple stakeholders (say it is a company-sized goal to create a new product or computer system)—then things are very different. The goal probably includes deadlines you must commit to. If that is the case, meeting those deadlines can become more important than meeting the exact vision. In fact, once multiple stakeholders with varied interests are being served like this, this is no longer just your vision, it becomes a *group* vision. And unless you are exceptionally good at setting and maintaining vision in the group (few are—Steve Jobs, CEO of Apple, comes to mind), the rules of the game change compared to creating your own goals. Core actions to achieve each milestone become less inspired ones, and more *managed* ones. Execution excellence becomes key, and Control-layer tools usually take over.

That's not ideal, but it is a fact of life for most organizations trying to create large structured outcomes. In such a Control-layer project, you will likely want to use formal project management methodologies to execute the project in a way that meets those deadlines. Formal project management methodology is beyond the scope of this book, and is a big study area in itself. If you are not already trained in project management, find skilled project managers in your organization to run that aspect of it.

### Always Take First Action

In all these cases, even for large projects, it still makes sense to identify a next action task to do immediately—one that you can do to give the goal a little jump-start. So either do it today, or put it on your Now Tasks list for action this week. For a small goal like "take up golf," it might be buying a book on golf, for example. For a large goal that leads to a project, it might be scheduling a vision planning meeting. Any small next step can help get a goal in motion.

# Take Some Action Every Day?

Many writers on goal setting say that even for smaller goals you should take some action on your goal *every single day,* even if you are not inspired to—that the discipline of doing so is needed to obtain your goals. Implied is that doing so will lead to at least some small incremental progress every day, and that will add up over time to the completed goal.

I have mixed feelings about that as a way to make progress on your *goals.* Certainly for *tasks,* ones that just require a series of steps, that will work. For example, if you are repainting your house, you might do a small section every day; over time it is done. But goals are different. Recall that in the introductory chapter of Part II, I pointed out that goals require a bit of magic to achieve; they are *not* just a series of steps and not achieved by merely applying willpower. So in general, after you do take your first action described above, I recommend from then on relying on *inspired* action for most of your goal progress. That's a better long-term strategy. Let me illustrate this with an example.

Writing a book is a goal many people have and a fairly difficult one to achieve. A common recommendation I hear is that book writers should write a little bit every day, and even force themselves to do it, no matter what—that by doing this they will steadily make progress on the book. However, as a writer, I can plainly state that formula never worked for me—it felt artificial, and the writing that resulted was insipid and lacking in depth. What *did* work for me was when I waited for bouts of inspired thoughts on the topic; when those hit, I could sit and write all day and late into the night. I do believe this is true for goals in general—that mainly *inspired* action will do the trick, and such inspiration may not arrive on schedule every day.

Now, it is true the do-some-work-every-day approach may help some people on some goals—but not because of the small bits of progress they make. Rather, for people who do not activate their goals every day, these small bits of action, if done positively, can be a form of goal spinning. Lacking a formal activation process, this daily action serves as the daily focus needed to coincidentally spin up the goal. As long as the action is done positively and with the goal in focus during the action, "organic" goal activation could be a result.

My problem with *relying* on this, however, is that taking uninspired action every day, and seeing few or no results, can lead to discouragement. In that case you may be focusing on the lack of progress—negative goal spinning. If that starts to happen, it is better not to do the forced action. Rather, just spin your goals every day with a positive focus on the vision until a surge of inspiration comes your way; otherwise, you could continue to get discouraged by ineffective actions every day.

So what should you do? I leave this to you. If you can make positive progress each day with daily scheduled activity, go for it. However, if you are finding forced activity is not bearing fruit, then don't. In either case, focus on spinning the goal each day and watch for truly inspired action ideas to present themselves to you.

One last point. With consistent goal activation, you should be led to your goal achievement consistently. However, if a goal seems to get stuck, perhaps it is a bit too big for you. Or, interestingly, it can even be too *small*. Take a look at the next chapter to see how this is possible and to learn some strategies for moving beyond your limits.

## Summary

I encourage you to take first action as soon as you create your goals.

First action helps knock a goal loose, it helps focus the mind. But after some first action, rely primarily on *inspired* action to continue through to goal completion. If you are activating your goals every day, you will see that inspiration for action arrives fairly regularly.

In addition to first action, you may want to do some action brainstorming—creating a list of action steps, for example. Perhaps even create a simple plan.

For larger goals with multiple stakeholders with varied interests, you will definitely want to create a project plan and use formal project management methodology to help drive deadline completion. At that point, however, the project will become more of a Control-layer exercise, and the vision will likely get dispersed across multiple people. You will need to work hard to maintain a group vision on such a project.

For your own goals, refer to your action plan often, but do not become a slave to it. Listen to your inspirations for new direction, and replan if needed. Rely more on inspired action than on forced action.

CHAPTER **14**

# Stretch Your Now Goals

How challenging a goal should you set for yourself? Normally, when first setting a goal, I say go beyond your comfort zone but not too far. Remember my conversation in Part I about the difference between tension and stress? Some tension is natural. The tension we feel when setting a larger goal may just be the result of our working a reasonable distance beyond our comfort zone. You see, we all get accustomed to the way things are, and even if we propose a simple improvement, our psychology may push back. It may experience some discomfort, which just might mean that we're advancing the right amount.

But you don't want to stretch so far that you demoralize yourself. Use the stomach test. If your stomach twists into knots when you consider the new goal, you may be pushing too far beyond your current beliefs. By beliefs, I do not mean moral beliefs, but rather habits of thought about what you consider is possible for yourself.

## Think Bigger if Needed

Even so, there is a value to expanding beyond your current beliefs too, if you can. That's how you grow. Strong and rapid advancement breeds pride and a sense of accomplishment.

And surprisingly, in some cases, going beyond your current beliefs may be the *only* way to achieve the goal you are seeking. Here's how that works.

Let's say as a goal you propose a modest 2 percent pay increase to yourself. It is a nice, safe goal that you believe you will have no problem achieving.

However, if your emotional reaction to that new goal is "This is not very exciting since it's so small," then it will be hard to achieve. Emotion and passion are a strong part of what makes goal spinning—goal activation—possible. If those emotions are absent, the goal may be even harder to activate and create.

So if the only reason you set a particular goal level is that it's all you believe you can get in your current situation, but you are not excited about it, then aim higher. Increase your goal to the point where you feel excited about the new level. Even if you don't know the action paths you can take to reach the higher level, aiming higher may be the only way to make it happen from a goal activation point of view. The test here is enthusiasm. If only a larger goal gives you enthusiasm, it is the better goal.

So go ahead and set the larger goal, even if you have no idea how you could get it. In fact, not knowing or seeing an action path to reach a goal can be an advantage in the following way. If you see no way to get to the goal, you can drop preconceived notions on the How, and just focus on the Why. Remember, your subconscious always responds to the Why, not the How. In fact, the How can be distracting; you can get lost in the details. And it can hold you back. If you only believe in goals for which you see a clear action path, you may be missing some exciting expansion.

Instead, if you focus on the Why—the reason you want the goal—it is more likely that the subconscious mind will fully kick in during goal spinning. That way, you are not distracted by studying and fretting over the steps to get there, at least not during goal spinning, where that focus does not help. Save the How for the planning steps—or even better, see where goal activation leads you before planning. You may be surprised by the creative new approaches you come up with.

Now, I just advised you to increase your goal to a level that may be beyond your current beliefs about what you think is possible. On the one hand, that allows you to get excited about the higher goal. But immediately another voice may kick in that says, "I could never do that!" If that voice kicks in so strongly that you get a net negative feeling about the goal, if your stomach is in knots—well, that could sabotage your subconscious from buying into the new goal. You now have no choice; you need to adjust your beliefs to fit the bigger goal.

### Pushing Past Glass Ceilings

You see, we create a glass ceiling for ourselves through the beliefs we hold about our abilities or about the world around us. And we do that without realizing it. I'm sure you have heard stories of people under hypnosis accepting silly limitation suggestions; for example, under hypnosis they are told their hand is too heavy to lift and then they cannot lift it off the table.

Similarly, we hold beliefs and mental models about ourselves and the world around us: how much money we can make, how prominent a position we can hold, or even the class of people we can associate with. Many of those beliefs define limits that don't need to be there; they lock us away from expanding. So the first step in achieving a new goal is to believe that it is achievable. If the only goal you can get excited about is one you currently don't believe in, you're going to need to change your beliefs about the goal.

To make a goal more believable, I do not mean you need to understand all the steps of how you are going to get there. All you need to do is know that, somehow *it is possible*. You just need to feel that it is *believable* that you could *somehow* achieve it. That's enough of a start.

Let's talk first about some accepted ways to overcome major self-imposed glass ceilings; they take further study, but they may be what you want to do. Then I'll show a simple method you can try now if you think your beliefs need just a little help.

## Adjusting Your Beliefs

People can gradually adjust the beliefs they hold about themselves by stretching their goals a little, achieving those, gaining confidence, and then stretching some more. That is the traditional growth path, but it can take time. For example, it can take years for someone to grow into a position of authority; they need time to gain the confidence to do so. I have seen some organizations accelerate that process, assigning challenging projects to individuals even before they are quite ready—so that they are forced to quickly grow into the new position—and then constantly raising the bar again before they get too comfortable. The military is like that, and companies like Accenture routinely do this also.

## Ways to Overcome Limiting Beliefs

However, in some cases, limiting beliefs are deeply held, and even over time individuals stay stuck at that glass ceiling I described above. Or they have no individual or organization to mentor them through a rapid advancement, but they seek that advancement nonetheless. If this sounds like you, you might consider using some of the new and well-established self-help and assisted-help techniques to advance your self-beliefs more quickly. There are many such approaches available, and I will survey a few of them quickly here. Go to this page on my website: MasterYourWorkday.com/RecommenedResources. There you will find direct links for each of these. Also, study the Recommended Resources section of this book.

First, if significant fears are limiting your advancement—say, you fear authority or fear asserting yourself—you might use hypnosis to overcome those fears. I have never tried it but understand it can work quite well. There are many professional hypnotherapists that specialize in this sort of thing; you should be able to find one in your area, or you might study a book on self-hypnosis.

For solving similar fears as well as a wide range of other limiting beliefs, a process called Neuro-Linguistic Programming, summarized well in the 1996 book *NLP: The New Technology of Achievement* by Steve Andreas and Charles Faulkner, is a comprehensive approach to moving forward. NLP was highlighted by author Anthony Robbins in books like *Unlimited Power*.

The Sedona Method®, which I will mention again below, has a strong but very simple technique for working yourself past your internal resistance to upward movement. Yet another is the Lefkoe Method, highlighted in the book *Re-create Your Life* by Morty Lefkoe.

There are a number of mind-body techniques available for *rewiring* deeply held limitations. A process called Psych-K is one—it uses muscle-strength testing to isolate and fix limiting beliefs. Another technique that has gained recent widespread prominence is the Emotional Freedom Technique (EFT), also called The Tapping Solution. It was first developed for helping trauma patients overcome their fears, but has recently also been found useful for relieving limiting beliefs in otherwise normal individuals. How it works is hard to describe, but the process is a combination of using verbal affirmations and physical tapping of acupuncture points. I know that sounds odd, yet I have seen people gain truly remarkable results from it. You can teach yourself how to do it; see the book *Try It on Everything: Discover the Power of EFT* by Patricia Carrington. There are at least thirty other books written on this popular topic.

## What If–Why Not

Each of the above approaches takes some effort to learn or requires outside help, and so they are usually directed toward more significant limitations. If instead you simply have some *hesitations* or *doubts* around new goals you are creating, I have a simple procedure you can use to find gaps in your beliefs and, in many cases, adequately fill them. It uses some simple questions and positive statements to get to the root issue and then "talk it down." I call this technique the *What If–Why Not* technique. In this technique you state the new goal and you look inside yourself for internal objections to the goal. You then, one at a time, talk down the objections in your own mind until you stop rejecting the goal.

Here are the What If–Why Not steps.

1. Write a very brief Vision Goal, perhaps with a challenging target, and advance the "size" of your goal to the point that you feel excited about the goal (but not too far past that point for now).

2. Adjust the language in your written goal to be like this: "What if I found a way to easily…" and then the Now Goal statement. For a personal example, let's say you desperately need a bigger home due to a growing family. So write, "What if I found a way to easily… get a house 50 percent larger than, but just as nice as, our current house." Adding the words "What if I found a way to easily…" as an introductory phrase removes a bit of the disbelief and tension from the goal. It also counteracts any self-limiting How worries you might be subconsciously entertaining and it leaves your mind more open to experiencing the positive outcome.

3. Now, read this statement to yourself. What does your gut say? If your gut responds pleasantly, "That would be nice. I look forward to it," then adding

the "What if I found a way to easily…" statement softened this enough for you, and you are probably fine with this goal now. Just keep the phrase, "What if I found a way to easily…" in the goal whenever you activate it from now on.

4. However, if you still feel a strong doubt about the Now Goal statement, enough that it sucks the energy or enthusiasm out of the goal, then take it to the next level. You want to clearly identify the objection or the source of the doubt. If you cannot put your finger on the objection, then say to yourself, "This won't work because…" and see if the problem that is bugging you pops out. In this example it might be, "This won't work because… we don't have the money for that bigger house."

5. Then, for that objection ask yourself, "Why Not?" in a way that can soften the objection. Ask yourself why the "What If" statement couldn't work. Then, look for a flaw in the negative logic of your objection, or a way around the objection. Write down any "openings" that could make the "What If" statement possible. Also think outside the box—think of solutions outside the original objection that could make it null and void.

This is important; find multiple openings that you can buy into as being *possible*. They do not need to be highly probable or even paths to your goal that you would want or might plan to do. I just want you to convince yourself that the new goal *is in the realm of possibility*. Start with easy-to-accept possibilities, even if they weren't part of your plans, and even if you have objections to the brainstormed solution.

So in this example you might write down, "Well, I suppose it's possible I could find a new, even better job at a much higher pay scale." Now, I know you have no intention to find a new job right now, but list it anyway. Or "My spouse might get a raise," or "Maybe there will be an unusual financing option that meets our monthly requirements," or "Maybe there will be a foreclosed house that exactly meets our needs at our current price," or "Maybe we can get an attached rental and pay for it that way." Keep listing as many openings as you can.

Thinking outside the box like this, you will find there are many possible ways to beat that objection. This is brainstorming, so don't say no to anything;

don't filter out any solution you may think is unfit. The point is not to make a plan that you will act on. Rather you want to list so many possible exceptions to the objection that you *overwhelm* your negative internal voice. Continue finding options until you soften your objection; continue to the point that you stop mentally rejecting the possibility of your goal. Keep doing this until you finally admit, "Yes, some combination of action or good luck or ingenuity really could lead to this goal being possible."

6.  Next, rewrite the portion of the Vision Goal that you were "stuck" on in a way that captures this possibility. For example: "I know I can find a way to afford a 50 percent larger home. I am a creative person and will easily find a smooth path to doing that; after all, I listed 15 ways to make it work, so I know this is possible. We will easily find a way to live in a comfortable, roomy, elegant, and lovely home that advances our happiness even more." Eventually you can remove the introductory portions of this vision statement. Knowing that something is possible will be implied in all your vision statements.

7.  Now, read the vision statement to yourself again. How does it feel? If you are no longer rejecting it, you are good for now. You can now focus on the enthusiasm of the goal, and use that enthusiasm when you do your goal activation every day. If, however, reading the new vision statement either now or later elicits another strong objection, repeat steps 4-6 until you soften that objection too. Repeat until you "give up" on the negative energy around the goal, and just accept it as possible. Again, this can slip over time; you may think of even more objections later. So if over time you ever find yourself doubting the possibility of the goal again, repeat the above.

8.  Live with the larger vision for a while until it feels right and is part of your mental model. If it is a very large or life goal, then use the "Locking in a New Belief" exercise next to really build your vision into your subconscious.

By the way, you might recognize the above as a version of a common sales technique where you, as a salesperson, address each objection of the buyer, one at a time, to show them the item may actually be just right or possible for them. That's exactly what you are doing; you are selling yourself on the *possibility* of this new goal. You are doing this so that your subconscious mind won't block it and so you can activate it during your goal spinning sessions.

## Other Similar Approaches

All of the principles of goal spinning and the steps for adjusting beliefs that I have described in this book were things I had been doing for years with great success. So I was delighted to see other books describe similar things. It should be no surprise that universal techniques are identified and used by others. So I was only slightly surprised to see steps very similar to those above on adjusting beliefs in the book *Psycho-Cybernetics* when I read it later for the first time. You may recall I have referred repeatedly to this book as one of the best on the power of visualization; and now I refer to it again.

In that book, Maxwell Maltz calls his version of adjusting beliefs "rational thinking." He has an entire chapter on this topic called "How to Succeed with the Power of Rational Thinking." Embedded in that chapter is a process to move beyond old, limiting beliefs. Maxwell says if you find yourself saying, "I can't" to a new goal, then ask yourself, "Why do I believe that I can't?" He then takes you through a series of questions similar to the Why Not process above. The point is that many of our limiting beliefs have little to support them if we challenge them from all angles. I encourage you to look at the book if you feel you'd like additional tools in your goal-success tool kit.

Another similar technique is called The Sedona Method, described in a book by the same name by Hale Dwoskin. He takes you through a similar question-and-answer session to soften and eliminate limiting beliefs.

## Rising Up the Emotional Scale

There is yet another source I encourage you to study if you truly want to make a regular habit of moving beyond your currently limiting beliefs. Jerry and Esther Hicks, whom I introduced in Chapter 12 as a primary source on the Law of Attraction, have written a series of books about how to achieve the things you want in life. The best book of her series is *Ask and It Is Given*. In that book they describes an emotional scale ranging from despair at the low end to exhilaration or joy at the high end. They say in order to reach our goals, we need to change the emotional set-point of our attitude about any given goal to as high a point as possible on the emotional scale.

They recommend we do this step by step, slowly, because it is hard to change a belief from "I can't possibly do this" to "I'm excited that this goal is easy to complete." They say that's too big a jump, so instead slowly work your way up the emotional scale by challenging the negative belief with slightly better beliefs, releasing a little resistance at a time. For example, the next level statement might be, "Well, there might be a way to do this." After that, the statement could be, "I nearly always find a way to make things work, so I'll bet I can find a way to do this." And so on, working at each level until the statement feels comfortable.

The point is to find relief at each level; if you feel relief at each level, then you're making progress. What I mean by "relief" is that you feel less tension about your ability to reach the goal; you want to see relief grow a little more each time you work on it. Jerry and Esther have a set of tools (called processes) in the second half of the book that I think are some of the best out there for changing limiting beliefs on any topic.

I have to warn you, though, the premise of where this information is coming from is definitely in the New Age category, and so, depending on your world-view, it may seem to be quite far-fetched. That said, the concepts in the book are spot-on and absolutely the best on the topic.

## Locking in New Beliefs

The What If—Why Not method will work for many of your goals. But if you have a particularly challenging goal, or a big one—for example, a life goal, such as changing your career, or finding a life-work scenario, or even larger—then after you complete the What If—Why Not steps, you probably need to do more to now lock in the new belief you just accepted. Otherwise, the new belief can fade.

Or if you find that doing the What If—Why Not exercise still leaves you feeling uneasy about the goal, you definitely will want to do more. And even if you feel good about your goal, the following may still seem attractive to you as a way to accelerate your goal attainment. What follows is an exercise I call *Locking in New Beliefs*.

### Using Visualization to Lock in New Beliefs

The point of this exercise is to create a script you can read to reinforce a new belief once it's been set. It will also provide more material to continue to spin up the achievement of your new goal, a goal that a belief may be influencing. Basically you are spinning up your new belief using the same principles we covered earlier in this part of the book, but with a little extra help. It is a set of statements around a number of specific aspects of the outcome that, together, can get the subconscious becoming more accustomed to the new belief, thus locking it in.

Doing "scripting," which is writing a detailed narrative of how you would move through your day with your new goal in place, is a common prescription from many success books that teach their own versions of goal spinning. Maxwell Maltz's Theater of Your Mind, which I mentioned earlier, is essentially this. Scripting is also the name of one of the processes in Jerry and Esther Hicks's book. However, most books do not provide sufficient detail on how to write the script, which leaves people hanging—it is my experience that many people have problems writing these scripts. My *Locking in New Beliefs* exercise below fills this void by providing a formula to create such a script.

You do this in two steps. In step one you brainstorm a list of all things currently in your work or personal life that *might be influenced by the new belief.* In step two you then write a new version of each, describing what their positive new state would be once your belief or associated goal was complete.

For step one, what should you put on that list? Well, some things on the list will be obvious, like the size of your paycheck for a financial-related goal. But also, think more broadly; think of things seemingly unrelated to the goal that could change too.

For example, let's say your goal is to get a major promotion at work, and the belief you just adjusted in the What If–Why Not work was whether you were "good enough" to ever get that job. You now believe you are, but you want to reinforce that belief. Here is what you will do.

First, you will list obvious parameters, such as the following::

- *How will my paycheck look?*
- *What will my new job title be?*
- *What new office will I have?*
- *What new staff will report to me?*
- *And so on.*

Next, also list slightly less obvious things:

- *How will interactions with my colleagues change?*

- *How will conversations with my spouse change?*

- *What sorts of e-mail will I start getting and sending?*

Just keep brainstorming this list. Try to get ten or more items listed.

Here is a generic list you may want to pick from to build the "How will it change" list:

| | |
|---|---|
| • *My attitude* | • *My spending* |
| • *My expectations* | • *My income* |
| • *My conversations* | • *My calendar* |
| • *My calendar* | • *My self-talk* |

- *My bank account*

- *My feeling when I wake up in the morning*

- *My thoughts when I go to sleep at night*

- *My thoughts when I walk in front of a mirror*

- *My thoughts when I see my co-workers*

- *My thoughts when I consider my boss*

- *E-mails I get from others*

- *Phone calls I get from others*

- *(Add anything else specific to the topic)*

See my website (MasterYourWorkday.com) for Microsoft Word and MindJet MindManager templates with this list already created, which you can enter your ideas onto.

Okay, so that's step one, making the list of things influenced. Step two is to write next to each item one or more very positive versions of how they might change, once your belief or goal has been achieved. Write it up. Find and include the positive feelings, and if possible, find the passion in each change. You'll find a complete example of this in the next section.

Use your computer text editor to write it so you can edit it a few times—so you can add more things and clean it up as you go. Once complete, print it out and add a reading-through of this script to your daily goal activation exercise for that goal. Each day, read the script and mentally picture the experience. Obviously you would only do this for really important goals, as it does take time to study this each day. And you may only need to do it for a while, until you feel fairly confident about the new belief; after that, you can switch back to your shorter Now Goal statement.

This is a very powerful tool for implementing the changes to your subconscious mind that you will need in order to start stimulating automatic actions in the right direction. Take it seriously.

Let me give you an example.

### Locking in New Beliefs Example

Brief Now Goal statement: "My personal sales this next quarter have increased by 35%, and I have maintained a balanced and satisfying work style." Depending on the industry you are in, that can be fairly hard to believe. So let's say you've done the What If—Why Not steps and you now believe it is at least possible. You are now going to use the Locking in New Beliefs steps to become more at home with this new belief.

Step one is to identify what aspects of your work and personal life are influenced by the goal. Step two is to write up how they will look once the goal is achieved. Here are the results of both steps.

1.  My paycheck: Nicely larger this month!

2.  My calendar or time: My clients are calling me, wanting to buy. I have sales meetings with them scheduled on my calendar. I have many closing meetings scheduled on my calendar. (Picture that.)

3.  Attitude of my boss to me: "Ted, good job—keep it up. You are an example to all of us!"

4.  Comments from my colleagues: "Wow, Ted, what's your secret? Can you show me how to do some of this?"

5.  Conversations I have with most others about the new success: "Yeah, sales are good. My contacts are all paying off. Most of my calls are closing; people just seem to want to do business with me. You guys can do this too—just envision how you want your sales to go, and then do the work."

6.  How my family is reacting: (Describe a positive reaction when you tell them, or when you take your spouse out to dinner or off for a weekend.)

7.  My feelings: It sure feels good to have a solid increase in sales. I like being in this comfort zone, knowing that I am set and in the flow. It feels like every contact I make just comes through.

8.  My expectations: These sales will continue to keep closing; I am on a roll and all the pieces continue to fall into place to close increasing numbers of sales. I just have to speak, and the sale closes, and this will continue into the future; this is amazing! I have now come to expect this with all contacts; it feels so natural for it to happen.

9.  My attitude: I am hugely upbeat. It is amazing how success at work affects all aspects of my life, including my attitude about life. I enjoy my weekends more, knowing I have met and exceeded goals all week. I feel comfortable taking time off for play.

10. E-mails to me: I am getting 10 to 20 new sales responses per day by e-mail. Whenever I look at my in-box, there they are.

11. My activities: I am helping with delivery of the sales, doing follow-ups, and filling out the forms. I am making sure production is on track for the sales. I am calling prospects, and the calls work. I will also be coaching junior sales folks on how to do this.

Again, this may seem a bit superficial, but it is amazing how a small amount of visualization can replace long-standing self-limiting issues.

Here is a nonwork example:"I have reached an ideal weight of 160 pounds" (the person is currently at 180 pounds).

Identify what aspects of your work and personal life are influenced by the goal, and how they will look once the goal has been achieved.

1.  My meals: Only reasonable portions end up on my plate; it just looks right and feels right to eat less. I am just not that hungry.

2.  My belt: My belt is locking 2-3 notches tighter; wow that feels good to see so much progress so fast!

3.  My clothing: My pants now bunch up under my belt due to extra waistband material. Ha! I am so happy to be buying SMALLER clothing now!

4.  My stomach: My stomach definitely looks flatter, tighter. I especially notice it when I wear golf shirts; they just seem more athletic now.

5.  My self-image: I see a trim, athletic man in the mirror.

6.  My posture: I am standing up straighter. I look more athletic.

7.  My attitude: I feel great and feel much more self-assured, knowing I am in unusually good shape for my age. My body is trim and firm.

8.  My expectations: I expect myself to choose the right foods automatically. I feel good about those foods; they just seem right.

9.  My conversations: "You guys can do this too; this is how." "I don't need all those sweets; they just don't do anything for me." "I tend to pick just the right amount of food." "I tend to pick healthy foods; this just comes naturally to me."

After you have been using the script for a few weeks or more, you may want to rewrite it with fresh ideas, so it does not get stale. Otherwise, after a while you may glaze over when you pull the sheet out to read each day. Continue to add passion in every statement you write; the Locking in New Beliefs method will work much better if you do this. Try to use wording that evokes your inspiration for this goal. Use emotive language that may at first seem a little silly, but that does in fact stimulate your emotions.

## If Results Are Slow

Using these techniques works. I have seen it over and over again. However, it can also take a while.

You know, I have read a lot of success books. Many I greatly admire because they are written with integrity and an honest knowledge that what is recommended can work. But I dislike many as well. The ones that especially bother me are books that cheerfully state all you have to do is XYZ and you will be a millionaire in no time at all. I think the authors of those books also have good intentions; they are trying to establish an upbeat, think-big attitude, which of course is helpful. However, to me, the overly positive writing gets tiresome, especially when promises of huge amounts of money arc at stake.

So with that in mind, there is no way I will tell you that this process is foolproof. I don't want to set overly high expectations for you. The processes will definitely help greatly, but there are so many variables that one can never know for sure.

For example, how long will this take for a given goal? A common thread in many of the books that teach similar visualization techniques seems to be something like 21 to 30 days of daily practice. I've had that experience with many goals, using these techniques, so I know it can be true.

But even though I have been doing these techniques for decades, many of my goals I just can't seem to knock loose. Usually, in those cases, I find I need to adjust the wording or adjust my beliefs about the goal. Or in some cases, the goal is just not right for me, and I do not realize that until I start to sense a pushing back inside, against the goal, in a way that I didn't detect before. In the next part of the book, Part III, we'll talk a bit about using your intuition to clarify the "rightness" of your goals.

Also, I want to re-emphasize how especially important it is to be flexible with your Target Goals, your numeric goals that seem so fixed and definite. These are the ones that are easy to miss for obvious reasons. Let me just say a little bit about Target Goals.

## Targets as a Game

Think of what the word *target* means. It comes from a sport like archery, or darts, or even gun practice, where you place a concentric ring target at a distance, and you aim at it. If you are new at the sport, it is rare that you hit the center. At the beginning, you may even miss the outer ring. With this metaphor of sports in mind, here are a couple of things to consider about your success with making specific Target Goals.

If you are playing a sport, you know it's a game; you don't quit if you fail to hit the center of the target right away. You know it will come with time and practice. I want you to feel that way about your numeric Target Goals. Sure, get passionate about them, but still treat them like a game.

Sometimes people hit the bull's-eye on the first try. You might with your goals as well. But usually you need repetition; you need practice.

You may find you need to change the way you shoot the arrow, or throw the dart, or aim the target gun. Expect some fine-tuning to get it right.

You will have spells where you are aiming very well and other spells where you are not.

Don't get discouraged; try to keep it fun. The point of a game is not to hate the game all the way up to the point you hit the bull's-eye and then finally declare that the game is enjoyable, now that you have won. Instead, you enjoy the game and its "play" every step of the way. You enjoy the first time you try and miss completely; you enjoy getting better. You are thrilled when you score better and better along the journey.

So use that same "game-like" attitude about your Target Goals. You will be happier if you do.

Also, regardless of the success experience, recall my earlier statement that the goal activation process itself can be quite satisfying. It feels good to spend a few moments each day picturing and mentally enjoying the things you want in your life. Write your statements in a way that you enjoy reading them, so that you enjoy the dream they create each time you review them. That feeling of enjoyment will spill over into your day, and will have an immediate positive influence on all you do, whether you see the results right away or not.

# Summary

When sizing your goal, aim beyond your comfort zone, but not so far as to be demoralizing. You need enough of a goal that you feel excited about looking forward to it. However, if you do not believe in your ability to reach a goal, it will not be possible to activate the goal. In that case, you need to change your habits of thought on the topic. I call this adjusting your beliefs.

If you feel you have significant internal blocks holding you back, there are many approaches available to rapidly make large adjustments in your beliefs about your abilities. Those include hypnosis, NLP, EFT, and others.

If you merely have some hesitations or doubts about a goal, I offer two techniques that can help. One is called the What If—Why Not technique, where you state a new goal and then "talk down" any internal objections you may hold against the goal.

The other is called Locking in New Beliefs—it is a way to create a script describing how your attained goal would look across many aspects of your life. You can activate it along with your other goals.

Goals may be difficult because they just aren't right for you. You may need to use your intuition to figure that out. The next part of the book, Part III, covers some ways to grow your intuition, to help align your work goals with who you really are.

PART II CONCLUSION

# Conclusion to the Create-Layer Solution

By now I suspect you see that the Create-layer solution requires a different approach or energy than just tracking and working tasks. There is a bit of magic to it, particularly for goals for which simple action steps just aren't sufficient.

Why is there such a need for this? The topic of goals has been confusing for most people. Industry's current focus on numeric targets and the lack of focus on vision leaves many cold. The resulting difficulty in achieving goals leads to people falling back on Control-layer brute force techniques to try to push their goals to reality. Brute force or willpower has become the standard approach, and those workers that fail are seen as not having willpower, as being weak. The way some people talk about the goal process, there seems to be almost a judgment element added to it; or a moral-character element. It is as if only really good or unusually strong-minded people can set and achieve goals. Only those that are ready to pay their dues are allowed admission to the goals game.

But it doesn't have to be that way. Once you identify why the confusion exists, you can use goals to your advantage as easily as anyone else can. Once you understand the difference between Target Goals and Vision Goals, and start to create complete Now Goals, you will start to see that your goals are achievable. And especially once you start to use the Create-layer skill of activating your goals, and putting them into pull mode, you will see them start to be achieved with less gnashing of teeth. You'll see that obtaining what you want in life is your birthright, not a test of character. It just requires following four steps for each of your goals.

Here are the four steps again.

Step 1:   Create your Vision Goal. As you know by now, a Vision Goal is essential—I showed you in Chapter 10 a simple formula to create it.

Step 2:   Identify your Target Goals and add them to the Vision Goal. Nearly all goals need Target Goals, and Chapter 11 showed some fine points on adding them. Once you've added them, you now have the two core pieces of your new Now Goal statement.

Step 3:   Activate the Now Goal. This is just as important as writing a good Now Goal statement, and the most important ongoing step after initially creating the goal. Chapter 12 presented a thorough explanation of why goal activation—goal spinning—is needed and how to do it.

Step 4:   Take first action. This is where you start to engage your goal. Chapter 13 covered how to do that.

If you have a series of small goals, you can combine the Now Goal statements all on one page; that way, it will be convenient to activate them, one after another, in one quick sitting. Larger goals with more description may require separate sheets.

And for tougher goals, you may need to go beyond these four steps and change your self-limiting beliefs so that you can accept them enough to do the goal activation successfully. That is what the What If—Why Not technique, shown in Chapter 14, is designed to do.

As you can see, creating Now Goals will help achieve your goals, but there is a little work required to put them in place. The hardest part of that is goal activation, because you need to do it every day. And the changing beliefs exercises may feel a bit artificial to you. So if you are hesitant to try these techniques, I certainly understand. But if you *are* hesitating, I also want you to ask yourself, "What is the alternative?" Let's talk about that.

# What's the Alternative?

If you are still unsure about this, not sure if you want to take the time to do all the Now Goal steps, I want to ask you, what's the alternative? Daily activation of a well-written Vision Goal is, in some cases, your only choice. If you have been pursuing a particular goal for years, your lack of spinning up the goal's vision may be why your goal iscurrently stuck.

Goal spinning makes intuitive sense. For example, most of us know the power of negative thinking, that if we develop a bad attitude about something, our likelihood of reaching the goal will be low. So I do not think any of us want to encourage a negative attitude. But some goals, even without a negative attitude, seem really hard to obtain. No matter how hard we try, how hard we work, they seem to remain at arm's reach.

In those cases, what really is our choice? We can try to continue to push through them, trying every possible angle to achieve them. But some goals have no remaining logical or traditional ways to achieve them after we have tried all angles—goals like selling to the unsellable clients, or getting picked for the promotion from a field of hundreds. Goals like these can seem as if they need a magic element.

I say, if pushing through a goal does not work, try something new. Use the techniques in this book to put your goals into pull mode. Focus on the vision and then activate your goal so that your subconscious mind effectively pulls the solution to you. It cannot hurt to try.

And this describes a larger picture. If we don't activate our goals, then we are left to our default beliefs and behaviors. As mentioned earlier, those come from our childhood and adult "training," and from our current good and bad experiences in life. If we rely only on that, we just keep repeating the same outcomes.

Default behavior may also come by letting others spin up your goals for you. Who spins up goals for you? Your parents do it every time they "advise" you. Your friends and peer groups do when you target your own behavior to match what you think they want to see in you. Your boss does when he sets goals for you that may not match your own. The media do every time you watch and buy into a show or advertisement that defines how your behavior should be.

Better to spin your own goals; by doing so, you live your life with purpose and intention. This may be your first opportunity to really change what may feel like a stuck life situation. So if I were you, I would activate as many goals as possible.

## Best Hard Work You Can Do

Here is another way to look at this. What is hard work? If someone like your boss, mentor, or parent tells you they want you to "work hard" and be successful at your job, what does working hard look like?

Facing frustrations along the way, and working long hours in a disciplined way, is one traditional description. Facing the tough stuff, pushing past obstacles, and engaging your willpower are all typical descriptions.

But I wonder if frustration and obstacles need to be the core part of the equation.

What does hard work really mean? For knowledge workers, the definition of work is "applying focused attention to a work subject." That makes sense, doesn't it? For most of us, work equals focusing attention. So hard work means being diligent or disciplined in how you focus your attention.

I say, focusing your attention *most productively* is your real challenge, not focusing on obstacles for long hours. For example, wouldn't it be better to spend most of your time focused directly on achieving your positive work goals? If focusing your attention to activate your goals is as powerful as I say it is, activating goals may in fact be the best definition of hard work, because it may be the most important and productive work activity you can do to create outcomes.

Some say this sounds too easy, lazy even. But I suspect anyone reading this book is already familiar with hard work, putting in long hours, and sacrificing family time to get ahead. You don't need someone to convince you to work harder; you need someone to show you how to work *smarter.* Perhaps this is one time when working smarter really pays off.

In fact, taking time every morning to activate your goals *is* hard work. While it only takes five or ten minutes, it feels time consuming because it seems disconnected from "real" activity to reach the goal. That can make it difficult to continue every day. I am sure you will feel you have more pressing things to attend to when you start your day. But in reality, the best hard work you can do may be doing that—creating a discipline of continually visioning new and existing Now Goals as you progress through your career, and then activating your Now Goals every day.

In the next part, Part III, I will focus specifically on this idea of progressing your career through the visions you create about your work. I call that Connecting Your Workday Now.

# PART III

# Connecting Your
# Workday Now

The Workday Mastery Pyramid

CHAPTER **15**

# The Overlapping Circles of Life and Work

Recall that the theme of this book so far has been to improve and optimize the experience and productivity of your Workday Now, which is that period of time that includes both your Immediate Now at work and what you see coming in the next week or two. The point is to improve your experience of that key period, such that you start to attain what I call Workday Mastery, an experience at work of being productive and effective, and essentially happy and satisfied with work. We started that in Part I of the book by talking about how to clean up any chaos at work so you are not overwhelmed by everything that is on your plate. And in Part II, we continued that by showing you an effective way to create goals and outcomes.

In this final section, Part III, I want to discuss how you can *connect* to your work so that work is in alignment with who you really are, bringing greater productivity, satisfaction, and ease to your work and life. By doing this, you will change your Workday Now (and beyond) to be a much fuller and more satisfying experience. It is the ultimate step on the path to Workday Mastery, and represents the top level of the Workday Mastery Pyramid.

Here is one way to visualize connecting your work to who you really are. Imagine two circles. One represents you, your likes, your dislikes, your inner

221

drives—your core; it represents who you really are. The other represents your work or career and the activities within your career. Imagine these two circles drawn on a piece of paper.

For most people, they are far apart. What most people do in their work is far disconnected from what they value in life, from who they really are. The thoughts they think about themselves, the emotions they feel, and their image of what they want and value in life—all seem miles away from the image of what work could be or is. Many people feel they are faking their way through their work, that it has nothing to do with what they want out of life beyond being a source of food for the table.

I want you to use the processes in this book to bring those two circles closer together. Maybe they will eventually fully overlap, maybe they will just touch, but progress is possible. This section is about doing that. It is about connecting your work and your career to who you really are.

What does that mean? Well, for one thing, it means finding passion in your work. It means finding ways to bring the things you believe in, deep in your life, into your career. It means, while at work, operating from your core, so that your work reflects the best of your values and joys in life. You will never be the fully productive and effective professional you want to be unless you do that. The most impressive and satisfied professionals are those that integrate their work with who they really are.

To start bringing those two circles together, you should ask yourself some questions about your current work. Why do you go to work? Is it purely for the money? Do you enjoy work? If you do not enjoy work, is your current rationale for work just to pay the bills? Is it to get ahead to a position that you think you will enjoy later? Or is it simply to get to retirement, when you plan to really enjoy life?

If you do currently enjoy work, ask yourself, "What are my aspirations for more?" And if you do not enjoy work, ask, "Are there ways to improve this situation?"

You see, the first step to connecting your work with who you are is making peace with your current work, and finding ways to appreciate it more. So one of the perspectives we will take in this section is to look at your current Workday Now experience and see how you can improve it. Improving it is an important step to connecting your work and career to you. In my mind, creating your workday to be congruent with who you are is the highest level of managing your current workday.

## The Power of Your Vision or Purpose

Combined with improving your current situation, I will also talk about finding a larger personal vision or purpose to connect your career with—which may take you beyond—your current job. You see, more than anything else, the previous part of this book, "Creating Your Workday Now," showed you the power of *vision*. As you saw there, it is vision that makes outcomes and goals possible. It is vision that turns lifeless paper goals into living, breathing, inspired goals. You learned that all your goals can thrive if you start with a vision first, and that the vision should then be activated to make it happen. You saw that execution excellence is certainly necessary, but that vision will always be the starting point.

Now, in Part III, I want you to take vision beyond the level of individual goals. Vision adds inspiration and meaning to your entire workday and *life* as well. I want you to see vision as the way to define and create your work and life experience. It is said that vision can create worlds; that is almost a cliché these days, but it is nevertheless true, because a profound vision can, at a minimum, create *your* world, the one you experience.

When vision is applied at your overall career level, I call that *purpose*. In fact, when discussing this at the career level, I use the words *vision* and *purpose* somewhat interchangeably.

Why the word *purpose?* At the career level, vision usually represents adding meaning to your work—adding the Why to your work, the purpose. And that adds a lot.

Remember all the implications of vision from Part II? Finding a vision means finding inspiration, excitement, and passion. Recall that my larger definition of vision said vision is a *description of an outcome that conveys a sense of how the new outcome transcends the status quo—in a way that engenders inspiration for action.* So in your career that means finding how your career will move you forward in a profound way; and the vision itself, once established, actually provides the impetus for consistent, inspired action forward. A career vision, if strong, propels you forward through your career. It puts your career into pull mode—your work becomes a calling rather than just a job. That is definitely something we all aspire to, isn't it?

## Looking Ahead to Part III

Connecting your life and your work, the theme of Part III, requires working with vision, applying vision to your overall career, and then making it happen. Here is an overview of how each chapter in this section helps you accomplish that.

### Connecting to a Larger Vision or Purpose

The best way to start is by creating a larger vision for your work and career, one that feels just right. Doing this can be hard because our thoughts of a larger vision or purpose are often clouded by what others think—society, parents, and our friends (keeping up with the Joneses)—so you may need help with this.

That's why in Chapter 16 I review the common sources of a larger vision or purpose in a person's career, and how to discover them. If you currently cannot point to anything now that you would call a career vision or purpose, this chapter will give you material to brainstorm with and some ideas of where to look to find a larger work vision.

### Connecting with Yourself

Next, Chapter 17 provides more tools for identifying that larger work vision by discussing how to better connect with *yourself*—the inner you. Doing so allows you to hear the still, quiet voice within, and that voice is your most reliable source of what you really want to be in life. In that chapter I talk about different ways to connect with yourself. It involves learning to listen inside, connecting with your intuition and ultimately your heart; it really is about listening to your heart in ways you may have never done before. My hope is that once these skills are being used, they will lead to some insights, either small or large, about your career and vision.

### Connecting to Your Life's Work

Chapter 18 builds on the previous chapters in two ways. First, with a larger vision in place, this chapter will help you create a sense of what your current *life's work* is; that is, it will help identify your next job role, one that incorporates that larger vision or purpose. The idea is your very next role should be one that leverages who you really are into who you can become. I want you to identify work that is a reflection of your innermost loves, interests, and drives.

Chapter 18 then provides a way to reach that life's work by using the same skills you learned in the Goals portion of the book, only on a larger scale. At the end of Chapter 18, you will write up a vision statement for your career in a way that allows your career to match who you really are. You will do that in a manner similar to what you did for your Now Goals in Part II of the book. You will then activate that vision just like you are doing each day with your smaller goals. And, as with those, you will be putting that Vision Goal into pull mode to make it easier to reach.

Once your career is in pull mode, you will start to find that your work pulls you through the workday, rather than you having to push yourself through each day. As your new vision-based career starts to crystallize, your work becomes that *calling* I described above—it becomes a profession or activity that is calling you forward at all times. And at that point, in my opinion, your work stops being "work" and becomes more of an inspiration, maybe even your mission.

### Connecting to Your Mission

In fact, Chapter 19 discusses the idea of *mission*. Finding your mission is a frequently discussed topic of many career- and goal-oriented books, yet I think it is still largely misunderstood. In Chapter 19 you will see that I feel that finding your mission is not, as many books imply, your first step for enlarging your career. Rather, the activities I list above—finding a purpose, getting connected, and defining your life's work—are all more important first activities. Yet finding your mission can be a profound discovery once accomplished, and it can deeply affect your career choices. I will explain that paradox in a satisfying way in that chapter.

■   ■   ■

So enjoy Part III. It is a fitting conclusion to this book on mastering your workday and an appropriate way to cap the discussion of the Workday Mastery Pyramid. Recall how in the Introduction I stated that it parallels Maslow's pyramid—his hierarchy of *human* needs? Well, this part of the book concludes the climb up the hierarchy of *workday satisfaction* needs; it truly does represent the top of the Workday Now experience. You see, Maslow's theory stated the peak of life's journey is self-actualization, a state of embracing one's full personal potential. Similarly, finding vision and purpose in your career such that it lines up with and connects your job to who you really are is the peak of your work journey. It also maximizes your personal potential—in this case, your potential to enjoy both work and the other aspects of your life. So have fun with this section and enjoy the insights it brings.

CHAPTER **16**

# Connecting to a Larger Vision or Purpose

The first step to connecting your work to who you really are is to create a vision of work larger than yourself. What do I mean by a vision larger than yourself? It is anything you can point to that gives meaning to your work. Sometimes the larger vision is about seeking a better or expanded self; becoming more skilled and more effective. Other times, the larger vision is of making a better world for those around you, and feeling proud of being part of making that so.

If your current work vision is of improving yourself, it's probably about being a person that is smarter, more skilled, more effective, and probably more abundant in money, friends, and influence.

If your vision is of making a better world, it might be about improving your family or community. Or it might be about improving humanity, perhaps through developing new products that make people better off, building something important, or helping with an engineering accomplishment or scientific discovery. Or you might envision providing service to those in need. Your vision could be to work in a significant way for a company or organization that does any these things.

Or your picture may be more general, to be happier or more spiritually connected. Though happiness is usually an assumed outcome of any of the above, a truly wise person realizes that happiness can come independent of changes in life, that it can come from the inside. And if you have a strong religious belief or spiritual practice, you may get all the meaning and vision you need for work from that.

Any of these visions, and more, can add meaning and richness to your work.

## Why Connect to a Larger Vision or Purpose?

Making such a connection to a larger vision in your career is essential. As you advance in your career, you desperately need to connect with things like this that are larger than your current self. Doing so pulls you forward into the larger and growing you. You will want that in order to be happy with work and life. This will give you a constantly improving Workday Now as you move forward; the goal is to achieve enjoyable, fulfilling work in your current workday.

It almost goes without saying that we should always be moving forward in life. Forward movement sets up a sense of momentum that something better is always coming. It is human nature to always be reaching for more and expecting more. Forward movement is what defines us. A vision of a larger, more positive future pulls us forward, and gives us energy in our Now.

A larger vision or purpose also provides a framework for many of your smaller goals. Once in place, nearly all your other work goals can and will plug into that vision. It can provide the positive impetus, the reason, for each of those smaller goals. Connecting to a larger vision or purpose provides a source of passion; it can give you a reason to get up in the morning. It can put energy in your voice, and a lift in your step; it can give you a focus in life.

### A Major Definite Purpose

Connecting to a larger personal vision is also to some degree about finding your *Major Definite Purpose,* a phrase you may see a lot when you read goal-oriented success books.

The first place I saw that phrase was in the classic book *Think and Grow Rich* by Napoleon Hill, which I have referenced several times in this book. I have seen that phrase, meaning the same thing, in many other success-oriented books since then.

The point in that first book, and in modern ones, is similar to my emphasis of this section. You want to find or identify a burning purpose that drives you forward, which occupies your mind nearly always at work. You want to find a purpose that gives you passion and inspires your action, and becomes the vision around which all your goals will orbit.

From the perspective of Part II and activating goals, finding such a purpose is a worthy goal, as there is nothing like a unified, overarching life vision to get the wheels of your subconscious all spinning in a positive direction. Can you imagine how many things the subconscious could arrange for you if you were all day long spinning visions aligned with a single purpose? In other words, imagine what things you could create if all your subconscious spinning wheels were spinning in the same direction. That's the ultimate power of having a *Major Definite Purpose.*

## Why Connecting to Your Purpose Is Important for Your Workday Now

So as you can see, once you do connect with a purpose, even if to just a small degree, it will help greatly in improving your Workday Now. And improving that is important. You see, many of us assume "enjoyable, fulfilling work" is something that is coming later in life, if ever. But I want you to improve your current work experience *now,* your experience in your current Workday Now. That means the mental image you hold of today and the near future should be satisfying. Rather than assume a happier job is always in the *future,* over the Now Horizon (some weeks, months, or years out), I want you to quickly get to the point that even while expecting more, you are happy with your present work, with the things you are doing in your present Workday Now. I want you to feel satisfied and fulfilled, enjoying the momentum forward *now,* while on the way to an even better future.

Why the emphasis on Now? Because you will never get to a happy, better future if your current life experience is unhappy. Your hours at work represent one-third or more of your 24-hour day, perhaps half or more of your waking hours. You bring your workday happiness, or lack of it, home with you. Your overall sense of happiness and satisfaction with life is hugely affected by it. An unhappy workday has a huge influence on your overall life.

If you are constantly spinning in your Now an unhappy existence, you will spin up more of the same in the future. You will be negatively spinning much of the day. So part of reaching your goal of having satisfying work is to find a way to make your current work satisfying. Connecting your work to a vision or purpose larger than yourself is a key part of making your current work more satisfying. That is what we are going to do in the pages ahead.

So if you do not currently have one, use the upcoming discussion to help pick a purpose or vision. In that discussion, I will list most of the common sources of a larger purpose or vision in the work world. Review that list; perhaps something will grab you immediately. If not, then just pick the best choice and play with it (see the section at the end of this chapter titled "It's Okay if You're Not There Yet" for more discussion of this). Once you find something that resonates with you, write down a sentence that you think integrates it with your current or desired inner drive at work, and try it on for size.

Also, as you take a look at the typical sources for larger visions ahead, see if any allow you to generate new ideas. By the end of that section, I hope you will have written down a few vision ideas and are starting to think about what you want to focus on. Then look at what you wrote down and ask yourself, "Does it feel right?" Noodle on it for a while and rewrite it many times if needed. Put it away and come back to it in a week and see how it feels.

If you currently already have a vision or purpose larger than yourself that you are quite happy with, then at this point feel free to skip to Chapter 17, "Connecting with Yourself." Or read on here for possible ideas of even bigger visions.

## Finding a Purpose in Your Existing Work

We all have a tendency to look elsewhere for an improved work life, but before you start looking outside your current activities, and possibly for a new job, know this: nearly anyone can find a larger purpose in their existing work. I encourage you to start there for two reasons. One, it is easier and quicker; changing jobs takes time and effort, and it could delay your satisfaction unnecessarily. The second reason is this: if you cannot find inspiration in your current job, you probably will not find it in your next job either. You will be spinning up an unhappy next job with your current attitude.

Luckily, there are usually many ways to find a satisfying vision right in your current company.

### Study Your Company's Formal Vision

One way is to think in terms of what your company provides, and then be proud of your part in enabling that, no matter how small. To start on that, note that many companies have a formal vision or mission statement (or both). If leadership is good in your company, they have "advertised" that vision inside your company's walls to try to build loyalty and dedication. I encourage you to find that company vision, study it, and see if you can "buy into" it as your own. You may be surprised at what you find there once you reflect on it; you may see a side of your company you never noticed before.

Most companies were founded on a larger vision, one that is not hard to buy into once you see it. It is just that as they grow, most companies have either drifted from that vision or it is out of sight for the average worker who is buried in day-to-day work. So finding it can be a nice surprise. This can be an easy and quick way to locate a larger vision to focus on for a while. And once you embrace it and start to talk about it, you may be surprised at the attention you get from higher levels of management. You see, nearly all senior managers want to honor their company's vision and feel a bit guilty when they find themselves too busy to do so. So when they see a more junior employee embracing that vision as part of their job, it can inspire them to consider you in a favorable light.

### Product or Project Teams

Even if you are not inspired by the overarching vision of the company, your inspiration might still be found within your company, but at the product or initiative level. You might get very enthused about working on a new product or project team. I have found project teams to be a great source of inspiration and motivation for team members. A sense of camaraderie and purpose often develops on those teams, and many team members say their participation gives them a new energy about their work.

If your company has such teams but you are not working on them, try to get an internal transfer to one that you like. Also, many such teams do not require a transfer; most large companies have cross-departmental part-time teams or committees that study or enact improvements within the company. Find one that deals with a topic you care about and then get passionate about it. Or create a new initiative yourself; you may be inspired to create a new direction in your company, to be an agent of change. All these can lead to finding a vision within your current workplace.

If you cannot find the larger purpose in something connected with your current organization, you can still build a larger vision that is outside it, and then find a way your current job contributes to it.

How? If you are learning some skills on your current job, you can honor that as "gaining experience for future roles," which can be a fine purpose to latch onto. Just make sure you can give vision to the progression you are making, and how it is leading to an advancing *you,* leading to your larger vision. Once you formulate that future vision and start to fine-tune it, you may find ways to tweak your current job to more perfectly match the skills you intend to grow. I have seen young employees chase seemingly mundane jobs with unexpected passion. Only later would I realize why: they had a precise plan for using the role to learn a specific new skill that they had later plans for. You, too, may be able to do that in your current job.

It is much quicker to improve where you are than to have to wait for a career change. You will find it will be easier to find your next job if you first make peace with your current one. If you are looking for a career change, avoid the temptation to "give up" on your current company. Avoid the tendency to get cynical about your current role. It is often popular among colleagues to chat about how bad the company is, how management doesn't get it, and so on. If you buy into that, it will be hard to find *any* purpose in your current situation. If you make it your habit of thought, you will be negatively spinning and you may never find a new, better job.

So as an exercise, do this: spend some positive time today brainstorming ways to find a larger vision or purpose right now in your current company. I'll bet you can.

# Advancing Your Career Can Be Your Larger Vision or Purpose

Once you are committed to a profession or company, the most common larger purpose you can connect to at work is in advancing your own career. While too often people make this all about power or money, let's talk about how this can work in a very positive way, one that lends itself to a larger vision.

## Non-Management Advancement

First of all, career advancement can come in various ways. Typically we think of advancing into leadership roles in management as the primary form of advancement, but that is not the only route to career advancement.

For example, advancing your skills so that you become the "thought leader" in a particular field or industry is a solid vision as well. This means becoming the go-to expert for questions about a field or discipline, and it can be a very valuable larger vision to seek.

In my Accenture consulting work in Silicon Valley, something I saw at the high technology companies such as Sun, Netscape, HP, and others, was a formal career track that honored technology expertise. This career track awarded raises and positional honor to individuals who excelled in their technology achievements, at levels equal to management promotions. These positions required no management of others; rather these were held by technology professionals, the experts on key engineering or scientific inventions that represented the core knowledge behind their products. The point was to allow these individuals time for focused work and thought leadership on advanced technology. Being the best in a field can be a true source of career advancement, and something to strive toward as a vision.

One way to say this in your upcoming life's work vision statement (something you will create in Chapter 18) is "I grow and excel in my engineering [or other] skill levels to the point that I enjoy significant recognition and rewards as a thought leader in my company."

## Management Advancement: Greater Position

More typically, though, career advancement is often measured by rising to higher management positions, the emphasis being on leadership of other people.

Unfortunately, too many people look at this as gaining power or money. However, a power perspective is usually a fear-based one, reflecting internal self-talk such as, "I am tired of being pushed around; now I get to be in control for a change." And a pure money perspective lacks vision as well.

Instead, I hope you look at it as expanding your positive *sphere of influence*. What do I mean by that? If you believe in your skills, capabilities, ideas, or message, or in your ability to improve others' lives in some way, then one way to expand your vision is to expand the range of people and organizations you are reaching with those skills and that vision. That larger sphere of influence is what advancement in management positions can bring.

Many people think that positional authority is what you gain in a more advanced position. But really, it is your ability to influence more people from that position that is key here. It is your ability to move more people toward an end goal; that's where the power lies. This is the difference between leadership and management. The best leaders rarely use their positional authority (the ability to give orders), but instead see their role as an ability to positively influence. You see, merely imposing positional authority can perhaps create short-term results, but in the long run it more often breeds resentment. In contrast, using the power of your position to expand your positive influence actually *inspires* action rather than *forces* it, and it creates long-lasting loyalty among staff and colleagues.

I encourage you to aspire to skills that command a larger sphere of positive influence, and then to positions where those skills can be used; to me, this is the best career advancement vision you can have.

A vision statement that captures this might include the line, "I continue to advance in my management roles such that my increasing sphere of influence has a growing positive impact on my business, and on the world around me."

## What Does Advancing Your Career Mean to You?

Also, ask yourself what the term *career* advancement means to you. Does it mean advancing within your company, or rather within an industry or profession? These days, company loyalty means less and less, so industry or professional advancement often makes more sense. As corporations become less and less loyal to their employees, and as employees become more mobile, you will want to analyze any position advancement within your company in terms of how it might play in other companies within your industry or profession.

Also ask yourself, does an advancing career mean advancing in one industry and profession, or possibly across many? In my case, I have changed industries and professions seven times so far, and have been able to advance my career all along the way. Here are the specifics: I started as a mapping soil scientist for the U.S. government, then became a civil engineer building commercial buildings, and then a software engineer. From there, I advanced to become the manager of the United States Peace Corps' entire IT department. Then I became a management consultant for Accenture and a then VP there. I next created AAA's Project Management Center of Excellence, and finally (so far) became an author and speaker. Each step was a fairly major change in both industry and profession.

For me, I saw such career advancement as primarily a learning experience independent of my field. My larger vision was about increasing my effectiveness and sphere of influence, about being able to effect positive change. My learning the details of each new industry was merely another source of challenge and accomplishment to me. Combining the skills of the various industries gave me great insight into common issues inside the work world, and that helped me build the vision that led to writing my books.

Perhaps you can see ways that a variety of experience can build a vision for you too.

## Learning Skills and Increasing Challenges

Speaking of gaining new knowledge and skills, skill advancement is a worthy larger vision in itself. Particularly in your younger work years, much of your work will be learning experiences, and much of your satisfaction and passion will come from the knowledge that you are learning and expanding your capabilities for use in later positions. And believe me, that is enough during the early stages of your career.

And even for more established workers, if you feel your career has flattened, it is never too late to decide to start learning new skills and to make that your current larger vision.

For example, for many people who say their larger goal is to make money, I really think their goal is to learn the *skill* to make money at will. This is a skill in itself and could be worthy of a larger purpose, as long as you connect more fundamentally meaningful ends to it as well.

Facing down increasingly difficult challenges in your work successfully can be part of a larger vision as well, as long as you see that as a positive skill-building exercise that will place you in a position in the future to have a larger influence, or to get closer to your goals. Many people write their purpose as "gaining positions of increasing levels of challenge and responsibility."

For some people, being the very best at something is the vision. The general statement, "I want to be the best darn [insert role] ever!" is a fantastic larger vision, because it represents passion and growth, the main components of a satisfying career path and vision. To be the best at something usually implies increasing skills and a dedication to choosing to constantly improve. This is a moving target, of course, so just be ready to pick a new vision once you reach your current goals.

### Other Sources of Vision and Purpose within Your Career

There are various other ways to find purpose and vision in your career advancement.

You might find it in longevity with or loyalty to your company; great pride can come from that. "I am proud and delighted by the years of service I have given as a committed employee of this company. My long presence here has made a significant contribution to the success that the company is today, and will continue to be tomorrow."

Your larger purpose may be the relationships you form at work. You might get such a thrill from meeting the people you come into contact with on the job that expanding that is your larger vision. "I deeply honor the growing number of meaningful and connected relationships I make at work."

Or it might be in the creativity you express. Product development and scientific research lead to important discoveries that can benefit the world, and this can lead to your sense of a larger vision. "I will create a product that positively impacts large numbers of people greatly."

Any of these and more can be sources of purpose within your advancing career.

It really only matters whether your selection provides you with positive inspiration. No one can judge your decision other than you. But ask yourself this: can you create a positive and emotive (and honest) vision statement around it, one that pulls you forward in your career? Can you get excited while viewing yourself in that new place? If the answer is yes, you've got it.

# Finding Your Vision or Purpose in a New Job

In the end, though, if after a fair amount of looking, you cannot find a larger personal purpose in your current role or somewhere else in your company, it may be time to start planning a move to another place where you can. If you are going to do that, you might consider the following types of organizations as a next place to work since they tend to have strong vision foundations.

## Startups and Nonprofits

Startup companies are some of the best companies to work for because their small size and speedy growth make for rapid and fluid dissemination of the company vision to all members of the rank and file. And startups usually are at the cutting edge of business or technology, so their visions are often quite exciting. They also usually offer rapid promotion paths.

I have worked in several startup companies, and the enthusiasm in staff for the corporate vision is usually amazing. Stock options and IPO potentials obviously help, but in most cases, the true enthusiasm comes from being part of an exciting and important new business vision. The fact that the vision came from someone else does not matter; as long as you have bought into it, it can become your way to connect to a vision or purpose larger than yourself. For example, I worked several years at a software startup called MicroDynamics, and while the IPO never materialized (and the company no longer exists), the experience was amazing. You might write a purpose statement such as, "I work in an exciting startup that provides an inspiring vision and opportunities for rapid advancement."

Nonprofit and service organizations are also a fantastic place to borrow someone else's vision and make it your own, or to join a group that shares your current vision, and expand on it. By definition, these groups tend to be vision oriented; after all, it is satisfaction with the larger vision that stimulates the founders to forgo profits in exchange for pride in the organization's outcomes. Working for one can be hugely satisfying and a genuine source of your larger vision.

For example, I was the Director of IT for the United States Peace Corps and it was a profound experience. The Peace Corps, as you may recall, was the agency formed by President John F. Kennedy to promote service by Americans around the world. Even though I was stationed in the Washington, DC headquarters, well away from the overseas action, I felt a close part of the overseas activity. It was very clear that our role at headquarters was to support the volunteers, who faced difficult challenges on the front lines. Dedication to that mission permeated the organization, giving many there a shared sense of larger purpose.

A wide variety of nonprofit or service groups have formed around visions of a better world through work on the environment, social work, politics, and religion. All provide excellent sources of a vision larger than yourself, whether you already share their views or seek to learn new ones to adopt. Your statement might be, "I work for a service organization that improves the world by [insert your favorite cause]."

And don't forget, the United States military also offers similar paid volunteer opportunities providing purpose and vision at all levels of the various branches of the armed services.

## Picking a New Profession

Rather than picking a new company or organization with a vision you like, you might want to pick a profession that in itself represents a larger purpose as part of its day-to-day activities.

The natural example is a role as a nurse, doctor, or other health care professional; or a firefighter, police officer, or EMT. All these roles have an implied vision to save lives, and for many that gives deep meaning and purpose. Naturally, jobs in these professions, when pursued for the right reasons, can lead you to a larger personal vision almost immediately. Granted, many currently in those roles lose the vision as they get caught up in issues at work. But with the right attitude, you can keep or pull that vision back in a role like that.

Even government positions have the potential for linking to public service in a way that defines a larger vision. While many in those positions focus more on the security of the job over the meaning, a large number do find and hold the vision of service their jobs provide to the public. The best positive example of that is perhaps being a teacher. Teachers usually work for local governments and there are no better examples of a profession with a larger vision or goal, one of improving and advancing our community's youth.

I would find people who work in these roles, learn about them, maybe visit some facilities, and if you find one that inspires you, write a vision statement that has you moving into such a role.

## Developing Your Own Business

Certainly, as discussed above, your career advancement within established companies may be the extent of your business vision. But at some point the upside of starting your own business may loom larger than the security of working for others.

Simply creating and growing your own business and seeing yourself succeed in it can be a purpose in itself. It gives you confidence in your ability to create something larger than yourself.

Or even better, you may have a business idea around a product or service that you are enthused about because the product will better the community or the world in some way. If you believe in it and the good it will provide for your customers, then, in my mind, that is one of the best larger visions to have because every sale you make not only makes you money, but adds to your sense of directly bettering the world.

And even if the product is not life-changing—perhaps it is just an ordinary thing—it can still be a source of vision.

These benefits are true whether you run a side business or plunge full-time into your endeavor.

When you do go full-time, it is an even greater pleasure to know that you no longer need to depend on others to support your family and yourself; it is a huge step forward. It frees you from one of the largest dependencies we all have: depending on others to survive. Knowing that you are making it on your own can feel like a huge accomplishment. Of course you will still be dependent; this time it is on your customers. But at least you can have control over that relationship. If you provide an excellent product and service and one that they want, they usually respond predictably.

Watching your business grow can be a vision in itself, knowing that your efforts are solely responsible for that growth. But as I said, an even bigger vision gain occurs when the product or service represents a larger vision in itself. Perhaps it makes life easier for many people. Maybe it represents a product breakthrough. Maybe it actually saves lives. To me, there is no work vision or purpose better than having a business that delivers a life-changing service or product, and I encourage you to find one.

I certainly had that experience with the Outlook productivity book I wrote, which quickly became the best-selling title among the many Outlook books available. Every day I receive e-mails from readers saying the techniques in that book have changed their lives. To get such feedback is incredibly satisfying.

With that in mind, perhaps writing a book is something you should consider. Writing a book is not for everybody, but it is easier than most people think. And it lends itself to certain personality types, those who are knowledge-oriented and enjoy the written word as a mode of expression. It is of course hard to make money on a book, and it will eat up all of your spare time for many months, but the boost in self-confidence of such an accomplishment is easily worth that price.

## Looking Outside a Business or Career

While advancing your business or career may be all the larger connection you need for now, for many of us that is either not enough or not appropriate.

First of all, developing your own career may not feel very selfless, and selflessness is something that many feel is an essential component of a "vision larger than ourselves." It is almost in the definition.

Or maybe you have reached the peak of your career and want to extend you vision more toward helping others. Or maybe you have a passion that has nothing to do with work but that is so satisfying you have no need to look to work for any sense of forward motion; this is one place where work is just a paycheck supporting a larger outside vision.

Whatever the reason, there are multiple ways to connect with your purpose outside your career.

### Developing Others' Careers

One source of satisfaction that goes beyond your own career (but is often exercised within it) is to help develop the careers of others who work for you or with you. Whether as part of an official mentorship program, or as just taking an unofficial interest in a junior staff member's career, it is a worthy source of purpose and vision. The senior managers that I've known who do this in various companies often say that mentoring a junior staff member was one of the most important things they did at their jobs. In a way, it brings out the teaching instinct in many of us, something that is satisfying but often hard to express in the business world. I recommend the book *Greater Than Yourself* by Steve Farber for a parable-like story of why this is so important.

### Family

Certainly family is one of the most common ways to connect to a larger purpose. Being a provider for your family gives a source of meaning, usually with love at its basis, and any time you put love into a vision equation, it expands the intangible payback immensely. Supporting a family is the larger purpose most often cited by most people when asked what they are working for.

It can also be a source of one's balance and stability. Family life often brings out the best in people, building skills that counterbalance the competitive workplace energies with patience, warmth, compassionate leadership, and more. Family is a common focus for anyone who seeks more out of life than just work.

For people who feel that their lives or their work gains have already peaked, thinking ahead to improving the lives of their growing children is often their main purpose. The statement "I want my children to have what I could not have" embodies this sentiment.

For many of us, regardless of our work, enjoying the existence of our families and our roles in them is a primary life purpose. It represents the love of life embodied in a few key souls. It represents our closest community. It gives expression to our best inner qualities of love, dedication, and courage. It is our source of an expanding heart. It is our source of personal growth. That is the larger purpose role that family plays for many of us.

Of course, if family begins to feel like a ball and chain, then you have lost that, haven't you? If that has happened to you, I urge you to find the love there again and gain the support it gives you. It is always there. Once you do, family expands your heart. Love of family adds warmth to every business transaction. A glance at a picture of your family on your desk during work adds depth to your decisions, your discussions, and your work experience. It adds integrity as you place this larger purpose in the back of your mind with every business action. Family represents love, and love is in so many ways the missing element in many businesses.

For all these reasons, family certainly can be a higher vision or purpose for many of us while at work, and you may want to write up your purpose or vision almost entirely in terms of your family. Such a purpose might be, "My number one priority is providing for my family such that they have all the things needed in life to be safe, happy, constantly growing, and well-cared for."

But many of us do not have immediate families. And many who do also need something larger to add to their goal of supporting their family. For many, supporting their family is a given, but they want to accomplish much more than that. You will find your own place on that continuum.

## Community

Right next to the influence of family on work is something less common these days, but also an important possible source of purpose. It is the belief in and support of your *community.*

Decades ago it was popular to form community service groups like Kiwanis, Rotary, and others, whose purpose was literally to do good deeds for the community. Members bettered themselves through networking and having fun.

Such groups have lost popularity, and it is more and more up to the individual to find meaning in their community. I met a business owner in a town in northwest Washington state. He started and ran a small coffee and bakery shop. We got to talking and he told me how much he loved making a contribution to the local community with his business. He shared how he wanted to be part of and nurture the community experience. He was without a family, so in a way the community was his larger purpose.

I think this is more common in a smaller, rural community, where one-of-a-kind businesses can provide much-needed services that are completely lacking, for example, when a doctor moves into a town that has none. For that matter, a mechanic, a banker, or a dry cleaner can provide an essential community service, and your role in providing that service can be a major inspiration.

But even in large cities, the local grocery, hardware store, tailor, barber, or hairdresser all make a contribution. There is an appreciation that grows between the patrons and the owners. When people talk about their positive experiences with this vendor or that, that then becomes one part of the substance of their lives. It becomes a thread in the fabric of the community. If your business contributes in that way to the community, your workday contribution can feel enormously important, and you will want to nurture it. Keeping it alive and well fed can become the higher purpose for you in your work. So a vision or purpose statement might be, "My business provides an essential community service that is recognized by many, and that brings me a strong ongoing sense of contributing to my local area."

## Professional Organizations

If you work in a profession or industry supported by associations or other professional organizations, in some ways such organizations can become a community as well. Industry groups, standards committees, trade associations—all of these groups can become a source of a higher purpose at work.

While most people join these as a way to network and advance their careers, once you become active in one, your perspective can change. Volunteers in these groups start to see the contribution the group makes in advancing the profession or trade as a whole, and a larger purpose can emerge that is very satisfying.

I've witnessed people in companies I work for become active in industry groups solely for the purpose of improving the industry, and that is perhaps the best way to use this in a "larger purpose" role. A vision statement along these lines might be, "My role in this professional organization contributes to the expansion of my profession as a major source of improving our society and the world."

### Volunteer Organizations

As in the "places to work" discussion above, *volunteering* for a nonprofit or service group can provide a source of higher purpose. The selflessness of volunteer work is liberating. And if you are lucky enough to be in a role or organization where you directly see the results of your volunteer actions, it can be fantastic.

You do of course need to pick and choose your organizations. Many non-profit groups exist solely to make money for the owners, so use your judgment on which ones feel right to you.

### Outside Passions Such as Sports

Activity in some personal passions like the arts or sports are nearly impossible to get paid for, so you will need to pursue them outside and in addition to your regular source of income. Nonetheless, because of your deep enthusiasm for them, they can provide the larger vision you need to keep your life satisfying and constantly moving forward.

For most of these, the end game is enjoying the activity itself and improving your skills in that activity. Being active in amateur sports can easily go beyond just having fun and rise to the level of a vision or purpose larger than yourself. Improving to the point of being the local champion in a given sport may be the end game. Winning competitions and then mentoring others both contribute to a sense of reaching a larger you, and that could be your vision, especially if you start teaching others and gain from that sense of purpose.

I took up flying sail planes for a while and could not wait for the weekend to go flying; what a fantastic feeling to be soaring over the earth on wind power alone! At the time I felt like if all I did was that, I was in heaven, and I enjoyed the steady increase in skills each time I flew. I moved on from that to other interests, but it was my vision for a while at a time when I needed one. I hear golf is like that for many people.

Some of these passions, like the arts, represent a connection in itself; the feeling of connection is the purpose. Many people feel they are "in the flow" when they are performing or creating. Some sports may provide the same. In fact, a number of books have been written about how during running or other sports people can get into "the zone," where all things come easily and automatically and a sense of rising above the ordinary takes over. See *Finding Your Zone,* for example, by Michael Lardon. Such an experience is often called the "runner's high," and many runners live for that.

I am sure you have activities like this that, if expanded, could capture your main larger interest, and provide a vision or purpose larger than yourself.

### Religion and Spiritual Growth

I put this last not because it is least important, but because it is the most subjective. For many people, their higher vision or purpose is a religious or spiritual one, and it pulls them forward in life and work, and does so as well as or better than any work, social, or family vision can. A religious vision can serve as the underlying spark for just about any area of life. If you are strongly religious or spiritual, don't feel like your main vision needs to be the more business-like ones I listed above. In my mind, the most profound and most admirable visions are the spiritual ones. So by all means if you hold one, honor that part of yourself by incorporating it partly or fully into your vision. Ultimately, that will be your biggest vision.

## Visions to Question or Avoid

Before moving on to the next chapters, which are about how to implement these visions, let me first give you some advice about some visions to avoid. You see, some visions I call "false" visions—they are created and pursued for the wrong reasons. Let's talk about that.

### Filtering Out Fearful Choices

First, when thinking about options for a larger vision, I recommend you filter out fearful or "shouldful" choices. What I mean by that is, we often make career and purpose choices based on something we are running from, or someone we are afraid of, or "shoulds" we have been convinced we should follow in life. We do this instead of the better way: basing choices on a positive inner drive or a positive digest of life experiences. I want you to avoid the fear- and shoulds-based choices.

For example, how many people who say they want to be a doctor say it because their parents or friends say they should, instead of from a deep inner desire to help sick people feel better? Similarly, too many law school applicants think first of how important it sounds to say, "I am going to law school," or later, "I am an attorney," instead of following their true aspirations. There are many other career choices like this that are made for the wrong reasons.

This happens because many of us have old fear-based tapes playing in our minds from years of shoulds and shouldn'ts being thrown at us, and these tapes can lead to decisions that don't make us happy.

So as you walk through this section, do a little soul-searching and ask yourself where the initial feeling of a larger vision is coming from. Is it coming from an authentic positive inspiration within, or are you reacting to old fears and shoulds? Lean toward the inner, positive, and inspirational impulses.

### Money as a Vision—Is It Enough?

I have cautioned in Part II about using money as a vision. So without dwelling too much on that again, let me just say this briefly. Setting a primary goal of having a million dollars, for example, is usually a hollow goal. Unfortunately, many get-rich-quick books, and even legitimate success books, remind us that if we think big, we can pursue anything we want, and so why not start at the top with a nice large money goal as our primary focus.

However, I suspect that intuitively you know money alone does not play very well as a "Vision Larger Than Yourself." Regardless of such success books (or perhaps because of them), I'll bet that in your gut you know there has to be more to a life's work than just making money, and that any larger purpose around work will most likely transcend focusing only on the size of your paycheck or bank account.

But of course, all of us want increasing money; money is so key to funding basic needs and to enabling so many of our larger aspirations, even service aspirations. So yes, as I mentioned in the Create-layer section, I also feel some reference to money can and probably should be included as one or more of your Target Goals in any set of life or higher work goals you may create. Just make sure you have a larger vision that the money Target Goal rides on.

### Investments as a Larger Vision or Purpose?

Some people ask if being a successful investor qualifies as a vision or purpose larger than just making money. Certainly investments on the side have no conflict and fit the category as a side goal, as long as you hold a larger vision. But can being a full-time investor be your larger purpose, or is that just the same as having money as your primary goal? I tried it for a short while, and I now know I cannot do that; I need more substance in my career. But some people can. I suspect you might go into investing either after you have a fulfilled career behind you and you are semi-retired, or in conjunction with volunteer work or hobbies that fulfill your other goals, and use investments to fund those endeavors.

If you work in a salaried job, having investments on the side is important because they can provide a sense of unlimited upside for your money. If your salary is fixed, investments give you the hope that more money can come, and hope for more is always an important added component of any overarching larger vision.

There is another angle for using money as an element of a larger goal. As I mentioned earlier in this chapter, I think that many people who say their main goal is making money, perhaps in investments or some other business activity, really mean that learning the *skill* to make money *at will* is their goal. This is a skill in itself and worthy as a larger purpose, as long as you connect more personally meaningful ends to it as well.

What larger ends? For one thing, it builds confidence in yourself and removes fear of lack, and that is a strong foundation for even greater achievements later. Or you may want to teach others who need a money stream to fund other activities how to do it, and you can feel deep satisfaction from that. Or the purpose could even be enjoying money making as a game, and then finding true meaning by spreading the wealth to many along the way, thus enjoying their happiness.

For example, I knew an investor who developed a very successful system of investing, made his millions, and then went on to teach that system to people whom he enjoyed working with. He described the teaching experience as being the best of his career, much better than making money (though I suspect he would not have traded it). The lesson is, find a way to make gaining money part of a larger vision.

If any of these goals matches your inner positive drive and feels large enough for you, by all means pursue it. If it ever starts to feel hollow, though, or not fitting to you, just move on; you can always raise the bar for your goals at any later time.

### Living for Retirement

While we are on the topic of money, you might ask, "Is working for a happy retirement a worthy larger purpose?" Let's talk about that.

First of all, there is nothing wrong with setting that goal, as *one* of your goals. But as your *primary* larger work vision, it is lacking. It gives no meaning to your current activities other than living for later.

To see why, let's take the extreme (but common) approach to this. The way many people approach retirement is this: "I will work hard at a job I don't really enjoy, but that is okay, because when I retire I will enjoy life then."

Not only does that shortchange your current work and life, but it may not turn out that way. As I mentioned earlier in this section, unless you find a way to be satisfied in your current work, and all work advancements after that, you are likely to have an unhappy retirement too. Recall the power of negative goal spinning.

I'd rather have you build a capacity for satisfaction in what you are doing now, a capacity that will carry over, no matter what you plan to do in retirement, and no matter how you fund it. A larger vision about work will provide that capacity. You are then much more likely to have a happy retirement. A vision that includes a happy current work life *and* happy retirement is best.

# Summary

Holding and pursuing a vision or purpose larger than yourself is essential to experiencing a satisfying and fulfilling Workday Now. Doing so pulls you forward into the larger and growing you. Forward movement sets up a sense of momentum, a sense that something better is always coming. Forward movement is what defines us, and gives us energy in our Now.

If you do not yet have a vision or purpose larger than yourself applicable to work, be sure to take time to study the common sources of that in this chapter. If you find one, fantastic—start applying it in the chapters ahead. If you do not, then consider the following.

## *It's Okay if You're Not There Yet*

You may be thinking, "Let's get real; I have nothing like a passionate vision yet. I am too early in my career to even consider a major definite purpose." Or, "I have never found anything like that and have given up looking."

If so, that's fine. In my early years when I considered this, I felt a bit uneasy with the idea that to be successful one needed to determine their major definite purpose. I felt I was too young to commit to a definite purpose yet. It seemed so unlikely that I would ever get that passionate about something having to do with work. And if it were to ever happen, I felt I needed more time to find it. And further down the road, even more experienced workers are usually resigned to a less-than-happy work life. "After all" they say, "work is called 'work' for a reason."

I know a lot of people feel that way. So that's why for those of you like that, the intention I have for this chapter starts out a little less ambitious. I am simply hoping to help you find a way to *connect* with a larger purpose. By that, I mean identify something in your work or life that will inspire you to whatever degree while at work, that will create an aspiration to reach for, but that is not necessarily yet a burning life desire.

For example, perhaps you find a project at work that gets you excited, and you want to become part of it. You may not see it as your career direction, but you can still find yourself getting passionate about the objectives of the project.

This more humble vision may be all you can expect, particularly if you are new to the workforce. Early in your career you are likely to be still searching, testing out purposes held by others, adopting them and seeing how they feel. You might be testing the vision of your company to see how you feel about it.

So whether you are new to the workforce or a bit jaded about larger visions, if this sounds like you, all I ask at first is that you find a way to connect inside with a deeper, more meaningful idea about why you come to work. Use the ideas in this chapter to slowly work in that direction. That will be enough for now.

### It Will Change

Also, if this is the first time you have thought about your larger work vision, do not worry about getting it "right." I guarantee that you will change it many times through your career and even several times in the next days or weeks, as you do the exercises ahead. As you mentally toss around this idea of a larger vision, you will be matching it up against your inner world and your life. That will stimulate some reflection, and many more ideas will emerge over time. And even once you stabilize your vision for some months or years, in the long run, as you set and then achieve your larger goals, you will set new goals that are larger than the ones before. As you go through life, your life experiences will add to your picture of what you want out of work and life, and periodically entire new sets of goals will emerge. Your worldview will change.

This is perfect; it is just the way you want life and work to be. So don't think you have to permanently identify your larger vision now or get it exactly right. You do not have to pick something and then commit to it for the rest of your life.

### Making These Visions Happen

Once you pick a larger purpose that resonates with you, that you can connect to, now is the time to start visioning it. In Chapter 18, "Creating Your Life's Work," you will do that. There you will be using tools similar to those in Part II to create a work goal around your vision, and to activate it.

But first, I want to cover another important "skill" for work, a skill I call Connecting with Yourself. This skill is essential to enliven the inner guidance you will need once you start pursuing larger visions, especially visions that go beyond well-trodden paths. That is the topic of the next chapter.

CHAPTER **17**

# Connecting with Yourself

I admit, the phrase "connecting with yourself" may sound a bit odd. You may be thinking that some pop psychology content is about to be thrust upon you, or perhaps even more challenging, a personal spiritual belief will be unveiled.

But the purpose here is much more benign; I merely want you to take a moment and consider the simple yet meaningful advice to trust your internal guidance more and more at work. Many of us are so burned out by the urgencies of business, or jaded by our information overload, that we forget to listen to our own inner messages. The benefits of doing so are huge and very practical, even in the workplace—no, *especially* in the workplace. If you do learn to hear and trust your internal guidance more, it will nearly always take you to a better and more meaningful work result—at a minimum it will make work easier and more enjoyable.

In this chapter I am going to discuss what I mean by connecting with yourself, discuss many of the workday benefits of doing so, and then talk about how to do it. I will focus a lot of attention on the idea of *business intuition*—what it is and how to increase it. I think you will find this chapter very interesting, even if the phrase "connecting with yourself" does scare you a little.

# What Does Connecting with Yourself Mean?

One benefit of identifying a larger vision or purpose that inspires you, as described in the previous chapter, is that it also helps you connect with yourself. What do I mean by connecting with yourself? The exact experience of this in the work context can vary. It ranges from a vague sense of understanding yourself and how you best relate to your work, to a feeling of being in the flow, with work achievements coming effortlessly. The latter end of that range is not as typical of course, but is possible. You should be happy if you can say that you are satisfied with who you are and how you move through your work, that you see life and work as an ongoing and ever-expanding journey, and that you are an eager and mostly satisfied participant in that journey. That's a nice start, and there is more.

I also think a truly connected person hears the inner messages of their soul and uses them to guide their work. They define themselves not so much by the world around them but by the smooth conversation with their inner vision, where aspirations are clear and motivating, and both achievements and failures are registered and learned from. A truly connected person has a clear, quiet voice from within that helps them in real time; it is trusted and usually correct.

How does all this look on the outside? You've probably met people at work who seem very confident in their roles. They seem to glide or even soar through the workday. They seem like they are comfortably in the right place at the right time. It may be they even seem more successful, that the right solutions come easily when needed. They seem to be in a place where appropriate business decisions and actions come almost automatically. They've got good ideas and they are tuned into the business and people around them. They do all this relatively effortlessly; sometimes they barely seem to break a sweat.

Such people may just be very experienced at what they do. But mainly I think they are both well connected to their work, and well connected to *themselves.* In the Workday Now model, it is all about boosting the quality of their Immediate Now, their I-Now. It is about boosting the quality of their own human attention, so that it is clear, attuned, and in touch with the outer and inner world. It is also about connecting through there to their heart.

However you define it, I think you will agree that "getting connected to yourself" as much as possible is extremely useful, both in personal and business life. While you may not reach the degree described above, I think even a little of this is helpful for a happy life and a successful work life and career.

# The Benefits of Connecting with Yourself

There are some specific benefits that come from a stronger internal connection. They range from improving the quality of the work vision you create to improving your attitude at work. Such connection also helps you make better business decisions. Let's explore that range.

### Connection Helps You Identify a Larger Vision and Life's Work

Ultimately, a good connection to yourself is the only way to go if you are trying to find a larger purpose or vision that matches you well, as discussed in Chapter 16. It is also key if you are looking for your life's work, as I describe in the next chapter. Most people I talk to who have found inspiring life-purpose work did so by trusting their gut, their intuition, and their heart to find it, explore it, and understand it. Think of what the word *inspiring* means; it means "being filled from within with passion and excitement about something." Inspiration is clearly one result of opening a connection to yourself—being able to hear your inner messages and allowing them to guide you to fulfilling work.

### Connection Leads to an Effective Workday Flow

Perhaps one of the most familiar bits of jargon around the connected state I have described above is the idea of *getting in the flow.* This was a popular concept starting in the 1990s, and I think it still describes well the experience I refer to here.

I'll bet that you can recall periods at work (and play) when you were mentally clear, where all life's actions just seemed to fall into place, and work and life proceeded effortlessly. This is being in the flow.

We usually write these periods off to chance, situation, or perhaps preceding events that made us feel good; or to just a lucky day. But it is actually a well-studied phenomenon, and something worth striving for.

The reigning expert on this topic is Mihaly Csikszentmihalyi from the University of Chicago. He wrote the 1990 book called *Flow: The Psychology of Optimal Experience*. In that book he indicates that episodes of these experiences can be cultivated to be more constant. In other words, we can train ourselves to live a life in the flow. He describes flow as a state "where people typically feel strong, alert, in effortless control, unselfconscious, and at the peak of their abilities. Both the sense of time and emotional problems seem to disappear, and there is an exhilarating feeling of transcendence."

If you study his work, you will see he is describing what I call an exceptionally clear I-Now experience, the Immediate Now within the Workday Now model. Really, he is talking about increasing the quality, nature, and focus of our attention, our point awareness. After all, life is just a series of now experiences, so if we improve our ability to experience, we improve our lives.

Such a clear experience of *flow* as described by Csikszentmihalyi is, to me, one strong form of connection to yourself, and a very useful one for improving your work experience.

The benefits of this in real time at work are obvious. Day-to-day tasks are accomplished more easily, and decisions resulting in better outcomes are made.

### Connection Directly Improves Your I-Now

Even if you don't immediately recognize the long-term career impacts of self-connection, in the short term you can certainly see the effect on your attitude and enjoyment of work. Recall the theme of this book: to improve the quality of your Workday Now, right now. Well, self-connection will do that too by directly improving your I-Now experience.

You see, we often operate as if our current Now experience is a result of our memories of the past and our visions of the future; if we have fond memories and a bright future, our Now experience is good. Many of us spend a lot of time trying to create those bright memories and futures, to make our current lives better.

We should do that, of course, but I'd like to also propose that there is a more direct way. I feel that we color our experience of the past and future with a filter built into the I-Now mind. No matter what really happened in the past, or what really is scheduled for the future, we actually interpret the past and future differently based on how we filter them in our thoughts and feelings right now, in our I-Now. You've seen the extremes of this; you wake from a bad sleep, face the day tired and cranky, and then everything looks bad all day. Such a coloring of experience happens all the time, usually more subtly, but it still happens.

So if we improve our ability to experience life in the I-Now, to remove the negative coloring we often unnecessarily add, we can improve our day-to-day experiences greatly. Just the attitude change alone will positively affect how we approach the work on our plate.

How do you get there? In the sections ahead I am going to cover some ideas on how you may get connected to yourself. They vary from simply paying more attention to your intuition, to structured practices like meditation. I hope you will find something useful in the range of approaches I suggest, something that will help you increasingly work at what I call the Connect layer of work.

## Connection Leads to Better Gut Decisions

One of the benefits of being connected to yourself and clearly hearing your inner messages is that it helps greatly when making business decisions.

These days, with the complexity of the business world, decision making is harder than ever. How do you teach someone to make good decisions at work? Business schools provide analytical processes for interpreting data, and some general business training. But do they provide reliable training on how to make day-to-day decisions? No, this is not adequately taught in business schools, even the best ones.

I think that is reflected by where our business leaders do get their training. If you look across America's largest companies, very few of the CEOs come from Ivy League schools, so clearly, academia does not provide leadership skills. I think the best decision making comes from leaders who can think effectively from their gut. Learning how to develop accurate gut decision making is a key component of being a good manager, even for someone who only manages their own work.

This is of course not just me talking; gut decision making is becoming a commonly recognized talent. Even the publication called the *Harvard Business Review on Decision Making* has added a whole chapter called "Gut Decision

Making," so at least the Ivy League schools *recognize* the phenomenon. Many other references and organizations are recognizing it as well.

Many people think such natural decision makers are born with this skill. Others think it can be developed only through years of on-the-job experience. However, I think you can develop good business intuition in other ways as well. How? Well, I think it's an inside job. While experience is important, I say decision-making skills may have even more to do with connecting with and understanding those gut messages you get from within, from connecting in general more clearly to yourself.

# Connection Improves Your Business Intuition

Another way of saying we have a good gut decision-making capability is to say we have good business intuition. I am a big believer in this. The thing I value the most of all *my* skills is my intuitive decision-making capability. Among logic, my experience, my writing skills, and my intuition, for me, intuition wins big time. If I had to enter a totally new business area tomorrow, one that I had no experience in whatsoever, I feel strongly I could succeed in short order, due to my business common sense—my business intuition.

I feel that a large part of connecting to ourselves at work is learning to hear and trust our own intuition, specifically our business intuition. I say the best managers use intuition as a key part of their decision-making process. Having a solid intuitive skill greatly improves your work outcomes, success, and satisfaction.

### What Is Intuition?

What is intuition? There is a side of me that dislikes using the term *intuition,* since it has so many connotations to it. My definition of *intuition* is simply a gut- or heart-level knowing of something, arrived at without primarily using rational thought. It might be a feeling I have to act or not act, or a decision that I make without knowing why I made it. I know it happens when I cannot trace my decision back to a specific set of facts, or line of thinking. In other words, intuition can be the result of making connections using information that is not sitting in the forefront of your mind.

It's not that people who use business intuition do not also use facts or rational thought in their work; it's just that rational thought does not seem to be the primary input for the intuitive knowing experience. And certainly the idea is not to listen *exclusively* to those intuitive impulses. As famous psychic Laura Day says rather poignantly, "Don't listen *only* to your gut-level impulse, for it may just be indigestion." So any businessperson who uses intuition almost always considers that information along with facts, rational thinking, and sensory input. It's just that those other items often do not add up clearly in the business world, and so intuition will often be a major or even the final deciding factor. Intuitive information provides valuable insights, particularly in this over-clocked and over-connected world, a world in which it is nearly impossible to consider all the facts logically.

You may have already experienced for yourself many cases of generating successful intuitive hunches in business. If so, you probably need no convincing of how useful, even powerful, intuition can be in business.

But in case you have not had those experiences, or doubt intuition even exists, you are not alone. The trouble with even successful hunches is that their success is easily written off to chance, coincidence, outside circumstances, or wishful thinking, and so are easily dismissed. Few people like to call their hunches "intuition."

Yet you will probably be surprised by the overwhelming extent to which intuition is already recognized in the business and scientific world.

First of all, if you have ever taken a Myers-Briggs personality test, which is often given in management training, you probably know that "Intuitive" is recognized as one of the four major types of work personality styles.

Business leaders consistently describe how they use their intuition for their decision making. In fact, the most impressive leaders are those who are able to decide quickly, confidently, and move on, rather than spending long moments thinking every decision through, studying the facts exhaustively. Business life usually moves too fast for that, so leaders who think well on their feet, that is, those who make good intuitive decisions, are the ones who succeed.

## The Importance of Intuition in the Scientific World

The importance of intuition in the scientific world is widely recognized as well. In fact, one good way to point out the value of intuitive insights is to reference the large number of scientific discoveries that have been attributed, by the discoverers themselves, to their intuition. Since the information did not exist anywhere prior to the discoveries in the cases I'm about to mention, we can eliminate many of the chance alternative sources of the information (but not all, of course). Here are some examples.

The most famous such intuition-sourced discovery is the double-helix structure of DNA. James Watson said it came to him in a mental flash, without rational thought at the moment.

Nobel laureate Melvin Calvin said the carbon path in photosynthesis came to him "in a matter of seconds" while sitting in his car waiting for his wife.

The ring structure of organic compounds came to Friedrich August Kekule von Stradonitz in a dream.

Similarly, Mendeleev invented the periodic table of elements after having a dream and awakening with the image of the nearly complete table in his head.

Thomas Edison believed he received many of his ideas independent of himself. He said, "Ideas are in the air" as if ready to be picked rather than reasoned out.

There are scores of examples like this. I'll bet that you can find business examples where intuition has provided almost amazing information. Just ask around your office, and you will find people who successfully rely on intuition for important business decisions nearly every day. Rarely is their impact as dramatic as these scientific discoveries, but even the small successes are important.

By the way, I do not want to imply that rational thought had nothing to do with any of these famous scientific cases. On the contrary, nearly all were preceded by days, weeks, or months of thinking on the topic. It's just that in nearly every case, rational thought reached a dead end, and an intuitive insight was the only way to move past that dead end. The intuition was prodded by the previous work.

This is absolutely true in the business world as well, where decision makers rarely have nearly enough data to make definitive choices, but will nonetheless review data before making the leap of a gut-based decision. It's the mixture of fact and intuition that is so powerful.

So the question is, can we reestablish our connection to our intuition in the business world, and thus benefit from that connection to ourselves? I believe there *are* systematic and proactive steps you can take to reconnect with your intuitive self. Let's talk about these steps in the next section.

# Ways to Connect with Yourself

Whether for building your business intuition, for identifying your larger vision, or for finding your life's work, a common solution behind all of these is what I generally call getting connected. As I said before, the exact experience ranges from a vague sense of understanding yourself and how you best relate to your work, to a feeling of being fully in the flow, with work achievements coming effortlessly. The latter end of that range is not as typical, of course, but is certainly possible.

However you define it, I think "getting connected" is essential for a successful work career. Let's talk about how to do it.

## Finding Balance in Life as a Way to Connect

First of all, if you have an unbalanced life, you are unlikely to enjoy a good connection. So I feel compelled to list here the usual set of "how to lead a balanced life" bullet points. That said, balance can only be defined by ourselves, and some of these bullet points go beyond mere balance and directly to connection.

For example, exercise is usually considered an essential part of a balanced life. But it is also one that may go beyond mere balance, because many have stated that running and other endurance sports are a direct way to get in the flow. Many who run regularly say they feel in the zone—well connected—and say that carries over into the workday.

Yoga can be another exercise that does more than simply balance life; many find it is nearly meditative in its connection ability.

Getting adequate sleep is of course important for balance. And finding activities that help you recharge are key. Finding vacation time is critical.

And of course finding time to spend with friends and family, and being in healthy relationships—all these things help your work–life balance.

While these things are essential, I believe we all need to go beyond simple balance-of-life prescriptions to activate connection with ourselves. And if these things do not bring you more clarity at work, you definitely need to do more.

### Finding Purpose in Life as a Way to Connect

Next, doing what I described in the previous chapter—connecting to a larger purpose or vision—is also a method of connection. That's because doing so is likely to move your attention away from day-to-day minutiae, and onto a more passionate focus. Since we know from Part II that what you put your attention on grows, this leads to a happier, more connected life in general. If you can recall when you were last jazzed about a project or some larger goal, you know how just having a passionate focus bleeds over into all aspects of life in a positive way. Such passion, particularly when combined with the other connection techniques ahead, helps you connect with yourself. Without such a purpose, many of us get in a habit of complaining and engaging in "victim talk," where we find ourselves constantly mulling over the small or large negative aspects of work and life. There is no faster way to cut off a connection than that.

## Developing Your Business Intuition as a Way to Connect

While I said earlier that better intuition is a *result* of connection, improving intuition is also a way to *improve* your connection. Once you improve your intuitive skills, all the benefits of being connected can follow. So how do you improve your business intuition?

Many say that what we call business intuition is really just the "knowing" that results from years of experience in a given business area. And I think that can be true—for many people in business, their gut decisions *are* based largely on a nearly unconscious synthesis of years of business experience. The gut decisions come from subconsciously considering the situation at hand and comparing it to previous experiences from similar business situations. They cannot point to the specific experience or even the comparison process; they just know "in these cases, I'd do this" and they are usually right.

So one answer to the question of how to improve your business intuition is to accumulate more work experience in their field.

## Intuition Transcends Mere Years of Experience

But while I think synthesis of previous experiences explains how many people make their gut decisions, there is much more to true intuition that goes beyond mere years of experience. Intuitive insights and decisions often come from a deeper place inside us that transcends distant memories or synthesis of experience.

A July 27, 2009, *New York Times* article talked about the fact that many very young U.S. soldiers with little combat experience stationed in Iraq were able to sniff out danger using gut-level hunches. The article stated, "Experience matters, of course: if you have seen something before, you are more likely to anticipate it the next time. And yet, recent research suggests that something else is at work, too." The article went on to say that those studies showed that subtle sensory input below the level of the conscious mind sent signals to the soldiers, allowing them to avoid danger. So perhaps intuition has to do with subtle sensory perception.

In fact, there are cases where business intuition seems almost psychic in nature, apparently predicting things no one could know. There are a number of such stories in the book *The Intuitive Edge* by Philip Goldberg about businesspeople whose nearly psychic predictions routinely give them a business edge. One example is Conrad Hilton, the hotel chain owner, when he was attempting to buy the Stevens Corporation in an auction in his early business years. He awoke the morning of the auction with the figure $180,000 floating in his head, and so submitted that as his bid, even though his calculations told him a much smaller number would have won. As it turned out, his bid beat the second highest bidder by only $200, and he won the property. That investment later secured him a nice $2 million profit and a jump start to his career. Luck? Perhaps. But perhaps what we usually write off to luck is business intuition at work; we all see people make similarly amazing business calls apparently out of the blue.

## How Can We Explain It?

If we are to improve our business intuition, we need to know where it comes from, and how to explain it. Again, as with anything that operates in the mind in an unseen way, how you explain such intuition, and how you increase it, will probably be subject to your universal view of life, your worldview.

Religious people may say that many of our true intuition experiences are messages from God. Similarly, proponents of New Age or spiritual thought might say true intuition is the result of tuning into a higher spiritual self or source. Psychologists will say that the subconscious mind is the source.

I can easily subscribe to any of these views, and I truly believe that all of them are possible. But since this is a business book, I will once again lean to the psychological explanation. Intuition can be almost completely explained by the subconscious mind at work, especially the type of intuition we usually see in business: making accurate business decisions based on limited information.

You see, the subconscious mind does a fantastic job of synthesizing our experiences, *even ones we do not notice,* and then feeding subtle information back to the surface mind when needed, in real time. The subconscious is one source of the thought impulses that we get all day, and perhaps our wisest source. Of course, an argument can be made from any worldview asking, "Who or what feeds the subconscious mind—could it be from more than our five senses?" I leave that to other writings.

While we can explain intuition as coming from the subconscious mind, not all of us have a well-established connection to those finer levels of the subconscious. That's why I think some people make better gut-level decisions than others, regardless of years and types of experience. The study of the Iraq soldiers showed that clearly some had the gut-level capability, and others did not. Can we improve that?

I feel one reason the connection to intuition is lost is that even though everyone generates intuitive information, most of us filter out much or all of our intuitive impulses. It's not that we do not have them—it's just that we do not *hear* them, or our habits of thought reject them. So finding a way to filter less may be the solution to improving our intuition.

**Learning Intuition Directly**

Some people say you can learn intuition directly. To do so, you might first ask, "What kind of intuition?

It is commonly said that there are four types of intuition, and you may experience one or more of them. The four are *hearing* thoughts as words or mental chatter; *seeing* a picture in your mind's eye; *knowing*, where you just know something but don't know how you know it; and *feeling*, where a body sensa-tion or emotion triggers intuitive knowledge that something is right or wrong. Each of these can be learned in different ways.

For example, if your form of intuition is that you experience gut feelings to do something, then you are probably best served by the last of the four types of intuition. And in that case, a way to improve it is to learn even more how to tune in and listen directly to your body. In the book *Find Your Inner Voice* by psychologist Karol Ward, the author extends her training and practice of the field of body–mind psychotherapy into a practical method for learning how to listen to the intuitive signals your body gives you. While I have not used the teachings in this book, they appear to be a very practical way to increase your intuitive capabilities. And they match very well with the terminology often used in business: listening to your gut.

*Knowing* something is true, without any outside input, is another mode, and is often described as a "sixth sense." A few authors acknowledge this directly with books on how to develop that ability. For example, one source for developing a sixth sense in the business world is the book *Practical Intuition for Success* by Laura Day. Day is a widely known psychic living in New York City who has written several books about increasing intuition based on psychic skills; you might find her work interesting.

Another author that resonates with me is Belleruth Naparstek, author of the book *Your Sixth Sense: Unlocking the Power of Your Intuition.* She discusses practical ways to increase intuition across a wide range of areas.

### Why We Filter Out Intuition

Why do we reject or not hear our intuitive information? Many of us from an early age were encouraged to think rationally, so we turned off the more illogical impulses over the years.

Equally likely, though, is that many of us are so busy during our workday that we cannot slow down enough to hear the impulses. You see, it is my experience that intuition appears in the "spaces between focused thoughts" and if we allow no spaces, we don't hear it.

For example, it is a common experience that the best intuitive information arrives when people are engaged in an activity that does not require focused attention, and often while the person is away from work. Many people report they get their best intuitive ideas while doing light, unfocused activity like walking, driving, or even washing dishes.

This brings me to the topic of using *think-time* as a way to improve our intuition and connection.

## Taking Think-Time as a Way to Connect

Many businesspeople find that they get excellent connected intuitive periods just by taking a little *think-time*. Gay Hendricks in his book *The Corporate Mystic* recorded the results of interviews with many corporate CEOs, who said that simply spending some time *thinking* every day helped greatly. Many of them had a remarkably similar approach of taking some door-closed time in the office, during which time they were not focused on anything urgent or on any deliverables, but instead were just taking light thoughts about the workday, perhaps simply staring out the window for a few minutes. They said this allowed their intuitive flow to open for them during those periods. It allowed these people to sort out the more important ideas from the noise of the workplace. Ultimately, it allowed them to make better business decisions.

### The Quiet Mind in Light Activity

Light activity, like walking in nature or gardening, often leads to the same experience. For example, I find some of my most intuitive ideas come during hiking, or even when exercising, shaving, showering or brushing my teeth; any activity where my mind tends to unfocus for a short while but is still alert. These are times when the mind is in between focused thought.

Interestingly, there is scientific evidence that supports this. In the November 2009 issue of *Wired* magazine, an article by Clive Thompson cites research at UC Santa Barbara showing that some wandering mind time can be very practical. Professor Jonathan Schooler's research there shows the brain's prefrontal cortex is activated during that time—that's the portion involved in problem solving. The article's author writes, "Your idling mind is likely doing deeply creative work, tackling your hairiest long-term tasks—projects you've been trying to address for months." Schooler suspects this "explains why so many 'aha' moments occur when we're drifting." ("Why an Idling Mind Is Mother of Invention," *Wired*, November 2009, p. 56.)

Light activity can open intuition for that moment, and so the trick to gaining from this is recognizing the value of the ideas when they come, and paying attention to them. The thing about intuition is it's quiet; it usually doesn't hit you like a freight train, but rather as just some quiet ideas mixed into your normal stream of everyday thoughts. So it is easy to miss. I finally made a point of keeping a notebook at hand so that when something that seemed interesting popped into my mind, I could write it down. I sometimes did not realize the value of it till later.

That's why doing this with *intention* can be valuable. Before a think-time session, decide what problem you are trying to solve or what insight you are seeking. Make a focused mental note of the topic and then take your think-time, perhaps even forgetting the original intention in the midst of the session, and see what comes up. I'll bet that you will find some answers in your stream of thoughts; your subconscious notes your intention and, below the scenes, starts to find the answers.

How is this different from brainstorming? In brainstorming, you keep the mind focused while actively moving from idea to idea. In contrast, think-time is similar but much less active; you only focus intently on the problem at the start and then see where the light thinking takes you. Napoleon Hill in his book *Think and Grow Rich* documented a technique he called "sitting for ideas," which was similar to this.

I use an intention technique like this when I hike. I take a vigorous hike many mornings a week up a small mountain near my home in California. I find those hikes to be a fantastic intended think-time for me. I'll start that hike and tell myself, "Today I want ideas about X," and then as I hike, fresh ideas relevant to the selected topic often come pouring in.

Some people find if they set this intention before they go to sleep, they wake up in the morning with ideas that are helpful for an answer. This makes sense since the subconscious mind is very active during sleep.

### Activate Your Goals So That Intention Is Always There

The approach where you ask yourself a question and listen for the answer can be hit or miss, though; we are often too distracted by current events to get the subconscious focused on a particular question introduced in the moment. We may quickly get lost in other thoughts.

Also, I suspect you will want to use intuition to get information about larger "how to get what I want" questions. That sounds like a *goals* topic, doesn't it?

So even better is to incorporate what I recommended in Part II of this book, which is to activate some goals and keep activating them every day over time. What that does is it keeps an ongoing, below-the-scenes intention active in the subconscious mind. Then when you take your think-time, the subconscious finally has the opening to deliver some ideas on how to achieve those goals. If you have done a good job of spinning up goals, then ideas related to achieving those goals are often the first solutions to flow forth when you take your think-time.

How does this work? Well, first, the goal activation helps channel the mind and keep the intention active in the subconscious mind so that the subconscious is pointed in that direction when you enter your think-time.

Second, goal activation (goal spinning) also helps set up the mechanical filtering of the subconscious so that it favors which thoughts make it to the conscious mind. You might have hundreds of minor wheels spinning below the surface, but the ones you actively and energetically spin every day win in the competition for your surface-level thoughts.

This is why your passion for something helps you achieve it. The frequent mental and emotional focus that passionate thought engenders impresses the subconscious mind, which then tends to favor intuitive thought on that topic. Could this be why people who seem to be nearly obsessed by their goals are usually the ones who achieve them? Some would say it is because they take more action, which is certainly true. But I think what I describe here is as much responsible as anything.

# Meditation as a Way to Connect

Taking this to a higher level, you might add meditation to your daily routine. I've been doing meditation for decades and can clearly link it to my better ability to make good gut decisions, both in business and personal life. It has increased my business intuition skills. I know of many other successful people in the business world who also do meditation and report the same.

You've probably heard of various forms of meditation or know people who practice it, but what is it really?

### Why Meditation Builds Connection

From the Workday Now perspective, the power of meditation is revealed by simply recognizing what we discussed in Part II regarding the value of attention. Attention is powerful. It creates and activates visions, and ultimately can create your world. Attention is probably the only truly limited resource you have. Unless you skip sleep or nonwork activity, you cannot increase the number of minutes of attention you have in the workday; however, you *can* improve the *quality* of your attention. This is not only useful for improving the quality of your work (clear mind, clear work), but also for connecting better with yourself. To hear your inner voice and make good business decisions, you want higher-quality attention.

Let me explain how meditation helps with this. In the Workday Now model, the I-Now represents our Immediate Now, which is whatever occupies either our focused or background attention at any given time. Normally we define the I-Now based on our attention—what we are "attending" to; it is our awareness of what's going on around us, and what we are thinking about, working on, or focused on.

But consider this. A capability of experiencing our attention separately from the usual objects of our attention exists. Attention itself can be a thing to attend to. Meditation is in fact just that. We do this by closing the eyes in a quiet place (to cut out sensory experience), and then use a technique to quiet the mental chatter, which removes the remaining source of attention focus. We are left with clear, unfettered attention for a few minutes a day.

This has two benefits. First of all, it allows our attention capability to rest in ways sleep does not, which leads to all kinds of mental benefits. And by the way, studies of at least some forms of meditation (Transcendental Meditation, mentioned below) show that during meditation the body experiences a metabolic rest deeper even than in sleep, which gives us a large number of physical benefits.

Second, though, is that this period of quiet but alert attention allows us to consciously experience and become familiar with finer, quieter levels of attention. And that is where intuition—that gut-level quiet whisper, often called the quiet voice within—comes from. By spending a few minutes a day still alert and listening but with the external and internal volume turned down, so to speak, we gain a habit of operating in this place. Then in normal activity, we are more likely to hear the quiet but wise messages that the subconscious sends us from that level all day long.

### How to Learn to Meditate

There are dozens of meditation techniques out there. The type I want you to find is any meditation technique that silences thoughts to some degree, and so allows you to connect more directly to your pure attention. This builds your connection to yourself, and builds your intuitive decision-making capabilities.

The kind I have done for decades is called Transcendental Meditation (TM for short), which has been available in this country for over forty years. TM is probably the most "legit" nonreligious meditation technique out there, with the largest organization behind it. Nearly all the hundreds of scientific studies done on meditation were done on people practicing TM; the scientific research on it is overwhelming (over 600 scientific studies have been done to date on TM). It is my first choice for anyone seeking a proven, reliable, and easy meditation technique, and you can find certified teachers nearly everywhere.

But there are many other secular techniques out there as well. Try looking in your local area for meditation classes, or check out your bookstore for an instructional book you feel good with.

Whatever meditation technique you choose, pick one that effortlessly quiets the mind. I am not talking about active meditations where you "think through" various topics, which keeps the mind engaged. The idea is to quiet and settle the mind and experience attention at quieter levels.

## Spiritual Connections

If you have a religious background, many western (and eastern) religions have meditation techniques similar to the ones above at their core. Any form of prayer that is not active, but rather designed to quiet the mind, qualifies as this sort of meditation. I knew a TM practitioner who later entered a Catholic monastery and he found the monks there practicing a meditative technique very similar to TM. Eastern religions are famous for their meditation approaches, with Zen Buddhism probably the best known.

Beyond or instead of quieting meditations, there are many other ways religious and spiritual people choose to get connected in more active ways. For religious people, active prayer and ceremony can be a phenomenally connecting experience. Every religious and spiritual culture has a tradition of using prayer and ceremony for actively connecting to God, and those that participate say the connection brings benefits to their entire lives. For many people, that connection can provide the personal insight I am referring to here, one that helps guide them through work and life. If you have that connection, I admire you and encourage you to continue with it. If you do not, but you are leaning that way, take a look at just about any religion you may already be close to. You will most likely find resources there for this that you might not have known existed.

Organized religion or meditation is not a requirement for spirituality, of course. More and more I am seeing people who connect directly with spirit, independent from religion, prayer, and meditation. I am meeting many people who say they receive direct advice either through journaling, reflection, or other means. What a gift that represents, to be able to have daily conversations with their inner spirit, particularly when it is in ways that answer the recipient's deepest questions. If this is consistent with your worldview, I encourage you to develop your own such source of connection. See the book *Writing Down Your Soul* by Janet Conner for one guide that may enable you to teach yourself to do this using journaling.

## Working from and Connecting with the Heart

Above I have outlined a number of ways or suggestions to get more connected to yourself, and the advantages they can have at work. Really, though, regardless of specific connection techniques, getting connected ultimately means working more and more from your heart. Much of what I described in this business intuition section is really just that.

You likely know what working from your heart means; you have probably done it often. It's subjective, of course, but for me it means a tangible, very positive feeling that arises when I turn my attention to some idea or activity and I know the "rightness" of it. It is usually a leading feeling. I am attracted to certain things, people, circumstances, and so on, and by going there I end up benefiting. By "benefiting" I mean, for instance, finding that the thing, person, or circumstance is leading to a very fruitful business outcome, or better, a solid and helpful part of my journey through life.

There are various forms of heart guidance for me. It might feel like enthusiasm, excitement, and even a true feeling of love or compassion. Or just a quiet, heartfelt knowing. It all depends on the topic and situation. Let's just call it a subjective, deep-seated positive feeling that allows me to know when some external thing is right. By "right," I do not mean right in the moral sense of the word (though that may also be true), but right for me and the world around me, for my success and balance with others, my growth, and my soul. Such things usually end up benefiting me businesswise as well.

Ultimately all of the tools and exercises above are about that; they are giving you the tools you need to work from your heart.

Working from your heart is both an outcome and a method of connection. We discussed some techniques to get more connected, and they will help you to more easily work from your heart. But you can also make a conscious effort to find more love in your life, and that may be your best method of connection of all. You see, once you open your awareness to the emotions of love and happiness, you also open yourself to the best of everything else around you. In the goal-spinning model, once you start spinning the general feeling of love and happiness, that spinning starts generating similar good things in other areas of your life.

For example, if you can recall the feeling of falling in love, perhaps for the first time years ago, you may recall feeling more connected to life, to the universe. If you have children or grandchildren, when you reflect on your love for them, you probably feel more connected to all of your life, including work. If you have a love for the outdoors, you probably find a greater connection to all things in your life while there. If you love music, dance, driving in the countryside, exercise, or anything else that makes you feel really good when you do it, all those things, by spinning up happiness, can bring connection back to you in a way that spills over into your workday.

Also, this is partly about balance, isn't it? If you find time to focus on the people, activities, and things you love in life, that restores your balance and just may open channels of intuitive connection for you.

My point is that while all the techniques I covered previously represent objective ways to connect, don't forget that the most essential and universal method of connection there is—love—is found by making a point of working from your heart. Find ways to bring more love and heart into your life, and your life will be much more connected.

By the way, if you are thinking this doesn't sound very businesslike, if it seems counter to the world of competitive business, you may be surprised at how widely this view is held. For example, there is a whole business book on this topic called *Love Is the Killer App* by Tim Sanders. That book points out how bringing the positive aspects of love into your business life has all sorts of monetary returns on investment; the book was a *New York Times* best seller, and I encourage you to take a look at it. Also, check out the book I mentioned earlier, *Happy for No Reason* by Marci Shimoff, another *New York Times* best seller, for ways to more easily create and spin happiness in your life. Finally, look at the book *The Radical Leap* by Steve Farber, formerly a VP with the Tom Peters Company; in that book Farber discusses the value of using love and heart in leadership.

Another book I recommend that underscores this concept is *The Speed of Trust*, by Stephen M. R. Covey. In that book, Covey points out that most of the inefficiencies of an organization—excess bureaucracy, internal politics, and micromanagement—all stem from a lack of *trust* within the organization walls. Trust is earned by demonstrating actions that produce results in the best interests of all. Working from the heart does that. It circumnavigates the typical game play and fear-based defensive postures that are unfortunately so common in large organizations. Covey's book shows how important it can be to work from the heart in the business world.

And finally, some very objective research shows that working from the heart increases your work performance. The Institute of HeartMath has done extensive research showing that when individuals have feelings of compassion, caring, love, and other such emotions, they increase their heart-rhythm coherence, which is reflected by smooth, ordered heart-rhythm patterns. Among the many benefits of coherence found in the research are calmness, good energy levels, clear thinking, and proper immune-system function. Stress reduction is a common side benefit as well. The institute offers simple ways to increase such coherence; see the HeartMath entry in my Recommended Resources section for links to learn more.

## Connection Is Not Acting on Fear

Before concluding this chapter, I need to mention what Connection is *not*.

I suspect you know that working from a connected level, that is, using intuition or following gut feelings, does not mean simply acting on *all* your impulses. Impulses can come from various places—some intuitive and profound—and others more base, for example, anger, jealousy, and fear. Perhaps the most important example of the latter is *fear*.

Sometimes people think that their fears are forms of intuitive insight. After all, if they have a strong emotion of fear, shouldn't they trust that, like any other internal message?

However, I believe that negative emotions like fear are different. They usually come less from inner guidance, and more from basal instincts. I am not saying not to listen to fear; I think it can guide you away from trouble and can be a good reason to avoid something. I just don't want you to use it as your *primary* input when making an important decision. My experience is that fear-based decisions and actions usually lead nowhere—or worse.

My counsel is, if you feel fear about a topic in an important work decision, find a way to dispel it first before making that decision. Even better, as in Chapter 12, use the fear to identify what you *do* want, and then turn your emotional energies to focusing on that in a positive way. In other words, make your key decisions from a place of balance, or better, from inspiration. Try not to make those decisions from a place of fear.

The reason for such counsel is that your emotions of fear are a huge block to finding your inner connection. The fight-or-flight impulse of fear works in a different and overpowering part of the brain; it is an instinctive rather than an intuitive part. In fact, fear is usually so disruptive it will cut off all access to creative intuitive input. That's why decisions made from fear are disconnected from your internal wisdom and thus are often wrong.

## Solution Is in Earlier Chapters

In fact, if due to a systemic negative work situation you find you are *often* in a fearful state, you will find it difficult to develop the connection I discussed in this chapter at all; the ongoing disruption just won't let it happen. If that sounds like you, then instead, use the earlier chapters first to prepare for this one.

For example, if you are under intense pressure at work because you have too much to do, either self-imposed or from others, you need to dig out first before trying the connection approaches I outlined above. The best way to do that is using the techniques in the Control section (Part I) of this book. If you have not dug out, I doubt you will find the time and mental space to do any of the connection exercises coming ahead anyway.

For many of us, fear comes from stretching our goals further than our beliefs can handle. Use the belief-adjusting techniques in Part II of this book (Chapter 14) if that kind of fear is affecting you.

Similarly, you may have a self-image issue that could be helped by those same tools. You will see in the next section that bolstering or creating a new self-image is a major component of creating your life's work, so feel free to explore that option.

Whatever the source of your current fears, if they are occupying a lot of your self-talk at the office, then work on them first, using the practical tools in the earlier portion of this book. Then start using some of the connection processes in this chapter.

## Summary

Connecting to yourself is an important and practical skill to improve your success at work. Doing so improves the quality of the work vision you create, improves your workday attitude, and helps you make better business decisions. It is an important step to attaining what I call Workday Mastery, an experience at work of being productive and effective, and essentially happy and satisfied with work.

Improving your *business intuition* may be the greatest outcome of getting connected. Working on improving your intuition is also a *method* of connection, whether that is done by more often simply honoring your internal voice, or by learning intuition directly through training.

Taking think-time is another way to connect and gain intuitive insights, and it is used by many corporate executives. At its simplest, it means just taking some door-closed time and thinking through the day's events or topics. It may mean taking directed think-time—choosing a topic and then sitting or walking quietly while looking for insights. The best way to activate think-time is to activate your goals as described in Chapter 12—you will find your think-time is much more productive if you do.

Meditation is an excellent way to build a connection with yourself. It has been used for years by many people in the business world with great results, many of which have been proven through scientific studies.

Both nonreligious and religious spiritual practices can also provide methods to connect with yourself in ways that greatly benefit your workday.

Ultimately, working from your heart is the best form of connection, and all the tools listed above can help develop that. Even better is to build your ability to work from your heart through your family and other relationships, or just by being more open to the happiness and love already in your own life.

Next, I want you to use the connection to yourself that you may have gained here to work on something very important—connecting to your life's work.

CHAPTER **18**

# Connecting to Your Life's Work

In Chapter 16 we talked about finding a vision or purpose larger than yourself. In Chapter 17 we talked about enhancing your ability to connect with yourself, so that your gut, your intuition, and your heart are guiding you through life and work, to a larger extent than before.

In this chapter I want to talk about the outcome of all that, actually finding work that puts it all together. The goal here is finding the work or job that reflects your sense of purpose and that lines up with what your heart is telling you that you should do. I call this *finding your life's work*.

If you wrote and accepted your larger vision from Chapter 16, and it was in fact in terms of your next job, well, you may already have identified your next stage of life's work. If not, or if you are not sure that was it, read on.

## Life's Work and Your Workday Now

Let's talk about *life's work* in the light of your Workday Now.

The essence of using Workday Now techniques is improving your work experience. In the Control layer, covered in Part I of this book, you learned Workday Now principles of getting chaos "managed down" so you can focus on what's important to you. In the Create layer, covered in Part II, you learned Workday Now elements and skills to create outcomes, create your goals.

Here in the Connect layer, the focus is on improving the quality of your I-Now, your job, and your career so that the entire range of your Workday Now experience feels aligned with who you are. The two circles described at the start of Part III, your circle of life and your circle of work, are overlapping.

Certainly, finding a work activity that matches who you are should do that. People who are doing their life's work are usually happy, productive, effective, and content. Since their work lines up with the larger vision they have for work and life, a sense of purpose permeates their workday. And since they are usually eager to take on more challenges in their field, a sense of expansion is often present.

Ideally, they are working directly on creating their current larger purpose or vision. Or they may be at an intermediate stage of that—building skills and experience, say, or building connections and networks. The important thing is that they have a purpose they are working toward, and their current position feels right on track, given the steps they see along the way to their larger vision.

That certainly describes an improved Workday Now experience.

## Why It's Important to Find Your Life's Work

So it feels *good* to be working at your life's work. But why is it *important?*

Well, first of all, you may feel an inner drive to do something important with your life. You may be driven from within to achieve, to make a difference, to explore activities that resonate with your inner being, with who you are. Finding your life's work fulfills that search. It fulfills a deep inner desire.

Finding your life's work will also boost your sense of self-worth and your sense of self-esteem. That's because once you find a passionate life's work, there will be no question in your mind whether what you are doing is right; you'll just know it is right. And that will lead to a sense of contentment with how you are expressing yourself in your job.

You see, self-esteem issues often come from a gut feeling that you are not contributing; that can occur if you are not in a role that suits your strengths.

Once you are doing your life's work, if you have felt self-worth issues before, there is a good chance they will diminish greatly.

Furthermore, perhaps for the first time, the meaning and sense of the word *integrity* will become apparent to you. What does *integrity* really mean? For some people it means honesty, not lying, and doing the right thing.

But I do not think of integrity as a moral thing; I think of it more as a state of mind. Think of what the phrase above, "doing the right thing," really means. It means doing the thing that is right—but right for whom? Ultimately, right for you, at the highest level. To me, that is the definition of your life's work: doing work that is right for *you*. You will know you are doing your life's work when it fills you with a sense of integrity, of being true to yourself. And this is the type of integrity that you carry with you all day, knowing that your activity is now locked in and you are on your path.

And here is one more angle on this. One of the most important qualities of life's work is that it is an activity that you love to do. Doing what you love not only feels good, *it is critical if you want to keep your job or business.* The authors Jerry Porras, Stewart Emery, and Mark Thompson state this best in their book *Success Built to Last*. On page 35 of that book they state, "It's dangerous not to do what you love. The harsh truth is that if you don't love what you're doing, you'll lose to someone who does." Their point is that whether it is a job or your business, if you lack passion for it, the passion that a competitor shows will overrun your success. You absolutely must work at something you love just to stay ahead! In other words, you *need* to find your life's work

## Life's Work Is Constantly Changing

The term *life's work* sounds big, doesn't it? It sounds monumental, and it sounds *final*. It sounds like the ultimate career we pick for the rest of our lives, the one that captures our life purpose, our skills, and our inspirations.

But as I said earlier, in reality, your life's work is a changing thing. It is the work that is absolutely right for you *at this moment*. In fact, I think the only accurate phrase is "your *current* life's work" because your life's work will change over time, perhaps rapidly. And you can grasp it at any stage of your life.

As an example, let's start small, very small. Let's say that a high school girl has taken a summer job. She now works in an ice cream shop and she thoroughly enjoys scooping ice cream for her customers. She feels happy and content, she is learning how to work the cash register, she is learning how to work with the public, she meets many happy people every day, and she truly likes what she does. She does her work well, and her customers are happy. She leaves work satisfied with the day, and she looks forward to work each morning. Maybe she has a thought of getting into the food business in a bigger way later in life, but she cannot imagine any better work for herself *at this moment* in her life. I would say she is currently doing her life's work.

Granted, this is a fairly small example. Most of us have matured to much higher aspirations. But this helps you see that you can be in your current life's work at any stage of your life.

At any stage of your life, determining whether you are in your life's work depends on how big a gap there is between you and your job. By "you," I mean your current vision of yourself, your skills and aspirations, and maybe even your personal larger purpose in life. On the other hand, there is your current job. If the job is serving the self-vision well, and the gap is not too big, then you're there. If you feel happy with the balance between the two, if you feel like the two circles are overlapping or getting closer, and you feel you have integrity in that role, I think you can say you are enjoying your life's work.

But even in this case, know this: you and your vision and aspirations will grow, and so you need to grow your work activity as well, or you will no longer feel that you are "in your life's work." In a year or two the aspirations of the girl mentioned above will probably rise so much that she cannot imagine herself continuing working in an ice cream store. Essentially we need to surf our aspirational growth curve to stay in the game. That's what keeps life interesting!

## Identifying Your Life's Work

If you are not currently active in what you would call your current life's work, then you will want to get there. Getting there is a three-step process: 1) identifying the elements of it, 2) writing a vision statement for it—your life's work statement, and then 3) creating it in your life. Let's talk in this section about step 1, identifying your life's work.

## How to Identify

Taking the time and energy to identify the elements of your life's work is important; you need to decide what it looks like. You want to know what sort of job, career, or activity you are pursuing. You cannot rely on just falling into something without deciding what you want. And when you take steps to create it, what you are creating should be well defined.

This may in fact be the same thing as the larger vision you identified earlier, if that vision identified your job. However, your vision may have been more general; if so, then this section is where you put that larger vision into a work format for your next job.

Identifying your life's work can be done using a few routes, and you should use all of them. First, use your intuition and your heart to sense what your new career will look like. If your intuition is strong, sometimes it alone can lead you to your work. But whether you think it can or not, I also encourage you to also do the two exercises that follow.

Exercise 1 is to spend some time reviewing your work history and identifying work roles, activities, and passions that have worked for you before, that you have enjoyed and succeeded with. Many of these probably share components of your next life's work role. Exercise 2 is to then integrate any new vision you now have in a way that honors your current strengths and preferences, and expands beyond them.

But let's start first with using intuition—your heart or your gut. This, I think, is the first and best way to guide yourself to your life's work. This is why the "Connecting with Yourself" chapter preceded this one. You see, I believe your soul is always striving to fulfill some mission in life by leading you intuitively to life and work activities that will do so. I believe if you listen to your intuition, to your gut or heartfelt decision making, you can lead yourself right to your life's work.

And more importantly, as your definition of life's work changes over time— and it will as you grow—then your intuition will guide you to the next role, and the next, and the next, perhaps before you even realize the growth has occurred. Nothing beats finding and trusting your own inner messages for finding and keeping your life's work on track.

To this end, when your intuition sends you messages about what your next life's work role should be, write them down, honor them. Take them seriously. Use them as part of your input for next steps. And then combine that with the following exercises.

### Exercise 1: List Your Favorite Past Job Qualities

While your intuition may help you find your work, you may also have to seek more details on what works best for you. So Exercise 1 is to make a list of the things in life and past work experiences that you enjoyed and were good at, and to use them later when you build the vision of an ideal life's work by writing your life's work statement. After all, the idea of your life's work is work that you thrive in, that you enjoy, so it *does* make sense to review what made you happy, satisfied, and appropriately challenged in work and life in the past. Those things will probably correlate with your strengths, and finding them will help guide you to finding your current life's work.

So in this exercise you will take the best of every job, skill, hobby, and activity you have or have ever done, and extract the core components of what you loved about them. I suggest lining them up with the categories shown next. This exercise will take some time to do, especially if you have had a long career; so set aside adequate time.

By the way, this exercise of listing the best qualities of your past jobs is exactly what the "Flower" exercise does in the book *What Color Is Your Parachute?* This book by Richard N. Bolles is by far the best book out there for helping you through a job-change process, and I have used that exercise in virtually every career and job change I have personally made. If you have been recently laid off, or if you are considering a job change, your first step should be to read that book (be sure to buy the most recent one; he updates it nearly every year).

Similar to Bolles's "Flower" exercise, below is a list of specific categories from which to brainstorm. With these categories at hand, mentally walk through your life, starting from school and early work experiences, and find those things that you very much enjoyed in your past that fall into each category. What things did you like about school in each category? What did you like about your first job in each category? What about your next job, and your next? Also look at any nonpaid work or even hobbies that you loved. Extract all the things that most inspired you—that you most enjoyed in your work and leisure activities. You may want to start this on paper by writing a short history of your work life, listing all your roles; then use that as a checklist against the categories below.

Once collected, in a new blank computer text document combine those experiences across all jobs against each category listed below:

- My Favorite Skills over my Entire Work History Are These: (list yours here)

- Favorite Geography or Locations: (list here)

- Favorite Interests:

- Favorite People:

- Favorite Environments:

- Favorite Values, Purposes, and Goals:

- Favorite Working Conditions:

- Favorite Salary: (this is probably easy; usually it is the highest one)

- Favorite Level of Responsibility:

See my website for templates of this list, including ones created in MindManager, to help you get started with your brainstorming.

Next, look through this list and circle or underline 5 to 10 items that especially ring your bell, even now. These are soon going to become part of your new life's work vision statement.

This should be enough to jumpstart your list of skills and preferences. However, if you want to create an even more thorough picture than this, there are two other ways I recommend to collect information about your core interests, passions, and strengths.

The first is to use the Passion Test from the *New York Times* best-selling book with the same title by Janet Bray Attwood and Chris Attwood. It is a reflective tool to help you identify what gets you most excited about work and life; knowing those passions will help define your new role. Finding your passions is critical to a happy work life. For a free Passion Profile test, go to www.thepassiontest.com/workdaymastery.

The other is a tool called the StrengthsFinder, which focuses on general work skills. This tool was highlighted in two books, the first being the 2001 book *Now, Discover Your Strengths* by Marcus Buckingham and Donald Clifton. Next was the 2007 book *StrengthsFinder 2.0* by Tom Rath, which updated the concepts. The books explain why identifying your natural talents is so important; they then connect you to a sophisticated online question-and-answer tool that will help clarify what your work strengths are and how to find them. (The online tool is free by entering a unique single-use code provided inside each Strengths book, so do not buy either book used.) If you want a more complete answer to Exercise 1, this is also a good next step.

### Exercise 2: List New Qualities You Seek

In Exercise 1 you listed all the things that worked in your past job and life experiences, and you indicated a few of those that you especially wanted to carry forward.

However, chances are you want to grow, you want to do even better in your next role, job, or career than you did in your past. So rather than just duplicating the last role that you liked, in Exercise 2 let's identify those things that take you a step or more forward.

First, look at your vision or purpose larger than yourself that you identified earlier. Find a way to work as much of that into your next role as possible. If that vision is just a little beyond where you are now, you might plan a jump directly into that vision for your next activity. If the new vision is a large change from your current work, your very next life's work might be an intermediate role that gets you closer. In this exercise, make a list of activity elements that could support that vision, or that could get you closer to that vision.

Do this by imagining yourself inside your vision, and then writing down the elements of that picture that are beyond what you have now.

Say you are a research engineer in a company now, but your larger vision is to be an engineering *college professor,* teaching and still doing research. So you are adding the teaching element, the college campus, a new lifestyle, and more. Record that list and how you want each of these new elements to look.

Or maybe you seek a larger role inside your current company. List the elements of the larger vision inside your company that you are seeking, such as having a larger staff, managing a product, or even having a seat on the senior management team.

Also list specific improvements you want or new preferences you seek compared to your previous or existing roles that are not vision oriented but are improvements nonetheless. For example, you may have different work hours in mind or a different size of company. Perhaps you have a different sort of boss you'd like to work for this time.

If you are having trouble making the list of new role qualities, try using the same category list that you used in Exercise 1 above to put together a picture of your new role, with details. Perhaps even think in terms of what *bothered* you about your previous jobs, and use those problems as opportunities to incorporate new elements into your upcoming career vision. Use those problems to identify the positive side of the issue, in terms of what you *do* want; flip the negative to the positive and list the positive desire.

The reason you are making this list is that in the next section we are going to use it along with the list from Exercise 1 to build your life's work vision statement for your next job. That statement you will use for goal activation, similar to what we did in Part II; you are going to be spinning up the full vision statement to create your new job.

### Tips for Creating or Finding Your Next Role

With that upcoming life's work vision statement in mind, I have a few recommendations for creating this new list of expansions you would like.

I cautioned before against using a "shoulds" approach when developing your larger vision. The same applies when choosing the qualities of your next job. In all cases, the way to know if you are inadvertently following old tapes from parents, friends, or society, or from past bad experiences, is this. Take a moment and think about the role, job, or career you are considering or the specific qualities of it you wrote down, and ask yourself, "How do these qualities make me feel?" Do the envisioned qualities bring you a feeling of happiness, lightness, and satisfaction as you picture yourself with them? Or is there a heaviness associated with them? Happiness is usually the right answer; heaviness is usually the wrong one. Use your gut.

Next, I want you to *think big* as you choose qualities of your next role or job because that leads to inspiration, excitement, and passion. Recall my discussion in Part 2, in the chapter called Stretching Your Now Goals—you need to think big enough to generate positive emotion. If your next logical step in your career does not generate emotion, then write down a level or two beyond that. Otherwise, your goal activation will not yield fruit.

### Be Ready to Flex

And finally, I also want you to remain flexible about whether the things you list are really going to be achieved exactly as you list them. You see, through my years of doing this, I have found that some things you can change through goal activation and some resist your efforts. For example, increasing your income level is something that I think *can* be achieved using the principles in Part II. Granted, you may hit belief ceilings you need to work on, but I truly believe you can break most of those.

I have also found that sometimes specific elements that I write down just don't work for me. Over time I realize they are not meant for me; they don't fit naturally into my life's work, or into my personality and strengths. And as a result, they are harder to get. You'll get a feel for what elements of your life's work you can influence easily through goal activation (and belief adjustment) and which ones seem to be resisted when you spin the goal. This will come with time and experience. The key is to be patient, aware, and flexible enough to yield to aspects of your life that seem to resist the goal setting level.

Why do some things resist achievement? It might be that the thing is not something you really want, but you have been told you should want it. Just be sure you really are excited about the thing. Or it may not match your strengths and so not work for you, or you do not have the innate talents required; try the StrengthsFinder test I mentioned above.

Another reason things might be hard to achieve is that they may not match your mission in life. Near the end of this part of the book, I am going to discuss my belief that we all have an underlying mission in life that will emerge over the years. This is an interesting section, but for now just know this: if the things you ask for are in direct conflict with elements of that mission, they will be harder to get. That said, I also think you will not have strong desires for things that are not in alignment with your mission; your intuition will not guide you to them. So this conflict probably will not come up often, unless you list the item due to a fear or a "should" from outside yourself.

So stay flexible on the elements of the new life work goals you set, and use your gut to tell you when you've pushed a rock up a hill long and hard enough and it is just not going there. It may be time to do a little soul searching and see if you should be looking at another rock, or at another hill.

Now that Exercise 1 and 2 are done, in the next section, you are going to consolidate them into a vision for your new life's work and then start to create it.

## Writing Your Life's Work Vision Statement

Now is your time to take the next steps to create your new role. You will use the principles of goal creation that you learned in Part II and apply them to this larger life's work goal.

Just like in Part II, the first step here is to write a narrative life's work vision statement that you will use to activate your goal each day. That statement will include the best of all the things you listed in the two exercises above, synthesizing them into a whole. This is really two simple steps.

Step 1: Study each element from the two exercises above and write descriptive and emotive language for each one that will help activate them well later.

Step 2: Now find a logical way to knit these pieces together into a narrative that reads well. Since you are going to read this vision statement once or twice a day, edit down the elements that you collected above in a way that flows well, creates a visual image, and fits on less than one page; a half page is probably best. You should be able to combine collections of elements together into single statements, just as I showed in the short vision statements in Chapter 11; that will help shorten the overall statement.

## Example Life's Work Vision Statement

Here is an example statement. It comes from the high-school ice-cream store worker I described above, but she is now about five years older. She attended culinary school for desserts, and has been working in a good restaurant as a dessert chef. She has developed a refined taste for gourmet desserts and has written the following purpose or vision larger than herself:

Larger Purpose or Vision:

> I will create nationally recognized food experiences for discerning dessert lovers.

She then completed the exercises above, and developed the following life's work vision statement.

> I am a master dessert chef and menu designer for a well-known, high-end restaurant chain. The restaurant chain is widely recognized for its creative cuisine and is located in most major cities (example: P.F. Chang's). I create the delicious dessert ideas that are placed on the nationwide selection. I am quite famous in the restaurant industry and among restaurant critics, and both praise my creative and distinctive approaches to well-known dishes. As a result, the restaurant receives awards often, and I am recruited regularly from competing chains. I enjoy a generous salary (at least $80,000) and receive stock options worth $10,000 each year. I adore my job—I feel like I have the best job in the world!

> The personal life my job enables is perfect. I live and work in or near one of these cities: New York City, San Francisco, Chicago, or Atlanta. My job enables me to have a delightful home that is at least 2,500 square feet in size, is located in a tree-lined suburban neighborhood, and is near good schools for my family. Since my job is mainly designing menus and not daily cooking, I am able to keep excellent work hours and have weekends off for fun with my family and friends. I am able to lead a balanced life with fun exercise, healthy and tasty meals, and exciting outdoor activities like bicycling, which I love.

The job gives me a lot of creative freedom. When I want to, I can choose to cook in any of the chain's restaurants, so I can enjoy the experience and gain insight into new menu ideas. I have a number of people reporting to me, so I can offload less interesting work and focus on new menu ideas. I take quarterly travel to a central training facility, where I train regional chefs on new dessert menus and receive feedback on existing menus. I am able to create new dishes often, and management gives me free rein to be as creative as I wish. I have a generous budget to experiment with. I also have a travel budget to take "tasting trips" three or more times a year, where I try out desserts at excellent restaurants in various interesting locations, including overseas—I love these trips.

Overall, I have what has to be the best job I can imagine. I am doing the things I love—creating fabulous new desserts—and am doing it in a way that brings me national recognition. In doing so, I am providing a delightful dessert experience for thousands of people, making them all a little happier each time.

## Principles to Keep in Mind When Creating Your Life's Work Statement

Some principles to keep in mind, which restate those from Part II:

- Create a picture in words. Tell a story that will allow you to see in your mind's eye how all this would look. Rewrite until you feel like the writing helps you picture yourself in the role.

- Express enthusiasm and use phrases that will inspire you when you read this every day.

- Use present tense—state the vision as if you already have it.

- Use positive phrases. For example, you would not say, "I want to no longer be bossed around." Rather, you might say something like, "I am in charge of my own activities; I have the freedom to create and execute my work in exactly the form I am inspired to do so."

- Feel free to include quantifiable Target Goals within the narrative.

And one more thing to add, which is new here. Many writers encourage you to answer this question somewhere in your life's work vision statement: "How am I helping to improve others, society, or the world with this activity?" If there is no obvious way that your new role does that, then list how *you* will give back, perhaps through charity or volunteer work. I feel that this element is important to add, both for your own sense of balance and from a larger spiritual perspective.

### Build a New Self-Image

Also consider this. If the new picture is quite a bit different from what you are doing now, then in effect, this life's work vision may be creating a new self-image for you, and that's a good thing. Let me explain.

We all know that self-esteem and self-image can have a large effect on someone's success.

One of the most interesting discussions of this aspect of self-image comes from Maxwell Maltz, in his book that I have already referenced a couple of times, *The New Psycho-Cybernetics*. Maltz was a plastic surgeon who witnessed over and over again how people's self-image determined their success and happiness. That's what led him to write the book, which is about the power of the subconscious mind and how we can transform ourselves if we choose to. As a plastic surgeon, he saw a wide variety of impacts of people's feelings about their physical appearance. He sometimes saw dramatically positive effects on success and happiness after even minor changes in appearance with surgery. The person's inner self-image improved, and that seemed to affect everything about their outer life.

Often what Maltz saw prior to surgery was an exaggerated sense of failure; the person's self-image was shattered due to their overreaction to a minor physical abnormality (a small scar from a physical injury, a slightly weak chin, a slightly large nose, and so on). They basically talked themselves into being a very inferior person due to seeing the physical problem day after day. I am sure you have seen people do this too—get overly sensitive about small details of their appearance. Perhaps you have done it at times yourself. In these cases, however, the people obsessed on the small flaw to the point of creating a significant self-image problem.

Maltz found that sometimes surgery in these cases improved that low self-image dramatically, but often it did not; in many cases, the self-image was too far gone. This was frustrating for him as a doctor, and he reached a point where he decided that surgery was not the main solution for many of his clients; it was the self-image that needed fixing. So he developed some self-image improvement tools based on the same principles I am showing here: building a mental image of what the person wanted to feel about themselves, and visualizing it. He found the tools worked remarkably well.

With those successes, he became so convinced that self-image was the most important underlying issue that he even started to make deals with some of his patients that he thought did not really need surgery. He told them to hold off on the surgery 30 days and instead use his mental technique of Theatre of the Mind (which I discussed in Chapter 14) every day for improving self-image. If after a month the patient still felt surgery was necessary, he would perform the surgery at that time. In nearly every case, after the 30 days the patient said they didn't need the surgery.

Maltz used that experience to build his extensive research on the power of the mind to expand inner and outer success. He came to some significant conclusions. Here is a quote from his book regarding self-image:

*All your actions, feelings, behavior, even your abilities, are always consistent with this self-image... In short, you will "act like" the sort of person you conceive yourself to be. More important, you literally cannot act otherwise, in spite of all your conscious efforts or will power. (This is why trying to achieve something difficult with teeth gritted is a losing battle. Willpower is not the answer. Self-image management is.)*

### Self-Image as Part of Your Narrative

So developing a new positive self-image that includes your new career is part of the activity in this section. As part of your statement, you are in essence rewriting your own self-image; and that can influence the elements your narrative will include.

Recall that the method in Part II was to essentially "pretend" that you had obtained the goal already. I asked you to live it so thoroughly for a few minutes every day that you actually experienced it in your imagination for those moments.

So in your life's work statement narrative, describe enough details so that a new "you," the new self-image, starts to emerge. Perhaps that is all about the job role. When describing that role, include phrases that will give you an impression of your new self-image in the role. It should leave you with a new vision of how you act at work, how confident you are, and how effective you are.

In addition to the work items for your new self-image, you probably want to also include statements that go beyond work and into how your personal life is transforming, too. Many success books have a checklist of things to consider when building a new "you," and you should consider if you want to include statements related to these in your new life's work vision. So to expand your new self-image, beyond the work list we already have, you might consider including the following:

- *My health and body look like this:*

- *My relationships look like this:*

- *My home looks like this:*

- *My car and other major possessions look like this:*

- *My vacations/travel/adventure look like this this:*

- *My hobbies, sports, or other creative expression look like this:*

- *My spiritual development looks like this:*

You may recognize this as being similar to the Locking in New Beliefs process in Part II. In fact, it is a subset of that, with the focus on self-image qualities. By the way, you probably won't include all of the items listed above; just work with those that inspire you. Include ones that you want to change and that could be affected by the new job or career you are creating.

### Wrapping Up the Life's Work Vision Statement

After you have spent a few hours or cycles writing and rewriting the life's work vision, at some point just call it done for now, and start using it in your goal activation (discussed next). Don't worry if it is not absolutely right. Your life's work vision statement will be a work in progress for months, maybe even years. With that in mind, make sure you save the file on your computer so you can edit it easily and reprint it often. I found myself editing mine every week for the first several months. That makes sense; as you read this to yourself two or more times per day, you are going to bounce it off multiple layers of your being, and new interpretations will arise. Go with it.

## Activating Your Life's Work Vision Statement

Just as in Part II with Now Goals, you will now activate your life's work vision statement by reading through it one or more times per day. For a life goal like this, I say read it first thing in the morning, and then last thing before you go to bed. Then, if you are inspired during the day, fit it in again. As before, as you read your statement, immerse yourself in the vision as if it were here now. Picture yourself inside the vision, as you read it.

Also like in Part II, this visualization is always done in your instantaneous now, your I-Now, meaning you should spend high-quality time envisioning the outcome in your imagination, being fully present during that process. So don't allow yourself to zone out during the reading. Also, don't allow this to feel like a chore. If over time you feel you do start to tune out or feel it is becoming a duty, then rewrite the statement to freshen it and make it compelling. I'd like you to *want* to read and hold the vision because you find it a pleasure to do so. If the vision is really the future that you long for, and if the writing is emotive and uplifting, that should be easy to do. If not, you should edit the statement to make it more so.

One way to make the vision easier to read and imagine every day is to add graphic images to your statement document. Some people include photo clippings of the things they are visualizing (if it is a tangible "thing"), finding them perhaps by searching for them on the web, and then using their computer software to paste those images right onto their script. Or if the item is less tangible, you can find and place *symbols* that represent the emotions of the thing. For example, you might place an image of a sun with a smiley face on it to represent happy customers, if that is a goal you wrote down.

If you have no easy way to put the images on the script page itself, then create a separate page or use a cork board, and place all the images together there, positioned in the order you read them in your script. Placing images of your goals on a page or board is commonly called a vision board. I glance up at my vision board as I hit each item while reading my script; it provides an extra level of imagery to my goal-spinning process.

You could create that board by clipping images out of magazines and pasting them on a larger piece of paper or cardboard. I create my vision boards on my computer using Microsoft PowerPoint since I know that program well, and since it links to a large database of clip art that anyone can borrow from freely. Any other graphics application can work too. This is just one example of how you can be creative and find various ways to engage your emotions when you read the vision statement.

When first getting started with your daily activation, pay attention to your reaction as you read your new statement. You may find the vision statement that you write out is hard for you to believe. If that happens, if you find yourself tuning out when you read the statement because it just seems too far-fetched to you, then you may want to use the tools provided in Chapter 14, "Stretching Your Now Goals." The two tools there are the What If–Why Not tool, and the Locking in New Beliefs tool. Consider using both of them should you doubt your own new vision. I'd rather have you adjust your beliefs than dumb down your goal to the point that it lacks passion.

Finally, if you are starting or expanding your own business and you feel you need help creating and activating the vision of your business using these principles, coaching is available from a company called OneCoach, founded by the authors of the book I referenced earlier called *The Answer*. In that book, John Assaraf and Murray Smith lay out a very complete set of steps for creating and activating your business vision. Many of their visualization steps are derived from nearly all the same sources I used to create my goal-spinning techniques, so they will look familiar to you. They then add useful business-skills advice and coaching, offering an integrated package. Find them at OneCoach.com.

## An Ongoing Journey

Next, as in Part II, start to look for inspired actions that will lead to your goal. What I have found is this: after activating my new life's work vision for some days or weeks, I often find in a somewhat random moment an intuitive insight for a strategy (set of steps) that can jump-start my progress toward that vision. Recall the think-time sessions I described in Chapter 17? That's often when these insights have emerged for me. This is the gyroscope effect in action. When those insights emerge, as soon as possible after that, I plan out the steps that match that strategy, engaging them as appropriate. The ideas are usually accompanied by a burst of enthusiasm, which helps carry me through the action steps; that's the flywheel effect in action.

This is exactly the sort of thing you are looking for next. You have primed your subconscious pump by activating your vision every day, and sooner or later you are going to see the core of an ideal action plan emerge that will manifest some part of that vision. Or you may run into someone who may be able to help you on your next steps, and since you are consciously or subconsciously looking for that, you'll recognize that opportunity immediately. To me, that is the best part of this process—when I get those bursts of eager ideas, or have those seemingly serendipitous meetings.

But that may not happen right away. If you are impatient, you may in fact be thinking that you want to hurry up and achieve the vision now. After a few weeks you may start looking around and wonder, "So when am I going to make progress on this?"

Being eager to "get there now" like that is natural and expected. However, note that the real reason for having a larger vision is as much for the journey itself as for the things you want. Having a larger vision or purpose, just beyond your reach, gives you energy and conviction. It propels you on. It pulls you forward. It gives you momentum and courage. It puts a lift in your step, creates an eagerness in your soul, and adds conviction to your voice. So enjoy the process and the benefits of traveling toward your goal, even before you have it. These are your best days, the days when you can clearly see what you want and feel that you are on your way there; enjoy the journey.

You see, once you achieve that vision, you will of course celebrate; creating your current life's work is the final act of your path to Workday Mastery, and you will feel that.

But believe me, once you do, you will also quickly raise the bar to the next level of vision to pursue. Again, that's because the pleasure is as much in the journey as in the thing you are reaching for. So learn how to enjoy the journey, starting now. Relax into the knowledge that you are on your way to your highest vision of life, and that each step in that direction, however small, can be a joyful one.

Where is all this leading? Well, over the years, you will take that journey through various life's work scenarios. You will achieve one and move on to the next, and you will think bigger each time you do. Throughout that process you may start to see a larger common element emerge. It may be that you see a pattern; you may see yourself tracking to a general positive overarching purpose. I call that your *mission*. Not many get a sense of it, but if you do, consider yourself lucky. Let's talk about that next, in Chapter 19.

## Summary

With the vision or purpose larger than yourself from Chapter 16 in hand, you will start to assemble a description of your next role. You will combine that with the results of two exercises, one to collect your favorite past activities and one to list your forward-looking job or role qualities. Putting all this together allows you to create your current life's work vision statement. In that statement you may actually build a new self-image—write a new narrative of your work and life.

You will then activate that vision using the tools you learned in Chapter 12 for activating your Now Goals. Over time, you will devise inspired plans and actions to achieve this life's work vision, just as inspired actions emerge over time for your smaller activated goals.

Creating your current life's work is the final act on your path to Workday Mastery. You have reached the peak of the pyramid. But it is still an ongoing journey. As you work more roles that you can call life's work, the concept of mission starts to make sense, as you will see next.

CHAPTER **19**

# Connecting to Your Personal Mission

Up until now, I have not referred much to the concept of a *mission statement.* You may have seen that term in other success-oriented books. It is also a common term in business, where it is used as a tool to help business management focus on the company's core goals. My usage here, however, will refer to your personal mission in life, which may in fact be expressed mostly through your work or business.

A lot of people are confused about the meaning of a personal mission and a mission statement. Following instructions from trainers or books, many people try to write one out, but when trying to, often don't feel the inspiration to do so, or get confused. That's okay, because I believe articulating it or writing it is *not* a necessary first step to pursuing various stages of your life's work. Not even an intermediate step. Some of us, perhaps most of us, may never get a clearly written mission statement created. And yet we still accomplish great things in life.

As a way of explanation, I will share with you my belief in what a personal mission is and how it behaves, and why the above is true. It is quite different from the business definition, and I think much more useful.

Here is my definition of a personal life mission.

*A personal life mission is the highest and most general vision or purpose that captures what you were born to do. Your mission is an ultimate sense of purpose that accumulates all the various visions and larger purposes you have pursued and will likely pursue over the years. It is a purpose that in the long run improves ourselves, other people, possibly our community, our country, humanity, the world, and, depending on your worldview, ultimately serves God or the Universe in that process. And our ability to really understand that purpose may not come until after years of life experience.*

That's a mouthful, so I am going to discuss all the pieces of it below, one at a time.

## Core Qualities of Your Life Mission

Let me start by describing what I believe to be the core qualities of an individual's mission; there are four of them. An individual's mission is 1) permanent, 2) always positive, 3) very general, and 4) discovered through experience.

1) Permanent

First of all, I believe we all have some purpose at our core, and that one of our life drives is to understand it and manifest it. If we are lucky, we do that. And if not, we always keep trying; it is one of the things that drives us forward.

You see, unlike nearly everything else we do in and with our lives, which I feel we can formulate and create according to our visions and goals, I believe our mission came with us when we were born and stays with us throughout our lives. It is part of the soul we were born with. You can use that term "soul" in a religious or nonreligious way; I leave that up to you. I just feel that we all have an *essence* that is us, a core that is who we are through our whole lives.

Now I realize there are various psychological theories about whether who we are is something we are born with or learn over time. I think we have qualities that result from both of those. What I am talking about here is something deep down that transcends all of that, and which may even be imperceptible to us much of the time. It is a slow-burn underlying impulse that keeps us moving forward in some characteristic way.

Mission is another topic whose explanation will vary based on your worldview. If you are scientifically minded, you might say it is in our DNA and that we have a genetic propensity or tendency to express our innate qualities in a specific way. If you are religious, you might say it is God's intent for you on this earth. If you are more generally spiritual or New Age, you might say it is the vibrational signature you were born with and carry with you, perhaps left by the stars or some other birth or prebirth influence.

No matter how you describe it or explain it, I do think it expresses itself in a rather stable, repeatable, and definitely subtle way, and that over time you may come to be able to put words around it.

2) Positive

I believe our missions must be positive, if for no other reason than that this seems to be the nature of life. If you look around you, everything alive is growing—plants, trees, animals, and humans—we're all trying to grow toward more and more in life. As individuals, we each have some role in making that overall expansion of life possible. So yes, I think the core mission is positive, not because everyone is a "do-gooder," but because expansion and growth is the nature of life, and you are part of life. One way to say this is that God or the Universe or nature—whatever matches your belief—put us on this earth with the intent to improve, to expand, and to make life for ourselves and others better in some way. So it is natural that your underlying life mission would be part of that somehow.

3) General

I believe your mission must be general, because it has to be, given all the choices we have through life, given our free will. Since I believe your mission does not change through your life, it has to be broad, if it's going to last your entire life. That's how you are able to exercise your free will, and embrace a variety of jobs, careers, and people, and yet still progress within your life's mission.

4) Discovered through Experience

I also believe that your mission isn't created by you, it is *discovered* by you. Its meaning emerges in your awareness usually after years of learning about yourself, your work life, your activities, and your tendencies. It emerges after connecting with and pursuing various life and work purposes and visions throughout your career. Along with that, it emerges after connecting with yourself or connecting spiritually. At some point I feel that it all comes together. We'll talk more about that ahead.

## Mission Guides Our Work Choices

I also believe that even if we cannot wrap words around your mission early in life, it still speaks to you your whole life. And that if you listen to your intuition, your gut, and your heart, then your underlying mission will guide your choices of activity and work. I believe that you know your work is right when it intuitively "feels" right—meaning it matches your core skills, preferences, and positive impulses, and ultimately your mission, in an intuitive and natural way, and as appropriate for your current stage of life. And to me, having that guidance is even better than being able to put words to a mission. Being guided by mission is the ultimate goal.

Let's look at an example to demonstrate. Remember the previous example of the ice cream shop staffer who was currently working in her life's work? She served ice cream in the best way possible and was happy in the process. But was that her mission?

No, the job itself is never your mission—that's too specific. However, because she is in a job that totally fulfills her, she might be able to describe her mission by asking herself, "What is it, at the highest level, about this job that just seems so right?" The answer in this case might be, "I am making people happy; I bring joy to their lives by helping them have a small but delightful food experience at that perfect moment in their day. I put smiles on faces every day. That makes them better people, that raises their level of happiness; I uplift people."

Now, that's a pretty good statement. It may even be her mission statement, though only time, maturity, and many more life experiences will really tell that. But it is well written in that it is at a sufficiently high level; it is not limited by a specific career or place or time period. And yet it captures perfectly what her delightful job does for the world.

## Mission Is Long-Lasting

The example above demonstrates why your life's work can and probably should change over time, even though your mission in life will stay the same.

That same ice cream scooper may later go to cooking school and learn how to be a chef and then uplift people's lives by creating inspiring, delicious food experiences (while being rewarded in the process). That same person may become a writer and write a book about how to prepare food and thus uplift readers who wish to believe in themselves as being able to learn to cook. That same person may later take that book on the road and become a motivational speaker and uplift people directly through her speeches about food. In each case the life work has progressed and changed, but the life mission has remained essentially the same.

And at each stage of her career, it is safe to say that the person in this example was doing her life's work. Now, to think that scooping ice cream could be considered one's life work may seem to minimize the meaning of that phrase. One usually thinks of life's work as the ultimate job, career, or activity that one should strive for. But you will always be striving, you will always be growing, and no matter how settled and definite a life work position or activity seems to feel to you, there will always be something beyond it. So don't diminish the concept of life work just because your current role seems small. It's all relative to where you are in building your skills, gaining experiences, expanding your vision, and projecting yourself forward.

## Mission Emerges Over Time

So there, I just described what a mission is, but you'll probably notice that up to this point I have still said relatively little about how and when you should try to create or write a mission *statement*. Isn't creating a mission statement normally the first thing done in most training on goals, and life work, and so on? Nearly all books on these topics insist on that.

Well, no. Again, I think your mission emerges over time. You discover it. I also think most of us are woefully unprepared to uncover it, especially at the early stages of our work history. It's a subtle thing and not usually easy to figure out; it's not a slam-dunk exercise.

Rather, over time, through observing your propensity or passion toward certain activities, and your skill and passion for certain work, you will come to know it. It will probably only emerge when observed over a number of years, perhaps decades, as you mature your personality.

And that delay is okay because, as I stated above, I believe that your soul (or essence, or born inclination) feeds your intuition daily, through your subconscious mind. It gives you information consistent with your underlying mission, nudging you in that direction. So if you can activate and trust your intuition, you are likely to stay on track, even without a written mission statement.

In fact, trying to write a mission statement too early can be counterproductive. My feeling is that it is better to let your heart and intuition guide you for a while, and not to try to force any activity to fit a supposedly static mission statement that someone perhaps said you "should" write. Your mission is not subject to the discussion in Part II about picking a goal and activating it. Trying to spin up an inaccurate mission statement may in fact get in the way. And you should not bother trying to spin even an accurately written one; it is already spinning, so to speak; it is already at your core.

## Life Experience Clarifies Mission

All that said, once you have matured in life and your career, and you feel the two circles of life are overlapping well, you may now in fact be able to wrap words around it. It may be interesting to do. Hopefully you have had a series of jobs, activities, and life experiences that you learned from. Hopefully they were ones that felt nearly "just right" and where you saw that the various contributions you made accurately resonated with you. And hopefully you now have a fairly mature intuitive connection and are able to trust that those insights are right. The essence of a mature intuitive connection is knowing how to discern which thoughts and feelings that your subconscious feeds you are soul-driven and right, and which are not. With experience, you will come to know that and will gain confidence in your internally identified mission.

So once you have been at this for a while you may be ready to make a stab at writing a mission statement. In fact, as soon as you feel you understand it, it does in fact help to write out your mission statement. Why? Once you have your mission confidently identified and written, it makes sense to activate *related goals* that more closely support it. So a written mission statement is useful to base your goals on.

How do you write it? Well, that is a very subjective thing. My only guidance is to examine your life and work experiences as above, and then stick to the qualities I described earlier. Let me rephrase them here in a way that may help during the writing: 1) it is consistent with your full range of life experiences, 2) it is very positive; 3) it is general enough that it remains relatively timeless; and 4) it makes sense at nearly every stage of your life.

## My Mission Statement

For example, my mission statement, which I realized was mine after examining years and years of various work roles is as follows:

*Helping large numbers of people uplift and achieve their life's goals and dreams through their work.*

That mission statement certainly works now. Looking back, I can see it also worked years ago, when I was the leader of a small project management methodology team buried deep in a large company. It worked when I was an IT manager mentoring a large team of workers. And it worked even when I was right out of school and learning the ropes of business, since all that I learned then made the rest possible.

That mission statement also applies to me looking forward, as I see my sphere of influence growing through writing more and more books and training more and more people.

And note that it is a general statement. The only word in there that isn't extremely general is the word "work." However, because I've known from an early age that a work focus was a core part of my life, it still feels accurate to me. So this mission, I feel, has been mine my whole life and has worked for me at every stage of my career.

And once again, this is my *mission;* the way I have expressed that through my *life's work* has changed at each stage of my work life, because the specific work activities have changed at each stage.

Writing your mission statement is purely optional. Don't worry about doing it right now if it does not feel right to do it. And if you do write it, don't worry about getting it perfect; if you get it wrong, you'll know it sooner or later. One day you will look at it and say, "This is not quite right." You'll then edit it and work with it for a while longer. Or you will decide to put it aside until you have gained more experience.

If you do write one, use it as a self-reflection tool. Don't try to use it as a should or a metric against which you measure your success in life. It is written purely as a general vision that you can take inspiration from.

## Summary

Your personal mission represents your highest and most general vision or purpose that captures what you were born to do. Your mission is an ultimate sense of purpose that includes all the various visions and larger purposes you have pursued and will likely pursue over the years.

The four core qualities of a personal mission are that it is 1) permanent, 2) always positive, 3) very general, and 4) usually discovered later in life.

If your intuition or connection to yourself is good, I believe your mission can guide you with fairly accurate work or role choices by inspiring your subconscious mind to favor some activities over others. That's why it is not critical to write out your mission statement—in fact, that may be a flawed activity unless done with great maturity. But with adequate experience and wisdom, you may feel inspired to do so. Use such a statement as a source of inspiration, not as a measure of your life success.

PART III CONCLUSION

# Thinking Big

In Part III you learned the last step of gaining Workday Mastery. You learned how to find a vision or purpose larger than yourself, and you learned how to turn that into a current life's work vision statement, a statement you are activating in your daily Now Goal activation sessions. Doing this, and then attaining your current life's work role, represents the top level of the Workday Mastery Pyramid.

The section then concluded with a look at personal mission—how it is a useful thing to consider. Even though we closed with mission, I feel the primary focus for most of our visioning work should *not* be on writing a mission statement. I think it should be on identifying your *current* larger vision or purpose for work, and driving that forward into your next vision and life's work activity, and then the next, and then the next. Don't worry if you can't call it your permanent mission; just keep advancing it. Life is all about experiencing more and more, expanding your abilities, and fulfilling more of your inner and outer visions.

For many of us, that may show up as more personal or material improvement, or improvement for our families. If you are deeply religious or spiritual, it may be about service to humanity or getting closer to God. It may be about expanding your learning, your knowledge. Whatever your largest visions may be, keep marching forward toward those larger goals. Keep creating even larger goals as you go, so that they consistently pull you forward. And think as big as you can, each step of the way.

Thinking big is important. I was once told that to "set" my larger vision I should pick the biggest thing I really wanted and then stop and ask, "How can I make it even bigger?"

In fact, one of my favorite exercises is to take a moment and ask myself this: "What would I do if I knew I could do anything, and not fail?" Think about that. What would *you* do? What would you envision if you knew you could not fail? What vision would you create for yourself?

For example, the last time I asked myself this question, I decided I wanted to create a university to train businesspeople on the ideas in this book and related material, a university that nearly all businesses would send their staff to. Now, I don't see a *practical* way to do that right now—or ever, for that matter. Starting a full-fledged university is a big feat, especially one of such quality that all would want to attend. It is several levels beyond anything I had in mind for the future. But that moment of my ignoring all roadblocks and instead imagining it as if it were done, with myself in that vision, had a remarkably liberating effect. It connected me with some inner creative knowing I didn't realize I had, and for a moment I rose above all my current restrictive beliefs, and I actually felt what life would feel like if those restrictions were gone. That felt very good, and that flash of inspiration has affected me positively since.

*What would you do if you knew you could do anything, and not fail?*

I encourage everyone to do that. It is instructive to momentarily remove all barriers like that, to think entirely outside the box; in fact, not just outside the box, but so far from the box that you can't even see the box anymore. What would you do if you knew you could do anything, and not fail? Imagine you have all the self-confidence in the world—that all the worries that currently haunt you are gone. Imagine you have all the money you need—that lack of money will never hold you back from any dream. Imagine you have all the help you need—that the people with the skills you need will come to you when you need them. Imagine that the time you need is there, the energy you need is there, and even the love and support your need is there. Imaging you cannot fail. In those circumstances, what is the thing deepest in your heart that you then would do?

Once you decide what that is, imagine yourself having it and then live your life in your imagination for a few moments, acting as the new you. What new decisions would you make? How would you feel? How would you live your life, day after day, year after year?

Don't dismiss this exercise. While I don't expect you to believe it, I do want you to pretend while you do it, because the experience of visioning bigger than you can possibly imagine is a very powerful experience. Why do children and many adults love magic tricks? Because those tricks challenge the normally rigid framework of reality. Why do we love larger-than-life movies? We all love seeing the often dreary limits of everyday life dissolved in a flash, even if for just an imaginary moment. Deep in our hearts we wish to be freed from our current unyielding present framework of life. We all wish that we could break free from our barriers, experience new wonders, and find new sources of joy and happiness. And when we experience that, even if for just an imaginary moment, it stimulates our creativity in a big way.

So please do stop occasionally for a moment, even now, and ask yourself, "What would I do if I knew I could do anything, and not fail?" Whenever you do this exercise, if you do it with conviction and with a wide open mind, you will find great and positive inspirations in the corners of your heart; ones that you didn't even know existed before. If you truly think big—bigger than you ever have before—then if even just 1 percent of your dreams come true, your jump in satisfaction will be enormous. So do this exercise, dream big, and feel that joy—if only for a moment—and let it inspire you to the next level of pursuit in life.

Finally, looking forward, don't pinch your dreams off because you think they are not possible, or because you have failed at a few before. Unfortunately, through the disappointments of our lives, most of us turn off our sense of hope and wonder and inner yearning for the best things in life and begin to expect less; we do so to protect our hearts. But what if we are wrong to do that? What if, instead of closing our hearts at every disappointment, we kept them open and pursued even more in life? What if we really could achieve even 1 percent of the biggest things we can imagine?

Please, don't close your heart off to the potential for what you really want. Think big, go after it, and keep your self-status and sense of self-worth strong enough that if you fail a bit—or even fall short of those larger goals much of the time—that you will still have fun trying again. Think big, imagine big, visualize big, and don't care if anyone sees you succeed or fail—just enjoy the journey.

■   ■   ■

One parting thought. Remember, it is all about vision. Think of this statement: everything that humanity has created in this world was an idea first, a vision first. Everything starts as a flash of inspiration. What does that tell you about the power of vision? Don't discount your dreams. Rather, embrace them and think of the possibilities that exist in those imaginings. Write them down, adjust your beliefs so you can believe in them, and then go after them. Activate them in your daily goal sessions, and look for an even larger you to emerge.

# Workday Mastery Toolkit

It has been a long and productive journey, hasn't it? You've learned quite a range of ideas, concepts, and tools, all on the road to Workday Mastery. In this book, you have spanned the three layers of the Workday Mastery Pyramid: a Control layer for vanquishing chaos and gaining order in your day; a Create layer for visioning and creating your goals; and a Connect layer for transforming your work into a calling that matches who you really are. These three layers build on one another.

You also learned an overarching solution framework—that of your Workday Now—emphasizing how knowledge of a simple "mental model" can help you to improve your entire workday experience.

As a wrap-up, in addition to the ideas we've discussed in the book, I want to give you a summary in one place of all the tools you need to put these ideas into practice. The tools naturally align with the three parts of the book, so that is how you will see them here.

# Tools by Layer

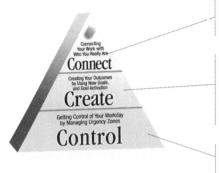

Life's Work Vision Statement
Personal Mission Statement

Now Goal Statements List
Now Goal Action Brainstorming
Now Goal Action Planning
Locking in New Beliefs Exercise

The Workday Mastery To-Do List
  • Now Tasks List
  • Over-the-Horizon List

## Tools from Part I: Controlling Your Workday Now

On the next two pages are the two main components of the Workday Mastery To-Do List you learned in Part I—the Now Tasks List and the Over-the-Horizon List. Recall that three levels of this to-do list were presented in Part I; the samples shown here match the most complete one, Level 3. Downloadable blank templates (including MindManager versions) are available at my website, MasterYourWorkday.com/ToolDownloads.

## Now Tasks List

As you may recall, the Now Tasks list is a form showing a one-page list of all the tasks you need to be thinking about in your workday. It was introduced in Chapter 2 and expanded on in later chapters. By the end of Part I the Now Tasks list included three urgency zones: Critical Now, Opportunity Now, and Target Now (all covered in Chapter 6), as well as the Significant Outcomes section at the top (discussed in Chapter 7).

Here is a sample of the full Now Tasks List (from the Level 3 templates), with notes on how to use each section on the form.

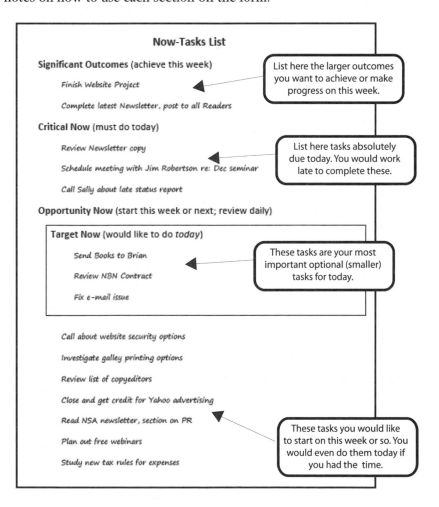

## Over-the-Horizon List for Defer-to-Review Tasks

In Chapter 6 you learned about the Strategic Deferral process, and specifically, Defer-to-Review tasks. You put Defer-to-Review tasks on the Over-the-Horizon pages. At its simplest, you use one page that you review weekly. Better, though, is to use the Level 3 templates, which include five additional pages to support the extended-review-cycle approach; that is shown below. As you can see, each added page has a longer review cycle.

Here is a sample of a completed Level 3 set, with notes indicating the optional pages.

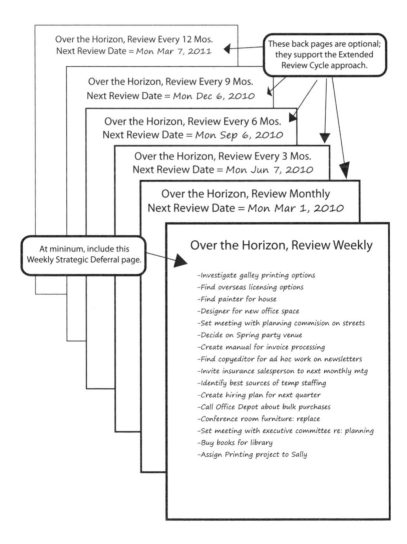

# Tools from Part II: Creating Your Workday Now

In Part II: Creating Your Workday Now, you learned how to create Now Goals. Most of Part II was dedicated to the 4-step Now Goal creation process. Here are the four steps again.

Step 1: Create your Vision Goal. As you know by now a Vision Goal is essential. I showed you in Chapter 10 a simple formula to create it.

Step 2: Identify your Target Goals and add them to the Vision Goal. Nearly all goals need a Target Goal component, and Chapter 11 showed some fine points on adding them. Once you've added them, you will have the two core pieces of your new Now Goal statement.

Step 3: Activate the Now Goal. This is just as important as writing a good Now Goal statement, and the most important ongoing step after initially creating the goal. Chapter 12 presented a thorough explanation of why it was needed and how to do it.

Step 4: Take first action. This is where you start to engage your goal. Chapter 13 covered how to do that. One option is to brainstorm a few actions for each goal, ideally using a mind map. Another option, for larger goals, is to create a small project plan (timeline).

At the end of these steps you typically ended with a list of Now Goal statements, which you activated all in one sitting. And Chapter 14 provided you with an optional exercise to help expand your beliefs about what you are able to accomplish, to help you set your sights on tougher goals.

On the pages that follow are samples of a Now Goal statements list, a first action brainstorming list, and a project plan, as well a sample Locking in New Beliefs statement and a generic list you can use in creating your own Locking in New Beliefs statement.

The Now Goal samples below were created using MindManager software, which I discuss in Chapter 13. However, you could create these in nearly any word processing application, or by hand. Templates for MindManager and Microsoft Word are included on my website, MasterYourWorkday.com/ToolDownloads.

## *Now Goal Statements List*

It is helpful to list all your smaller goals on one page so that you can activate them one after the other. One idea presented in Chapter 11 was to recreate this list each season with new goals you are working on and hope to complete that season. Here is a sample of one such page.

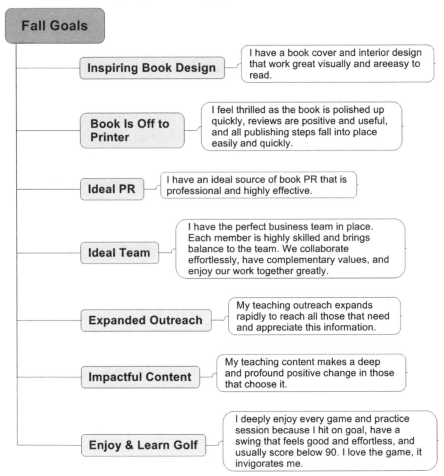

## Now Goal Action Brainstorming

In Chapter 13 I discussed optionally brainstorming actions. Here is one way that might look using the same goal form as above, just adding some action topics to the right of the goal.

## Now Goal Action Planning

In Chapter 13 I also discussed optionally creating a project plan (timeline) for the steps of a much larger goal. Here is how that might look. I used the optional JCVGantt add-in module for MindManager to convert the MindManager topics directly into a linked project schedule. You can of course use any application that creates timelines, like Microsoft Project, or even manually create a timeline in a graphics application or Microsoft Excel.

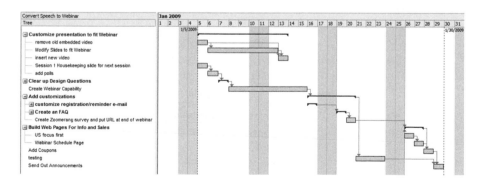

## *Locking in New Beliefs Example*

Chapter 14 in Part II was about expanding your beliefs such that you can take on bigger goals. I showed you how to create a list of ways that your Workday Now and personal life might change once those new beliefs or goals were in place. Reviewing that list daily during your goal activation process helps your subconscious embrace your larger capabilities.

Here is a sample of one such page.

1.  My paycheck: Nicely larger this month!

2.  My calendar or time: My clients are calling me, wanting to buy. I have sales meetings with them scheduled on my calendar. I have many closing meetings scheduled on my calendar. (Picture that.)

3.  Attitude of my boss to me: "Ted, good job—keep it up. You are an example to all of us!"

4.  Comments from my colleagues: "Wow, Ted, what's your secret? Can you show me how to do some of this?"

5.  Conversations I have with most others about the new success: "Yeah, sales are good. My contacts are all paying off. Most of my calls are closing; people just seem to want to do business with me. You guys can do this too—just envision how you want your sales to go, and then do the work."

6.  How my family is reacting: (Describe a positive reaction when you tell them, or when you take your spouse out to dinner or off for a weekend.)

7.  My feelings: It sure feels good to have a solid increase in sales. I like being in this comfort zone, knowing that I am set and in the flow. It feels like every contact I make just comes through.

8.  My expectations: These sales will continue to keep closing; I am on a roll and all the pieces continue to fall into place to close increasing numbers of sales. I just have to speak, and the sale closes, and this will continue into the future; this is amazing! I have now come to expect this with all contacts; it feels so natural for it to happen.

9.  My attitude: I am hugely upbeat. It is amazing how success at work affects all aspects of my life, including my attitude about life. I enjoy my weekends more, knowing I have met and exceeded goals all week. I feel comfortable taking time off for play.

10. E-mails to me: I am getting 10 to 20 new sales responses per day by e-mail. Whenever I look at my in-box, there they are.

11. My activities: I am helping with delivery of the sales, doing follow-ups, and filling out the forms. I am making sure production is on track for the sales. I am calling prospects, and the calls work. I will also be coaching junior sales folks on how to do this.

## *Locking in New Beliefs Generic List*

Here is a generic list of the most common aspects of work and life that might change that you can use to create your own such page if you like.

Downloadable templates of this generic list are available at my website, MasterYourWorkday.com/ToolDownloads

- My attitude:

- My expectations:

- My conversations:

- My calendar:

- My bank account:

- My spending:

- My income:

- My calendar:

- My self-talk:

- My feeling when I wake up in the morning:

- My thoughts when I go to sleep at night:

- My thoughts when I walk in front of a mirror:

- My thoughts when I see my co-workers:

- My thoughts when I consider my boss:

- E-mails I get from others:

- Phone calls I get from others:

- (Add anything else specific to the topic)

# Tools from Part III: Connecting Your Workday Now

In Part III: Connecting Your Workday Now, you learned how to create a life's work vision statement that you will activate daily. Most of Part III was dedicated to the background for building that statement, culminating in Chapter 18 where you created it. Then in Chapter 19 I discussed creating a short personal mission statement, one you can optionally create. Below are samples of each.

## Life's Work Vision Statement

In Chapter 18 you learned how to design and create a life's work vision statement, which you will use to activate your life's work vision every day. Here is a sample of one of these.

> I am a master dessert chef and menu designer for a well-known, high-end restaurant chain. The restaurant chain is widely recognized for its creative cuisine and is located in most major cities (example: P.F. Chang's). I create the delicious dessert ideas that are placed on the nationwide selection. I am quite famous in the restaurant industry and among restaurant critics, and both praise my creative and distinctive approaches to well-known dishes. As a result, the restaurant receives awards often, and I am recruited regularly from competing chains. I enjoy a generous salary (at least $80,000) and receive stock options worth $10,000 each year. I adore my job—I feel like I have the best job in the world!

> The personal life my job enables is perfect. I live and work in or near one of these cities: New York City, San Francisco, Chicago, or Atlanta. My job enables me to have a delightful home that is at least 2,500 square feet in size, is located in a tree-lined suburban neighborhood, and is near good schools for my family. Since my job is mainly designing menus and not daily cooking, I am able to keep excellent work hours and have weekends off for fun with my family and friends. I am able to lead a balanced life with fun exercise, healthy and tasty meals, and exciting outdoor activities like bicycling, which I love.

*The job gives me a lot of creative freedom. When I want to, I can choose to cook in any of the chain's restaurants, so I can enjoy the experience and gain insight into new menu ideas. I have a number of people reporting to me, so I can offload less interesting work and focus on new menu ideas. I take quarterly travel to a central training facility, where I train regional chefs on new dessert menus and receive feedback on existing menus. I am able to create new dishes often, and management gives me free rein to be as creative as I wish. I have a generous budget to experiment with. I also have a travel budget to take "tasting trips" three or more times a year, where I try out desserts at excellent restaurants in various interesting locations, including overseas—I love these trips.*

*Overall, I have what has to be the best job I can imagine. I am doing the things I love—creating fabulous new desserts—and am doing it in a way that brings me national recognition. In doing so, I am providing a delightful dessert experience for thousands of people, making them all a little happier each time.*

## *Personal Mission Statement*

In Chapter 19 I discussed creating a personal mission statement. Your personal mission represents your highest and most general vision or purpose that captures what you were born to do. Your mission is an ultimate sense of purpose that includes all the various visions and larger purposes you have pursued and will likely pursue over the years. The four core qualities of a personal mission are that it is 1) permanent, 2) always positive, 3) very general ,and 4) usually discovered later in life. Creating one is purely optional.

Here is my personal mission statement, as a sample.

*Helping large numbers of people uplift and achieve their life's goals and dreams through their work.*

## *For Further Assistance*

These tools will probably be enough to get you going. However, if you need further assistance, see the additional programs listed in the Recommended Resources section, next.

# Recommended Resources

## Workday Mastery Resources from Michael Linenberger

***Workday Mastery Seminars and Keynote Speaking.*** Boost your organization's productivity with on-site training on the Workday Mastery principles, or enjoy Linenberger's highly motivating keynote speech at your next event. In the seminars, Linenberger presents Workday Mastery productivity processes and walks students through hands-on exercises to firmly establish these workplace practices. Microsoft Outlook options are also available. For more information on these programs, go to MasterYourWorkday.com.

***Workday Mastery Coaching.*** We all sometimes need one-on-one assistance when implementing new teachings; Michael Linenberger offers in-person or phone coaching to fill that need. Designed to fit your personal situation, Linenberger will work with you to uncover your current workday problem areas and help you get your workday under control. You can even work with Michael on goal strategies and career counseling. Microsoft Outlook–based coaching options are also available. For more information, go to MasterYourWorkday.com.

***Workday Mastery CD Self-Training Set.*** Due out in spring of 2010 is Linenberger's Workday Mastery CD Self-Training set in which you will find all the core principles of *Master Your*

*Workday Now!* Accompanying the CD set is a printed workbook, including all book templates and exercises. This is a cost-effective way to receive training on the Workday Mastery principles, helping you overcome an out-of-control workday and boost your workday effectiveness. Go to MasterYourWorkday.com for more information.

**Daily Planner Binder.** One way to implement the Workday Mastery To-Do List presented in Part I of this book is to use the new Workday Mastery daily binder with preprinted pages for tracking all of the Workday Mastery task types. Available as inserts for existing binders, or as complete binder sets, these pages will give you a structured kick-start to implementing the Workday Mastery processes. The products are due for release in spring 2010; go to MasterYourWorkday. com to check on availability and to purchase.

**Total Workday Control Using Microsoft Outlook** by Michael Linenberger (New Academy Publishers, 2006, 2008). Throughout Part I of this book, I mention that one option is to use Microsoft Outlook to implement the Control-layer Workday Mastery principles. *Total Workday Control Using Microsoft Outlook* shows you how. It has been the #1 best-selling book on Outlook for nearly four years. Be sure to check for the latest edition of that book, as Microsoft is constantly updating their products, and I update the book to match those new releases. The book is available in bookstores and through online retailers, but consider buying the book bundled with my *Basic Configuration Training CD* described below, which is available only at my web shopping site: store.michaellinenberger.com.

**Total Workday Control Using Microsoft Outlook—Basic Configuration Training CD.** Designed to accompany my Outlook book, *Total Workday Control Using Microsoft Outlook,* described above, this training CD will help you get started with the Outlook implementation of Workday Mastery principles. It contains introductory, step-by-step videos on how to set up Outlook to match the Workday Mastery principles. The CD and CD–book bundle are available only at my web shopping site: store.michaellinenberger.com.

**Manage Your Now ClearContext Outlook Add-in Software.** Developed in a partnership between Michael Linenberger and ClearContext Corporation, this software preconfigures Outlook to implement the Workday Mastery To-Do List in Outlook. It also adds many useful features to Outlook, including in-box prioritization and project tracking. Go to www.michaellinenberger. com/clearcontext.html to download a free trial. Note: This is a special edition available only through my website.

# *Recommended Third-Party Resources*

The following third-party resources are what I consider your most important next tools in helping gain Workday Mastery. Nearly all tools below have been referenced elsewhere in the book (see the Index for specific page references). I have provided URLs below so you can study each of these more; even better, though, is to go to MasterYourWorkday.com/RecommendedResources, which shows the same list below, but with live URL links.

***MindManager software*** by MindJet. This software is a remarkable tool for generating and presenting ideas, and for implementing the Workday Mastery tools. It can be used to create the various worksheets cited in all three parts of this book. For example, in Part I you can use it to create the Workday Mastery To-Do List, including the Now Tasks list and Over-the-Horizon lists. For Part II it can be used to create your seasonal goals list. It can also be used for brainstorming action steps to achieve your goals, and for creating the Locking in New Beliefs script. It is good for generating project plans, especially when used with the add-in module, JCVGantt. And, finally, it can be used for creating your life's work vision statement, described in Part III. It is the one software tool I recommend most often to others. For a free trial download of the software, and for free Workday Mastery templates that work with the software go to MasterYourWorkday. com/MindManager.

***JCVGantt software*** by MindJet. This is optional add-in software for MindManager which allows you to create a linked project plan directly from topics in a mind map, something I encourage in Chapter 13. Go to MasterYourWorkday.com/MindManager for a free trial download to add to the MindManager software.

***The Canfield Training Group—Jack Canfield.*** Canfield's book *The Success Principles* is by far the best success book I have ever read, and I present many of Canfield's principles throughout this book. So it is no surprise that I am a big supporter of Jack's training. The Canfield Training Group offers life-changing programs that focus on living *The Success Principles*, raising self-esteem, optimizing peak performance, and breaking through barriers to greater success. www. jackcanfield.com.

***Brian Tracy.*** Brian Tracy consistently has one of the best approaches to goals and goal setting, and teaches an approach similar to the one in this book for activating goals. He is also one of the world's foremost thought leaders on personal and business success. Through his books and as one of the most sought-after success coaches, he has transformed the lives of millions. In particular, check out his books *Goals!* and *Time Power*. See his other books and programs at www.briantracy.com. Also, if you own a business, see Business Growth Strategies (BGS). BGS shows you how to increase sales and profitability in your business consistently, dependably, and controllably. Learn how you can become a BGS member here: www.bizgrowthstrategies.com.

**Happy for No Reason** by Marci Shimoff (Free Press, 2009). As I've mentioned, I think that experiencing happiness within yourself and bringing it to your work is very important. It is key to my Part III principles of connecting with yourself and finding your life's work. To support this, I highly recommend the happiness work of *New York Times* best-selling author Marci Shimoff, who also co-authored six of the *Chicken Soup for the Soul* titles and was featured in the movie *The Secret*. Marci has created this well-researched book, as well as a self-study course, which can help anyone raise their happiness level, no matter what their circumstances. Learn more and sign up for free Happy for No Reason coaching and newsletter by going to www. HappyForNoReason.com/workday.

**The Passion Test.** Passion is what connects us to purpose and vision, and this is a core message of Parts II and III of my book. Those who have discovered their passions and followed them have become the most successful, influential people of their time. However, it can be hard to find your true passion—there are so many outside influences that lead us astray. *The Passion Test* by Janet Bray Attwood and Chris Attwood provides a simple, powerful way for anyone to connect with their passions. Use the following URL and take a short quiz to find out where you stand in living your passions, then take advantage of the chance to get a copy of *The Passion Test* book to discover your own passions. Just go to: www.thepassiontest.com/workdaymastery.

**Success Built to Last** by Jerry Porras, Stewart Emery, and Mark Thompson (Plume, 2007). An insightful book that, among other messages, emphasizes that to be truly successful you must work at what you feel most passionate about—a key premise of Part III of my book. Stewart Emery, one of the coauthors of *Success Built to Last,* offers workshops and seminars on this topic and others. Find out more at www.stewartemery.com.

**Thank God It's Monday.** In Part III of my book I emphasize how important it is to love your work—that this is key to happiness with life. This amazing book by Roxanne Emmerich (FT Press, 2009) teaches how to transform your work life so that you are excited to come to work each day. Roxanne's unique strategies can make you more productive and profitable, and fully in love with your work! If you own or manage a company, consider bringing Roxanne in to transform your staff. www.EmmerichGroup.com or www.ThankGodItsMonday.com.

**The Lefkoe Method.** The Lefkoe Institute helps individuals who want to make lasting changes in their behavior or emotions (or both) in a gentle yet effective way. Using the Lefkoe Method, unwanted beliefs are literally unwired for good, which is essential to succeeding with my Chapter 14 on stretching your goals. Go to www.recreateyourlife.com/workday for a free trial of the method.

**The Institute of HeartMath.** HeartMath teaches techniques to keep your heart active in the midst of the busy world, thus increasing your satisfaction with work and life, as I encourage in Part III. The mission of HeartMath is to establish heart-based living and global coherence by inspiring people to connect with the intelligence and guidance of their own hearts. The HeartMath system is composed of research, programs, products, and technologies to improve health, well-being, and personal fulfillment. Go to www.heartmath.com to find a solution that will help you integrate your heart while in the midst of the stressful workday.

**The Speed of Trust** by Stephen M. R. Covey, with Rebecca R. Merrill (Free Press, 2006). This book provides a very nice reminder that business is not all about winning, closing deals, and smashing the competitor. Rather, it is about relationships—with your customers, coworkers, and colleagues—and the importance of trust In those relationships. This is core to my Chapter 17 message on working more from your heart. One observation that particularly struck me was that workplace efficiency and productivity greatly increase when people trust one another. This book is an excellent read that reignited my passion for a positive business world. www.speedoftrust.com.

**Steve Farber.** I have found Steve Farber's books to be effective, parable-style stories that emphasize the best in workplace leadership. His first book, *The Radical Leap: A Personal Lesson in Extreme Leadership* (Kaplan Publishing, 2004), is already considered a classic in the leadership field, and it speaks well to the role of love in business leadership—a message I discuss in Chapter 17. His latest book, *Greater Than Yourself: The Ultimate Lesson In Leadership* (Broadway Business, 2009), was a *Wall Street Journal* and *USA Today* best seller, and addresses the value of mentoring your staff so they become even greater than yourself, something I encourage in Chapter 16. Farber gives speeches on these topics and is the president of

Extreme Leadership Incorporated, an organization devoted to the cultivation and development of Extreme Leaders in the business community. www.stevefarber.com.

**The Answer** by John Assaraf and Murray Smith (Atria, 2009). This book offers an effective package of goal-attainment advice and practical small business planning insights, many of which match very well the principles in Parts II and III of my book. The authors have founded an organization called OneCoach to help small business owners succeed at both attaining their goals and developing effective plans for their businesses. Find them at www.onecoach.com.

**The Corporate Mystic** by Gay Hendricks and Kate Ludeman (Bantam, 1997). Hendricks is a self-development writer who in this book interviewed many of the country's best corporate CEOs. He investigtes how they apply higher principles of life to their work—principles like integrity, vision, intuition, and commitment. His research on how executives use "think time" to activate their intuition at work (highlighted in Chapter 17 of my book) explains one key way to better connect with yourself and your work. See www.hendricks.com for information on training to increase these capabilities.

**The New Psycho-Cybernetics** by Maxwell Maltz (Prentice Hall Press, 2002). Originally published in 1960, this book has sold over 30 million copies since then. It is by far my favorite book about tapping into the power of the subconscious mind to improve your life. You will see it referred to over and over again in my book.

**The Get-It-Done Guy.** I am always looking for consistent sources of good tips on workday efficiency. Stever Robbins is a great source. Stever Robbins delivers tons of useful advice on how to work less and do more. His tips are available in fun, brief, easy-to-listen-to podcasts, blogs, and articles—delivered with wit, humor, and substance. He helps you do what you do better and do it faster. Stever Robbin's book, *Get-It-Done Guy's 9 Steps to Work Less and Do More,* is forthcoming from Macmillan in August 2010. Stever Robbins, CEO Stever Robbins Inc., host of the *Get-It-Done Guy* podcast. www.steverrobbins.com.

**PhotoReading Program.** Efficient reading strategies can be vital tools for time management. I recommend "PhotoReading," which is a whole-mind approach to reading with speed, comprehension, and enjoyment. By using the PhotoReading system, you can easily get your reading done in one third the time you spend now without the stress of too much to read in too little time. It adapts well for all material from fluff to highly technical and from books to PDF files. Go to www.PhotoReading.com.

*The Sedona Method* by Hale Dwoskin (Sedona Press, 2003). This book explains the method of the same name, which teaches you how to release limiting beliefs through a system of self-inquiry. I cover the importance of releasing limiting beliefs in Chapter 14, and the Sedona Method can show you how to tap your natural ability to do that. This will free you to have, be, or do whatever is best for you now. Go to www.sedona.com for a free trial.

*Cynthia Kersey—Unstoppable* (Sourcebooks, Inc. 2005). In Parts II and III of my book, I emphasize the power of vision and passion for achieving your goals and thriving in your work. Cynthia Kersey is a master at teaching you how to do this. Through her books *Unstoppable* and *Unstoppable Women*, and through her effective *Unstoppable Challenge* coaching programs, she inspires you to find your own passions so you can succeed with your goals, and with life. For more information and to receive free getting-started tools, go to www.unstoppable.net.

## Other Recommended Books

*A Perfect Mess* by Eric Abrahamson and David H. Freedman (Little, Brown and Company, 2007). A well-researched work that argues that most efforts to "get organized" are not cost effective, as I discuss in Chapter 3.

*Ask and It Is Given* by Jerry and Esther Hicks (Hay House, 2005). The undisputed leader in the field of the Law of Attraction (LOA), Jerry and Esther lay out the principles of LOA in clear and practical terms. This book is my favorite in her series since the last half of the book contains an exhaustive set of step-by-step "processes" you can use to implement the teachings. This series is not for everyone, however, since the authors say it is channeled, and many readers will reject that premise. If you can get past that, however, the content is some of the best out there.

*Crazy Busy* by Edward M. Hallowell, M.D. (Ballantine Books, 2007). Dr. Hallowell was the first to identify overload at work as a source of ADD-like symptoms in workers. Here he discusses that, and strategies to overcome it.

*Do It Tomorrow and Other Secrets of Time Management* by Mark Forster (Hodder & Stoughton, 2008). This book discusses the concept of the Reactive Mind, the state in which we all overreact to needs and tasks the moment we see them. The author posits that we should wait and reconsider them the next day, so their true value is easier to assess. See Chapter 6 for my discussion of that, and consider Forster's book for a full discussion.

**Execution: The Discipline of Getting Things Done** by Larry Bossidy, Ram Charan, and Charles Burck. (Crown Business, 2002). This work focuses on organizations that succeed through emphasizing disciplined execution of their corporate plans. It represents a countervailing opinion to those that emphasize vision. See Chapter 10 for my approach to balancing these.

**Extreme Project Management** by Douglas DeCarlo (Jossey-Bass, 2004). The project management methodology detailed in this book emphasizes flexibility and nimbleness in planning, something I highly recommend for handling the rapidly changing business priorities in nearly all organizations these days.

**Find Your Inner Voice** by Karol Ward (New Page Books, 2009). This interesting book has a very specific focus. It shows you how to understand and listen to the messages your body and emotions send you about events around you. It can teach you how to use your intuitive gut feelings more accurately, as I recommend in Chapter 17.

**Finding Your Zone** by Michael Lardon, M.D. (Penguin, 2002). This book takes lessons from "finding the zone" in sports, and applies them to life.

**First Things First** by Stephen R. Covey, A. Roger Merrill, and Rebecca Merrill (Free Press, 1996). I enjoyed this book even more than the better-known book by the same author, *The 7 Habits of Highly Successful People,* due to its practical focus on time management.

**Flow: The Psychology of Optimal Experience** by Mihaly Csikszentmihalyi (Harper Perennial, 1991). Csikszentmihalyi is the reigning expert on the concept of *flow,* that feeling of being in the zone. I talk about flow in Chapter 17. This book explains its sources and ways to enhance it.

**Getting Things Done** by David Allen (Penguin, 2002). This book has become a near-classic reference for those seeking to get their overloaded workday under control. David elevated the "next-action" concept to a very practical level. I talk about using next-action tasks in Chapter 7.

**Love Is the Killer App** by Tim Sanders (Three Rivers Press, 2003). This volume makes a convincing argument that qualities normally associated with love can be applied in the harsh, competitive business world—with highly lucrative results. I discuss the value of working from the heart in Chapter 17.

***Never Check E-mail in the Morning*** by Julie Morgenstern (Fireside, 2005). Julie is arguably the reigning expert on personal organization; this book represents a collection of useful tips for getting your work organized, and complements my work in Part I.

***NLP: The New Technology of Achievement*** edited by Steve Andreas and Charles Faulkner (Harper Paperbacks, 1996). While more popular renditions have emerged for Neuro-Linguistic Programming (NLP)—namely those by Anthony Robbins—this book is the foundational volume on the topic; anyone considering NLP for breaking through limiting beliefs (see my Chapter 14) should read it.

***Now, Discover Your Strengths*** by Marcus Buckingham and Donald O. Clifton (Free Press, 2001). A useful guide that does what the title says—it helps you find your strengths so you can apply them in your job and career. Each book comes with a unique code that you can enter into the author's website to run an extensive online Q&A that helps you find your work strengths; this can be useful when following my recommendations for building your life's work statement in Chapter 18. The online tool is free by entering a unique code provided inside each book, so do not buy the book used.

***Practical Intuition for Success*** by Laura Day (Harper Paperbacks, 1999). This title follows Day's book *Practical Intuition*. Both books are about developing your own intuition (relevant to Chapter 17); this one is more business focused.

***Quantum Leap Thinking*** by James J. Mapes (Sourcebooks, Inc., 2003). James demonstrates multiple ways to change the beliefs you hold about yourself and to leap forward in life. This book was the first book I saw that clearly distinguished between creative tension (good) and stress (bad), a distinction I highlight in Chapter 3.

***StrengthsFinder 2.0*** by Tom Rath (Gallup Press, 2007). An update of *Now, Discover Your Strengths,* which improves on the earlier tool, this book can be useful when following my recommendations for building your life's work statement in Chapter 18.

***The 7 Habits of Highly Effective People*** by Stephen R. Covey (Free Press, 2004). Originally published in 1989, this is the landmark book that defines self-management best practices.

**The Fifth Discipline** by Peter M. Senge (Doubleday, 1990, 2006). A classic volume about creating "Learning Organizations," this book contains the best descriptions of, and practical business uses for, the concept of a mental model—a key foundation of my Part I Control-layer techniques.

**The Intuitive Edge** by Philip Goldberg (Jeremy P. Tarcher, Inc., 1983). Goldberg's thoughtful, incisive, and very well-researched book looks at intuition from all angles: what it is, how it's used, and how to improve it. I refer to Philip's work in Chapter 17.

**The Nature of Explanation** by Kenneth Craik (University Press, 1943). Craik was the person who invented the concept of mental models, a concept I rely on in Part I of this book.

**The Power of Now** by Eckhart Tolle (New World Library, 2004). Eckhart Tolle, in this very popular book, focuses on the importance of being present in our Now experience—taking it to a near spiritual level. I admire Tolle for drawing attention to this important concept, because he lays the groundwork for my book, where I also focus on the concept of the Now experience—but for a more pragmatic use. As you may have seen in my book, I use the concept of Now as a way to show how our attention is distributed while at work, and how high-quality attention in the Now is especially important when visualizing our goals. I encourage you to also look at Tolle's book to compare the two approaches to the Now.

**The Power of Your Subconscious Mind** by Joseph Murphy (Wilder Publications, 2008). Originally released in 1963, this quirky book includes a plethora of stories about people who have succeeded in numerous ways by applying the power of the subconscious mind—very relevant to my Chapter 12.

**The Science of Getting Rich** by Wallace D. Wattles (BN Publishing, 2008). First published in 1910, this book is the likely inspiration for countless success books written in the hundred years since it was released. For example, Rhonda Byrne stated this book was the inspiration for her DVD and book *The Secret*, and many think Napoleon Hill's *Think and Grow Rich* was based on it. It is the classic source of the premise that by using the power of your mind you can create what you want in business and life, as I discuss in Chapter 12.

**The Secret** by Rhonda Byrne (DVD, TS Production, LLC, 2006). This finely produced DVD documentary created a sensation around the concept of the Law of Attraction. It was released later as a book (Atria, 2006), which, by the way, contains additional material. I refer to the Law of Attraction in Chapter 12.

*The Success Principles* by Jack Canfield (Collins, 2005). This is by far the single best success book I have ever read. First of all, it is incredibly complete—nearly every success principle I have ever encountered, *and believe in,* is in here, and far more—it supports every aspect of my book. Second, it is remarkably well written, presented, and organized. It is a long book, but it is easy to move through it by picking sections you are interested in. And it is full of great stories that illustrate each principle. Read this book!

*Think and Grow Rich* by Napoleon Hill (Wilder Publications, 2008). First published in 1937, this is *the* undisputed classic success book; many contemporary success writers owe their core content to principles laid out in this book. Very relevant to my Chapter 12.

*To Do...Doing...Done!* by G. Lynne Snead and Joyce Wycoff (Fireside, 1997). A small, practical book about planning out projects on paper and then time-activating related tasks onto your to-do list. One of the first places I saw a discussion similar to the concept of next actions, as covered in my Chapter 7.

*Try It on Everything: Discover the Power of EFT* by Patricia Carrington (Try It Productions, LLC, 2008). One of the many books on EFT. Carrington does a good job of showing the wide scope of uses of EFT, including ones that may be more appropriate for the business audience. Consider EFT when using Chapter 14 of my book.

*Unlimited Power* by Anthony Robbins (Free Press, 1997). This book contains the most popular coverage of Neuro-Linguistic Programming (NLP) available. NLP is mentioned in Chapter 14 of my book.

*What Color Is Your Parachute?* by Richard N. Bolles (Ten Speed Press, 2009). In the past, when I was making job changes every five years or so, I read this book each time I did. It is a fountainhead of useful thought and resources about making a successful job or career change; and it is delivered by a very compassionate teacher. Richard updates this book nearly every year, so be sure to buy the latest version. I refer to this book in Chapter 18, when I describe ways to build your life's work vision statement.

***Writing Down Your Soul*** by Janet Conner (Conari Press, 2009). This is a very personal account of how journaling can lead to deep insights into yourself, leading to a better connection with your intuition—all relevant to Chapter 17, which is about connecting better with yourself at work.

***Your Sixth Sense: Unlocking the Power of Your Intuition*** by Belleruth Naparstek (HarperOne, 2009). Belleruth takes a more psychological approach to developing intuition than other sources I have seen; I like her style. This is applicable to Chapter 17.

# Acknowledgments

I am deeply grateful to the following people without whom I could never have completed this book (listed alphabetically).

David Abrio, Joe Burull, Mary Calvez, Sarah Clarehart, Phillip David, Jeffrey Detwiler. Dino Dichant, Floris Faber, Vivian Groman, Jennifer Hawthorne, Jason S. Huffman, Kathy Kaiser, Carol Kline, Jim Krenz , Wendy M. Larson, Amy Leschke-Kahle, Chuck Linenberger, Marc Linenberger, Judy O'Beirn, David Olkkola, Carol Reich, Daniel William Reilly, Kevin Roth, and Penny Sansevieri. And I give a very special thank you to Marci Shimoff, whose inspiration and support was immeasurable.

# Index

## A

AAA (American Automobile Association)  4, 235
Abrahamson, Eric  30, 327
Accenture  3, 4, 58, 185, 198, 235
accumulated accomplishments  40
action on goals
  brainstorming steps  188–190
  forced vs. inspired  188
  inspired  192
  planning  190, 315
  take action every day?  192–193
  taking first action  187–194
Activating Now Goals
  all about  159–183
  benefits of  159–160
  compared to positive thinking  178
  daily practice  183–185
  evidence that it works  171–175
  how long does it take?  178–179, 209, 295

how to  162–165
is it necessary?  176–178
life's work vision statement, activating  293–296
value for activating intuition  268
why it is needed  215–216
why it works  165–166
ad hoc tasks  86
Allen, David  84, 90, 328
Andreas, Steve  198, 329
*Answer, The* (Assaraf)  174, 294, 326
anxiety  14, 48
appointments  83
  defined  85–86
  for tasks  92
  vs. tasks  85–86
arts as source of vision  244–245
*Ask and It Is Given* (Hicks)  202, 327
Assaraf, John  174, 294, 326
attention
  power of  165–171
  using productively  216–217

Attention Deficit Disorder 46
Attwood, Chris 283, 324
Attwood, Janet Bray 283, 324

**B**

Ball, Lucille 42
beliefs
  fear from going beyond 275
  how they hold us back 197
  overcoming limiting 198
bicycle wheel 168–169
BlackBerry 94
Bolles, Richard N. 282, 331
bonus structures as goal incentives 134
Bossidy, Larry 328
brainstorming
  action steps 188–190, 315
  compared to intuition 267
Buckingham, Marcus 283, 329
Burck, Charles 328
Business Growth Strategies 324
business intuition 258–261
  developing 262–266
  fear as block of 275
  learning directly 265
  where it comes from 264
  why we filter it out 266
Byrne, Rhonda 175, 330, 331

**C**

calendar 83
  placing general task time on 91–92
  placing specific tasks on 85–86,
    92–93
Calvin, Melvin 260
Canfield, Jack 163, 323, 331
Canfield Training Group, The 323
career advancement
  in industry 235–236
  in leadership 233
  non-management 233
career as a larger vision 233–240
Carrington, Patricia 199, 331
cartoon maps 35

CEO Solution 71
Charan, Ram 328
*Chicken Soup for the Soul* (Canfield)
    324
chocolate factory 42
Clifton, Donald O. 283, 329
community as source of vision 242–
    243
company vision 231
connecting to larger vision, why impor-
    tant 229–230
connecting to your personal mission
    297–304
connecting with yourself 253–275
  benefits of 255–260
  business intuition as way to connect
    262–266
  by finding balance 261–262
  for better gut decisions 257–261
  heart, using to connect 272–274
  improvement in business intuition
    258–261
  improvement to I-Now 256–257
  methods 261–274
  think-time as method 266–268
  what it means 254–255
Connect layer 6
Conner, Janet 272, 332
Control layer 5–6
  as the foundation layer 6
converting e-mail to tasks 20
conveyor-belt model 47–49
  defined 39–40
*Corporate Mystic, The* (Hendricks)
    266, 326
costs of getting organized 30
Covey, Stephen M. R. 273, 325
Covey, Stephen R. 25, 174, 328, 330
Craik, Kenneth 36, 330
*Crazy Busy* (Hallowell) 45–46, 327
Create layer 6
  explained 126
creating outcomes 126–127
creative imagination 174

Critical Now 18, 20, 44, 47–48
  in paper planner daily pages 60
  management of 58–62
Csikszentmihalyi, Mihaly 328
curing addiction to e-mail 109–115

**D**

Daily Planner Binder, Workday Mastery
    322
Day, Laura 329
deadlines 20, 65–66, 191
  putting on Significant Outcomes 98
DeCarlo, Douglas 328
deferring tasks 69–70
Defer-to-Do 71–73
Defer-to-Review 73–77, 312
  Extended Review Cycles 74–76
delegation 95–96
developing intuition 262–266
developing others' careers as vision
    241
developing your own business as a vi-
    sion 239–240
*Do It Tomorrow* (Forster) 78, 327
due dates. *See also* deadlines
  avoiding them in goals 153–154
Dwoskin, Hale 202, 327

**E**

eBay 4
Edison, Thomas 260
EFT 198, 331
e-mail
  checking it on a schedule 112
  converting to tasks 104–106
  curing addiction to 109–115
  dealing with urgent mail 113–114
  filing 107–109
  flagging 106–107
  Follow Up flag in Outlook 106–107
  solution to overload 104–105
  trouble with 27, 78, 103–104
  why we check it too often 110–113

Emery, Stewart 279, 324
Emmerich, Roxanne 324
Emotional Freedom Technique (EFT)
    198, 331
emotional scale 202
Excel. *See* Microsoft Excel
*Execution: The Discipline of Getting
    Things Done* (Bossidy, et al.)
    328
*Extreme Project Management* (De-
    Carlo) 328

**F**

family as source of vision 241–242
Farber, Steve 273, 325
Faulkner, Charles 198, 329
fear
  as detriment to connection 274
  avoiding fear in career choices 246
*Fifth Discipline, The* (Senge) 36, 133,
    330
fight-or-flight impulse 275
file cabinets 91
filing e-mail 107–109
Finding a Purpose in Your Existing
    Work 230–232
*Finding Your Zone* (Lardon) 328
*Find Your Inner Voice* (Ward) 328
*First Things First* (Covey et al.) 174,
    328
Fisherman's Wharf story 34
flagging e-mail 106–107
Flow 255–256
Flower exercise 282
*Flow: The Psychology of Optimal Expe-
    rience* (Csikszentmihalyi) 328
flywheel effect 169–170, 295
Follow Up flag in Outlook 106–107
follow-up tasks 94–96
forced action 188
Forrester, Jay Wright 36
Forster, Mark 78, 80, 327
4-D system 68–69

Freedman, David H. 30, 327
FRESH Prioritization 79

# G

*Get-It-Done Guy's 9 Steps to Work Less and Do More* (Robbins) 326
getting in the flow 255–256
getting organized 29–30
*Getting Things Done* (Allen) 84, 90, 328
glass ceiling, pushing past 197
Gmail 106, 108
goals. *See also* Now Goals
  4-step process, summary of 129–130, 214, 313
  action on. *See* action on goals
  activating 159–183. *See also* Activating Now Goals
  as part of create layer 127–128
  as tasks 86–88
  contrasted with tasks 127
  difference from Significant Outcomes 96
  due dates and goals 153–154
  intangible 156–158
  just setting them is not enough 132
  lack of ownership 133
  managing for others 191
  new approach to 128–129
  problems with 2, 8
  seasonal time frames for 154–155, 314
  SMART Goals 2, 146–147
  sorry state of workplace goals 131–132
  spinning 159–161. *See also* Activating Now Goals
  stretching 195–210, 275
goal spinning. *See also* Activating Now Goals
  effect on subconscious thoughts 170–171
  on issues 180–181
*Goals!* (Tracy) 174, 324, 329
going-home test 51, 61

Goldberg, Philip 263, 330
golf, and visualization 172
government position as service 239
*Greater Than Yourself* (Farber) 241, 325
group vision 191
gut decisions 257–258
gyroscope effect 169, 294

# H

Hallowell, Edward M. 46, 327
*Happy for No Reason* (Shimoff) 182, 273, 324
hard work 216–217
HeartMath 274, 325
heart, working from 272–274
Hendricks, Gay 266, 326
Hicks, Jerry and Esther 175, 202, 327
High Importance flag in Outlook 114
Hill, Napoleon 173, 184, 228, 267, 331
Hilton, Conrad 263
horizon 39
hypnosis 172, 198

# I

ice cream girl example 279–280, 300
*I Love Lucy* 42
Immediate Now 129, 163, 254, 269. *See also* I-Now
importance
  intrinsic 53–54
  problems with 27–29, 61
in-box, overwhelmed 103
in-box stress 103
information noodling 111–112
I-Now 163, 164, 185, 254, 256–257, 269
  defined 129
inspired action 188, 192
Instant Messaging 114
Institute of HeartMath 274, 325
intangible goals 156–158
integrity 279
intrinsic importance 53–54

intuition
  business 258–261
  developing 262–266
  fear as block of 275
  for identifying life's work 281
  in Iraq soldiers 263
  learning 265
  where it comes from 264
  why we filter it out 266
*Intuitive Edge, The* (Goldberg) 263, 330
investments as a vision 247–248
iPhone 94
Issue Spinning 180–181

**J**

JCVGantt 100, 190, 315, 323
job qualities exercise 282–284
Jobs, Steve 191

**K**

Kersey, Cynthia 327

**L**

Lardon, Michael 328
Law of Attraction 174–175, 202, 327
Lefkoe Institute 325
Lefkoe Method 198, 325
Lefkoe, Morty 198
life balance as way to connect 261–262
life's work 277–295
  and the Workday Now 277–278
  changing nature of 279–280
  guided by mission 300
  identifying 280–287
  staying flexible with 286
  why important to find 278
life's work vision statement
  activating 293–296
  example 288–289, 318–319
  writing 287–293
Locking in New Beliefs exercise
  defined 203–208
  example 206–209, 316–317

reviewed 294
longevity as vision 236
*Love is the Killer App* (Sanders) 273, 329
low-priority items, problem with working first 27
loyalty as vision 236
Ludeman, Kate 326

**M**

Macintosh 16
Major Definite Purpose 228–229
Maltz, Maxwell 172–173, 202, 204, 326
Management by Objectives 146
Manage Your Now ClearContext Outlook Add-in Software 322
Mapes, James J. 24, 329
map of United States, as example of mental model 35
Maslow's Hierarchy of Needs 7–8
Master Mind groups 184
Master Tasks list 74
MBO 146
meditation 269–272
  as way to build connection 269 270
  attention, relation to 269–270
  how to learn 270–271
  in religion and spiritual practices 271
  Transcendental Meditation 270–271
meetings, declining low-value ones 92
Mendeleev 260
mental model
  as applied to goals 128–129
  defined 34–36
  the Workday Now as a mental model 37–42
Merrill, A. Roger 328
Merrill, Rebecca R. 325, 328
Microsoft Excel 17, 190, 315
Microsoft Outlook 4, 15, 17, 50, 63, 321
  Categories 108
  configuring notifications 114
  filing e-mails 107

*Microsoft Outlook, cont'd*
  for showing Significant Outcomes  97
  for Strategic Deferrals  72, 75
  High Importance flag  114
  using reminders for SOCs  99
Microsoft Project  88, 100, 315
milestones  99–100
MindJet  189
MindManager  17, 100, 189, 190, 315,
  323
mind mapping  189
mission  297–304, 305
  core qualities of  298–300
  defined  298
  discovery of  299, 301–302
  long-lasting nature of  300
  permanent nature of  298–299
  positive nature of  299
  statement  297
mission statement  297
  example  303, 319
  how to write  303
mobile tasks  94
money
  as a Target Goal  155–156
  as a vision  246–247
  for intangible goals  156–158
Morgenstern, Julie  329
Murphy, Joseph  330

**N**

Naparstek, Belleruth  332
*Nature of Explanation, The* (Craik)  330
Neuro-Linguistic Programming  198,
  329, 331
*Never Check E-mail in the Morning*
  (Morgenstern)  329
*New Psycho-Cybernetics, The* (Maltz)
  172–173, 202, 326
next action tasks  62, 84–85
  for Significant Outcomes  98
Nicklaus, Jack  172
NLP  198, 331
*NLP: The New Technology of Achieve-*
  *ment* (Andreas et al.)  198, 329

*Now, Discover Your Strengths* (Buck-
  ingham et al.)  283, 329
Now Goals. *See also* goals
  defined  147
  examples of  149–151
Now Goals list  154, 189, 314
Now Goal statement  149, 155, 314
Now Horizon
  defined  38–39
  tossing tasks over  70
Now Tasks, defined  51–52
Now Tasks List  18, 311
Now, why that word
  21, 229–230

**O**

OneCoach  326
operational tasks  86
Opportunity Now  18, 20, 48–49
  advanced  65–68
  daily review of  69–70
  fast growth of list  67
organization as a solution  29–30
Outlook. *See* Microsoft Outlook
over-clocked workday  14
Over-the-Horizon  18, 19, 44, 312
  extended review cycle  75
  for Defer-to-Review tasks  74
Over-the-Horizon tasks  43, 49–50

**P**

Palm  94
paper planner daily pages
  listing Critical Now tasks  60
  listing Defer-to-Do tasks  72
  listing Target Now tasks  65
paper system. *See also* Workday Mastery To-Do List
  converting e-mails to tasks in  105–
  106
  introduced  17–20
  weekly refresh  58
Passion Test  283
*Passion Test, The* (Attwood)  324

*Perfect Mess, A* (Abrahamson et al.) 30, 327

performance standards 128

phone tree 115

PhotoReading Program 326

planning action 190

Porras, Jerry 279, 324

positive thinking 178

*Power of Now, The* (Eckhart) 185, 330

*Power of Your Subconscious Mind, The* (Murphy) 330

*Practical Intuition for Success* (Day) 329

prioritization 27–28

procrastination 161

product development as a source of vision 237

product or project teams as source of vision 231

professional organizations as source of vision 243–244

projects
  as tasks 88
  difference from Significant Outcomes 96
  management 127, 191
  milestones 100
  plan or timeline 190, 315

Psych-K 198

purpose. *See also* vision
  at career level, same as vision 224
  in your career 223–224

**Q**

*Quantum Leap Thinking* (Mapes) 329

quick hits 79, 112

Quick Start 17–21

**R**

*Radical Leap, The* (Farber) 273, 325

Rate of Work 41–43

Rath, Tom 283, 330

rational thinking technique 202

Reactive Mind 78

*Re-create Your Life* (Lefkoe) 198

religion as source of vision 245

replies, e-mail 106–107

reticular activating system 163

retirement as a vision 248

reward/punishment model 24

risk management 182

Robbins, Anthony 198, 331

Robbins, Stever 326

**S**

Safeway 4

Sanders, Tim 273, 329

Schooler, Professor Jonathan 267

*Science of Getting Rich, The* (Wattles) 173, 330

scientific research as vision 237

scripting 204

*Secret, The* (Byrne) 175, 324, 331

Sedona Method 198

*Sedona Method, The* (Dwoskin) 202, 327

self-esteem 278

self-image 275

Senge, Peter M. 36, 133, 330

*7 Habits of Highly Effective People, The* (Covey) 25, 174, 330

Shimoff, Marci 182, 273, 324

short life of tasks 77–79

shoulds
  as a basis of goals 133
  avoiding 285

Significant Outcomes 96–100
  milestones 99–100

sitting for ideas 267

skill increase as vision 235–236

SMART goals 146–147

Smith, Murray 174, 294, 326

Snead, G. Lynne 84, 331

SOC Milestones 99–100

SOCs 96–100

*Speed of Trust, The* (Covey) 273, 325

spinning goals 159–161. *See also* Activating Now Goals

spinning wheel analogy 168–170

spiritual growth as source of vision  245
sports as source of vision  244–245
startups and nonprofits as source of vision  237–238
stomach test  195
Strategic Deferral  70–77
*StrengthsFinder 2.0* (Rath)  283, 330
stress  34
stress vs. tension  24–25
subconscious mind, as tool for goal activation  168
subconscious thoughts, influenced by goal spinning  170–171
*Success Built to Last* (Porras)  279, 324
*Success Principles, The* (Canfield)  163, 323, 331
Sun Microsystems  4

**T**

Tapping Solution  198
Target Goals
  as a measure  148
  defined  144
  identifying  147–148
  keeping flexible  151–152, 210–211
  that fit you  152
Target Now
  defined  62–65
  in Level 2 Workday Mastery To-Do List  64
  in paper planner daily pages  65
  required maintenance  65
targets  8
TARGET term for Defer-to-Do tasks  73
task management  83–102
tasks
  assigning  95–96
  delegating  95–96
  in physical piles  90
  keeping out of your head  89–90
  placing on calendar  92
  setting general task time  91–92
  short life of  77–79
  storing in one place  88–89

*tasks, cont'd*
  taking on the road  94
  why we work low-priority first  78–80
telephone, using more  114
tension vs. stress  24–25
*Thank God It's Monday* (Emmerich)  324
Theater of Your Mind  173, 204
*Think and Grow Rich* (Hill)  173, 184, 228, 267, 331
thinking big  195–197, 285, 305–308
think-time  266–268
Thompson, Clive  267
Thompson, Mark  279, 324
time management  91–94
*Time Power* (Tracy)  324
*To Do...Doing...Done!* (Snead)  84, 331
to-do list  18. *See* Workday Mastery To-Do List
Tolle, Eckhart  185, 330
Total Workday Control Using Microsoft Outlook—Basic Configuration Training CD  322
*Total Workday Control Using Microsoft Outlook* (Linenberger)  322
  methodology borrowed from  8
Tracy, Brian  25, 174, 323
Transcendental Meditation  270–271
treadmill model. *See also* conveyor-belt model
  defined  39–41
*Try It on Everything: Discover the Power of EFT* (Carrington)  199, 331
TV commercials, as a model for visualization  165–166
20-item rule  20, 51, 67–68
  Defer-to-Review as Solution  74
two circles of life  221–223

**U**

United States, map of as example of mental model  35
United States Peace Corps  3, 235, 238
*Unlimited Power* (Robbins)  198, 331

Unstoppable Challenge 327
*Unstoppable* (Kersey) 327
*Unstoppable Women* (Kersey) 327
UPS 4
urgency 25–26, 33, 37
urgency vs. importance 52–53, 61
urgency zones
  explained 45–54
  full management instructions 57–80
  introduced 43
  managing in 51–52
urgent e-mail 113–114

**V**

vision
  adding to goals 135–136
  arts as source of vision 244–245
  as the Create-layer solution 135–136
  as the source of all human-created
    things 308
  career as a source 233–240
  changing nature of 250
  community as source of 242–243
  defined 137–138
  developing others' careers as a vision
    241
  developing your own business as a
    vision 239–240
  family as source of vision 241–242
  government position as vision of
    service 239
  investments as a vision 247–248
  in your career 223–224
  in your company 231
  longevity as vision 236
  loyalty as vision 236
  of a group 191
  of your company 231
  product development as a source of
    vision 237
  product or project teams as source of
    vision 231
  professional organizations as source
    of vision 243–244
  religion as source of vision 245

*vision cont'd*
  retirement as a vision 248
  scientific research as vision 237
  size does not matter 138
  skill increase as vision 235–236
  spiritual growth as source of vision
    235
  sports as source of vision 244–245
  startups and nonprofits as source of
    vision 237–238
  volunteer organizations as source of
    vision 244
  why connecting to larger vision is
    important 229–230
  why it is usually lacking 136
vision board 293–294
Vision Goals
  defined 138–140
  formula for writing 139–141
  vs. Target Goals 145–146
vision statement. *See also* Now Goal
    statement
  for life's work 287–293
  in Now Goal 162
visions to question or avoid 245–247
visualization 164–165, 167, 172–173,
    174
voice mail 20
volunteer organizations as source of
    vision 244

**W**

waiting for list 95
Ward, Karol 328
Watson, James 260
Wattles, Wallace D. 173, 330
weekly review steps of Over-the-
    Horizon tasks 77
weekly task review 19–20, 20
*What Color Is Your Parachute?* (Bolles)
    282, 331
What If–Why Not technique 199–201
willpower 162
Windows Mobile 94

Workday Mastery
  as a mental game  4–5
  defined  1, 4
Workday Mastery CD Self-Training Set
        321
Workday Mastery Coaching  321
Workday Mastery Pyramid
  explained  5–8
  Introduction to the Create layer
        125–126
  sequence of  6–7
Workday Mastery Seminars  321
Workday Mastery To-Do List  44, 48,
        57, 310
  how to use  19–20
  introduced  17
  Level 1  18
  Level 2  64
  Level 3  74–76, 119–120, 311, 312
  summarized  118–120
Workday Now
  and Workday Mastery  4
  and your life's work  277–278
  defined  41–42
  introduced  2–3
Workday Now Horizon  37–38
workday overload  42
worrying, influence on goals  182
*Writing Down Your Soul* (Conner)  272,
        332
Wycoff, Joyce  84, 331

**Y**

*Your Sixth Sense: Unlocking the Power
        of Your Intuition* (Naparstek)
        331

To enjoy more Workday Mastery...
## Claim Your FREE
# *MASTER YOUR WORKDAY NOW!*
# TOOLS at
## www.MasterYourWorkday.com/ToolDownloads

Congratulations! You are now on the journey to Workday Mastery, and you will gain more control and satisfaction if you put the knowledge in this book into immediate practice. To keep you moving most effectively, I have created these free downloadable tools for you:

## Free Workday Mastery Quick Guide

This Workday Mastery Quick Guide summarizes in one place all the major processes you will follow when using the techniques in this book. Keeping this fantastic "cheat sheet" handy will speed you on your way to Workday Mastery.

## Free Workday Mastery Toolkit Workbook

The Workday Mastery Toolkit (found on pages 309 to 320) is available as a workbook download. The workbook contains all the Workday Mastery forms in PDF format. You can print some or all of this workbook and use it to enter your daily tasks and planning.

## Free Workday Mastery Toolkit Templates

The Workday Mastery Toolkit items are also available as downloadable templates so you can use your computer to fill them in. Both Microsoft Word and MindManager forms are provided (PC and Mac).

## Free Workday Mastery e-Zine

You will receive a regular Workday Mastery e-zine full of tips, tricks, and the latest breakthrough methods to keep the Workday Mastery system updated and cutting-edge.

## Video: Overview of the Workday Mastery System

This freee video overview is a great introduction to the Workday Mastery system. You can also use this video overview to share the concepts of the Workday Mastery system with co-workers, employees, friends, and colleagues.

## For these and other free tool downloads, visit
## www.MasterYourWorkday.com/ToolDownloads

(To access free downloads, users will be asked to register by providing their
first name and e-mail address. Offer subject to availability.)